The Divine Matrix

FAITH MEETS FAITH

An Orbis Series in Interreligious Dialogue

Paul F. Knitter, General Editor

Editorial Advisors

John Berthrong
Julia Ching
Diana Eck
Karl-Josef Kuschel
Lamin Sanneh
George E. Tinker
Felix Wilfred

In the contemporary world, the many religions and spiritualities stand in need of greater communication and cooperation. More than ever before, they must speak to, learn from, and work with each other in order both to maintain their vital identities and to contribute to fashioning a better world.

FAITH MEETS FAITH seeks to promote interreligious dialogue by providing an open forum for exchanges among followers of different religious paths. While the Series wants to encourage creative and bold responses to questions arising from contemporary appreciations of religious plurality, it also recognizes the multiplicity of basic perspectives concerning the methods and content of interreligious dialogue.

Although rooted in a Christian theological perspective, the Series does not endorse any single school of thought or approach. By making available to both the scholarly community and the general public works that represent a variety of religious and methodological viewpoints, FAITH MEETS FAITH seeks instead to foster the encounter among the followers of the religions of the world on matters of ultimate concern.

FAITH MEETS FAITH SERIES

The Divine Matrix
Creativity as Link between East and West

Joseph A. Bracken, S.J.

ORBIS BOOKS
Maryknoll, New York 10545

The Catholic Foreign Mission Society of America (Maryknoll) recruits and trains people for overseas missionary service. Through Orbis Books, Maryknoll aims to foster the international dialogue that is essential to mission. The books published, however, reflect the opinions of their authors and are not meant to represent the official position of the society.

Published by Orbis Books, Maryknoll, New York 10545, U.S.A.
Published in Great Britain by Gracewing, Fowler-Wright Books Ltd., Herefordshire, England

Manufactured in the United States of America.

Library of Congress Cataloging-in-Publication Data

Bracken, Joseph A.
    The divine matrix : creativity as link between East and West / Joseph A. Bracken.
        p. cm.—(Faith meets faith)
    Includes bibliographical references and index.
    ISBN 1-57075-004-1 (pbk.)
    1. Religions—Relations   2. Creative ability—Religious aspects.
I. Title. II. Series.
BL410.B716   1995
291.2'11—dc20   95-3202
                                                     CIP

Orbis/ISBN 1-57075-004-1
Gracewing/ISBN 0-85244-336-6

To N.
and other women friends
who have enriched my life over the years
this book is affectionately dedicated

Contents

A Note on Orthography

The problem of rendering non-Western systems of writing into Roman letters for English and other modern European languages is notoriously difficult. Joining many publishers who do not insert diacritical marks for words such as the Sanskrit *Śūnyatā*, this book also omits them.

Scholars and others who know languages such as Sanskrit, Pali, Arabic, or Japanese do not need the diacritical marks to identify words in their original written form. And persons who do not know these languages gain little from having the marks reproduced. We recognize that languages employing different orthographic systems have a richness and distinctiveness that are partially conveyed by the orthographics of diacritical marks. And while we do not wish to be part of flattening out the contours of our linguistically plural globe, the high cost of ensuring accuracy in using the diacritical marks does not justify reproducing them here.

Foreword

My colleague, Joseph A. Bracken, S.J., has written a substantial book in comparative theology. It operates on two levels. On one, it presents an hypothesis for comparing religious traditions West and East by bringing them into dialogue concerning the role of creativity. Bracken analyzes creativity as an abstract idea developed from the metaphysics of Alfred North Whitehead and supplemented by Whitehead's idea of the extensive continuum. Then the abstraction is made concrete by being used as an interpretive tool to understand infinity and related ideas in Aristotle, Aquinas, Eckhart, Schelling, Heidegger, and Whitehead himself, in the West, and certain important themes in Hinduism, Buddhism, and Taoism. By relating all these themes and thinkers to creativity, abstractly considered, it is possible to tell much about where they agree, disagree, supplement, or confound one another. Even where scholars or serious religious thinkers might disagree with Bracken's interpretations, the disagreements can be brought into dialogue by reference to the various ways the different positions specify, affirmatively or negatively, the abstract idea of creativity.

Bracken's contribution on this level is to the slow and fitful project of developing comparative categories by which it will be possible to understand and discuss the world's religions together. Creativity is only one such category, but obviously an important one. Bracken is quite conscious of the need for alternative metaphysical categories, and also for categories dealing with other themes such as soteriology and community life. His hypothesis about creativity is ready for discussion.

On another level, Bracken presents a much more fully developed theology of his own, extending Whitehead's inadequate discussions of God and creativity to the hypothesis that Whitehead's insights are better served by a special Christian trinitarian position. Briefly, Bracken argues that the three persons of the Trinity are to be construed as societies, in Whitehead's technical sense, sharing a common past, future, and mutual relations with one another and with the world of finite occasions, but united in one divine nature as their common "matrix" or structured field of activity. Creativity is infinite in all three divine persons, but determinate. Bracken thus joins Charles Hartshorne and Lewis Ford as thinkers who significantly develop Whitehead's position beyond his own texts, and he joins Ninian Smart and

Steven Konstantine in defending a contemporary Christian trinitarian theology, with subjectivity in each of the divine persons, and explicating that in the context of dialogue with the world's major religions.

Christian trinitarianism, of course, is not an idea that can be proposed, like creativity, as a relatively neutral comparative ground. It is a philosophical hypothesis specifically for Christian theology. On the other hand, precisely because of the other level of Bracken's discussion about creativity, his trinitarian hypothesis can be brought into fairly exact comparative connections with some of its alternatives. It constitutes an illuminating example of how abstract notions of creativity and divine infinity can be made specific and geared to the symbols of at least one concrete religious tradition.

For Christian theologians, Bracken has made an outstanding contribution to philosophical theology, irrespective of interests in comparison. Far better than most process theologians, or process innovators such as Hartshorne and Ford, he presents a contemporary metaphysics that addresses classical trinitarian claims about the Christian God. I commend this book to readers for both of its levels of theological argumentation, the comparative and the constructive. It advances the debate and should be widely discussed.

> Robert Cummings Neville
> Dean, School of Theology
> Boston University

Acknowledgments

Given the wide-ranging character of this book, it could not have been written without help from many individuals with more professional expertise in the subject matter of various chapters than I myself possess. In particular, I would like to thank the following persons who read different chapters in draft form and made helpful comments: James W. Felt, S.J. (Chapter 1); Tibor Horvath, S.J., and John H. Wright, S.J. (Chapter 2); Jonas Barciauskas and Miklos Vetö (Chapter 3); Andrew Reck (Chapter 4); Francis Clooney, S.J., Eliot Deutsch and John Grimes (Chapter 5); Michael Barnhart, Ruben Habito and David Kalupahana (Chapter 6); Maria Habito and Robert Neville (Chapter 7). Naturally, the views expressed in those chapters are mine, not theirs. But their comments and criticisms helped me to sharpen my argument considerably.

Likewise, special thanks are due to four individuals whose comments were not limited to single chapters: Huston Smith who initially engaged my interest in this project with his direction of a National Endowment for Humanities scholars' seminar on a related topic in the summer of 1990; Paul Knitter, my colleague at Xavier and editor of the *Faith Meets Faith* series in which this book appears, who read all the chapters and urged on me important revisions and clarifications; William Burrows of Orbis Books who likewise insisted on "reader-friendly" revisions; and, finally, Robert Neville, whose work in comparative philosophy of religions I have followed closely over the years and who graciously wrote the Foreword to this book.

Finally, I offer my thanks to John Perry, S.J., who as editor of the journal *Ultimate Reality and Meaning* gave me permission to use previously published material in Chapters 2 and 4 of this book: namely, "*Ipsum Esse Subsistens*: Subsistent Being or Subsistent Activity?," *Ultimate Reality and Meaning* 14 (1991), 279-92; and "Creativity and the Extensive Continuum as the Ultimate Ground in Alfred North Whitehead's Philosophy of Becoming," *Ultimate Reality and Meaning* 16 (1993), 110-19.

successor, is this compatible with the notion of divine perfection? Provided that at each moment the divine act of existence is complete and without defect, this would seem to be a legitimate interpretation of the perfection of the divine being. In fact, it would seem to be preferable to the opposite alternative, namely, that the perfection of the divine being is pure actuality without any admixture of potentiality, because it makes eminently clear that the divine being is also divine life. Life, in other words, seems to involve potentiality or growth, transit from one stage of existence to another. The divine being understood as pure actuality contains no hint of life since there is no movement possible within the divine act of existence.[26] Only with the presupposition of an ongoing transit from potentiality to actuality within the divine being can one speak of God as possessing life as well as mere existence.

Aquinas, to be sure, expressly rules out the possibility that in God there is anything like a conversion of potentiality to actuality. For, if God is the Supreme Being, then God must be pure actuality since only what is itself in act can move something else from potency into act.[27] Here Aquinas is following Aristotle's presupposition of an Unmoved Mover, that entity which directly or indirectly moves everything else but is itself pure actuality and thus unmoved. Even organic substances which possess a "soul" and thus may be said to move themselves possess a "part" that moves and a "part" that is moved. Moreover, the "part" that moves is itself ultimately moved by the Unmoved Mover.[28] And yet, as noted in Chapter 1, there is a certain inconsistency in Aristotle's thinking here. For, if, as Aristotle says in the *Metaphysics*, the reality of the Unmoved Mover is "a thinking on thinking,"[29] then this *thinking* is itself an activity which is ongoing and thus here and now incomplete. It cannot be complete without ceasing to be an activity and in effect becoming an entity (namely, a thought) with a fixed or static reality. There is necessarily, in other words, even within the Unmoved Mover a continuous conversion from potentiality to actuality, but in such a way that there is no danger of a cessation of this activity or its conversion into still another type of activity. For, "thinking on thinking" as an entelechy (*entelecheia*) or self-contained activity has already achieved its essential perfection or form even as it continues to exercise that perfection in successive stages of actualization.

Similarly, I would argue that Aquinas's notion of God, if reinterpreted as Subsistent Activity, demands a continuous conversion from potentiality to actuality. For, understood as Subsistent Activity, the divine being requires no extrinsic "mover" but rather moves itself from potency to actuality in virtue of its own intrinsic dynamism. I presuppose here the distinction between *cause* and *ground* (or *ontal source*) already mentioned in Chapter 1. That is, *cause* and *effect* are ontologically separate categories of being so that no entity (not even God) can, strictly speaking, be the cause of its own existence. On the other hand, if God be thought of as Subsistent Activity, then God's existence is grounded in the act of being, the activity

Introduction

Common Structures of Intelligibility

In contemporary interreligious dialogue, various approaches are used to enable individuals of different religious traditions to understand and appreciate one another's spiritual heritage. Simply listening to one another's stories and carefully observing the rituals which symbolically enact those stories have been quite effective in promoting respect for the inevitable diversity of religious beliefs and practices in the world today. At the same time, more theoretically oriented individuals find themselves looking for specific points of comparison between the various religious traditions. Their search, in other words, is for mediating concepts or common structures of intelligibility which allow them to understand in some measure the beliefs and practices of otherwise alien religious traditions. In the end, as Robert Neville comments, "a conception from some one tradition is extended, abstracted further, and purified of its particularities to serve as a vague ground for comparison."[1] Moreover, interreligious dialogue is often thereby promoted, as representatives of the different traditions debate the applicability of such generalized concepts to one another's world views.

Does this approach implicitly suggest, however, that in the end all the various world religions with their conflicting truth-claims will be reconciled with one another in the light of an overarching metaphysical scheme? Are they thus one and all just so many partial manifestations of a basically philosophical understanding of reality (much as the German philosopher Hegel interpreted various religions East and West in the light of his own notion of Absolute Spirit)? In reply, one would have to say that these generalized structures of intelligibility might eventually ground a single all-comprehensive philosophical system. But, for the present at least, all that they offer are relatively neutral points of comparison between differing religious world views. That is, they can provide a focus for conversation between proponents of rival religious world views whereby one's personal religious beliefs can become the subject matter of public debate and critical reflection.

The relatively new discipline of comparative theology, in other words,

1

seems to run the risk of privatization of religious discourse and of ideological imperialism on at least two counts. First of all, among theological conservatives who claim that their religion, and therefore their belief system, is either a privileged revelation of the deeper meaning of reality or in any case an autonomous, self-consistent way of life,[2] there is little opportunity for effective self-criticism in the light of other religious world views. The latter are inevitably seen as either false, meaningless or, in any event, patently inferior to one's own religious perspective. But, on the other hand, theological liberals who propose that all religions are culturally bound expressions of one and the same basic religious experience are indirectly guilty of the same tendency to privatization of religious discourse and to ideological imperialism. That is, because they claim that this universal religious experience is, strictly speaking, ineffable in that the object of this experience is humanly incomprehensible, they, too, tend to judge the religious experience and the belief systems of others in the light of their own experience and their personal belief systems. Since their only access to the Ineffable is through the medium of their own religious experience, they have no choice but to make that admittedly limited experience normative for the validity of the truth-claims of other world religions.[3]

Accordingly, appeal to some generalized structure of intelligibility, which may indeed be derived from one religious world view but in principle should not be limited to that same world view, at least allows proponents of differing world religions to move in the direction of objectivity. That is, they can argue about the suitability of that structure both for their own and for one another's world views. In the course of discussion, they should come to a new understanding of the philosophical antecedents and consequences of their respective world views, even if in the end they feel obliged to reject the philosophical category in question as not truly pertinent to their own tradition. Naturally, if that structure of intelligibility proves to be quite fruitful and provocative of new insights, then something like a rough philosophical framework for further investigation of the different religious world views may be at hand. But the fact that the philosophical category in question will inevitably be understood and applied differently in different world religions argues strongly against the possibility of a single metaphysical system acceptable to all parties for the theoretical understanding of their religious beliefs, at least for the present moment.[4]

In any event, within the present book, I shall set forth two such generalized structures of intelligibility; both have to do with a metaphysical understanding of infinity, albeit in different ways. The first is the notion of creativity within the philosophy of Alfred North Whitehead. Creativity, says Whitehead, does not exist in and of itself but rather is actual only in its "accidents" or instantiations.[5] It is, accordingly, not an entity, not even God as the Supreme Being or utterly transcendent entity. Rather, it is a process or, even more fundamentally, an underlying activity which serves as the ontological ground for everything that exists (including God within Whitehead's scheme of things). Not all Whiteheadians, to be sure, would agree with this last statement. Many look upon creativity as simply a general name for all the empirical instances of "concrescence" or self-actualization among "actual occasions" (momentary subjects of experience) within the world process.[6] Yet there are texts in Whitehead's master work *Process and Reality* and still other books which allow one to conclude that creativity is not just a nominal term for particular instances of concrescence among actual occasions but rather, as will be suggested in this book, a deeper underlying reality invariably at work in the self-constitution of those same entities.[7]

Connected with the notion of creativity in Whitehead's philosophy, however, is still another structure, namely, the "extensive continuum" as the necessary context for the operation of creativity. Whitehead defines it as that which underlies the whole world, past, present, and future in that it provides a "relational complex" in which all entities, both actual and potential, have their standpoint or niche.[8] Like creativity, therefore, the extensive continuum is not itself an entity but the necessary presupposition for the existence of entities. That is, just as entities presuppose an energy-source or principle of activity for their individual existence and activity, so those same entities also require a spatial context or ongoing structure within which they can co-exist in dynamic interrelation. As Jorge Nobo comments in a recent book on Whitehead's metaphysics of extension and solidarity, creativity and the extensive continuum together must be seen as "two differentiable, but inseparable, aspects of the ultimate ground of the organic universe . . . Accordingly, insofar as this ground is the whereby of all becoming, it is termed 'creativity'; and insofar as it is the wherein of all interconnected actual existence, it is termed 'extension.'"[9]

It will be my contention in this book that creativity and the extensive continuum are not only the ultimate ground of the organic universe within Whitehead's scheme of things but also equivalently at work in many world religions, albeit under different names. The Creation Hymns in Book X of the *Rig Veda* and the opening verses of the *Tao te Ching*, for example, make reference to a Great Void out of which reality as we know it emerged. Furthermore, operative within this Void from the beginning has been an energy-principle which is not itself an entity but the dynamism whereby entities emerge from the Void and are related to one another. Hence, both classical Hinduism and classical Taoism, as I shall explain in subsequent chapters, likewise seem to presuppose as the ultimate ground of the universe within their respective world views something like creativity and the extensive continuum operating in tandem as Nobo suggests.

Judaism, Christianity, and Islam, to be sure, as theistic religions, think of Ultimate Reality in terms of a personal or, in the case of Christianity, even a tripersonal God. Yet, as I shall try to make clear in the early chapters of this book, implicit both in the theology of Thomas Aquinas and, above all, in the mystical tradition of Christianity as represented by Meister Eckhart is the notion of the nature of God or the Godhead which is not itself a person but rather the ground or dynamic source of the personal being of God. Furthermore, the Godhead or the divine nature, I will argue, can be likened in its operation to the way in which creativity and the extensive continuum operate within the philosophical scheme of Whitehead. This is especially evident when one rethinks Whitehead's notion of God in explicitly trinitarian terms as I do in Chapter 4 of this book. No reference will be made in this book to the mystical traditions of Judaism and Islam although my limited reading in medieval Kabbalah and in the writings of Ibn 'Arabi allows me to conclude that the extension of my hypothesis to these other theistic religions would be at least prima facie plausible.

As we shall see in Chapter 7, however, classical Buddhism seems to resist analysis and classification in terms of my hypothesis, if only because the Buddha himself and his perhaps most celebrated commentator Nagarjuna refused to engage in metaphysical speculation about the nature of Ultimate Reality. Theirs was the purely pragmatic task of helping people to see through the illusions of this world (above all, illusions generated by metaphysical speculation about the ultimate causes of things, life after death, etc.) and thus to attain a deeper sense of peace in simply accepting reality for what it is, namely, as something dynamic and creative but for that same reason transitory and insubstantial. Yet at least some of the writings inspired by the teachings of the Buddha and certainly the *Mula-madhyamakakarika* of Nagarjuna, I shall argue, allow for a metaphysical reinterpretation in terms of creativity. That is, the deeper reason why life should be seen as dynamic and ever-changing is that all forms of life are short-lived manifestations of creativity. Yet, since creativity is thus presented as an *activity* immanent within the world, not as an *entity* transcendent of the world, it escapes in my judgment the critique of the Buddha and Nagarjuna vis-à-vis traditional metaphysical claims to knowledge of suprasensible Reality. Furthermore, as I shall point out in the latter half of the chapter, Kitaro Nishida, the founder of the Kyoto School of Zen Buddhist philosophy, seems to end up describing Ultimate Reality in terms which bear a distinct resemblance to the Whiteheadian notions of creativity and the extensive continuum.

Still another group of philosophers who resist any and all attempts at metaphysical analysis of Ultimate Reality are the Advaita Vedantins who by and large follow the lead of the celebrated Indian philosopher Shankara in his interpretation of the Hindu Upanishads. For them, *Brahman* (or the One) is the Infinite and thus beyond all human comprehension. Hence, to speak of it as an underlying ontological activity which is actual only in its manifestations is to render it finite and other than itself. Thus understood as a dynamic reality, it may perhaps be regarded as *saguna Brahman* or *Brahman* with attributes, but it cannot be made equivalent to *nirguna Brahman* or *Brahman* without attributes which corresponds to the true reality of *Brahman* as the Infinite. Admonitions such as these remind theoretically oriented individuals like myself that we are in the end working with models, not pictures, of Ultimate Reality. Models, as Ian Barbour comments, should be taken seriously but not literally.[10] That is, they offer valuable insights into the reality of that which for various reasons defies exact description and analysis, but they distort the reality under consideration if they are made equivalent to it after the manner of a photograph or picture. Hence, my representation of creativity as an underlying ontological activity which is actual only in its instantiations is at best a weak analogy for the true reality of the Infinite, which is by definition fully immanent within and yet totally transcendent of any and all finite reality.

And yet, when one seeks to understand how one and the same reality can be both immanent within and transcendent of all forms of determinate reality, what better model is at hand than the notion of an underlying activity which is actual only in its instantiations? For, as an energy source or principle of activity, it must be immanent within the entities which it thus empowers to exist. But, precisely because it is immanent as a principle of activity within all of them, it is equally transcendent of them all as well. It both is and is not each of the entities in which it exists. In this sense, it seems to correspond to the notion of non-dualism which is so prominent in philosophical elaborations of Hinduism, Buddhism and Taoism. David Loy analyzes in detail non-dual perception, non-dual action, and non-dual thinking and concludes that in each case the initial duality of the subject-object relationship has been overcome.[11] Yet, if there is such a non-dual experience of pure perception or sentience, for example, what does one therein experience if not an activity which is somehow foundational to both the subject and the object of perception? That is, prior to the realization that I have just heard a loud noise, there is simply the experience of noise apart from any reference to myself or the external reality causing the noise. This noise-making activity is the dynamic link between the subject and the object in the act of perception and thus transcends both of them even as it is immanent in both of them. Even more obviously, non-dual action takes place only when the doer becomes totally absorbed in the action which he or she is performing, and non-dual thinking occurs when thoughts are allowed to well up spontaneously from the depths of the unconscious. In each case, therefore, the duality of subject and object is transcended only in terms of identification with an underlying activity common to both subject and object.

Students of Advaita Vedanta, no doubt, will here object that *Brahman* as Infinite Being is totally at rest and thus devoid of any and all activity (*kriya*). In my first chapter, I try to anticipate this objection through careful analysis of Aristotle's understanding of motion and infinity and of potentiality and actuality in the *Physics* and *Metaphysics*. Motion for Aristotle is eternal and continuous since motion would be presupposed in the absolute beginning of motion or its total cessation. Yet, as something eternal and continuous, motion is somehow infinite since it has no intrinsic limits. Admittedly, Aristotle primarily had in mind here the unending motion of the outermost celestial sphere. But I shall argue that this same implicit sense of infinity likewise applies to all immanent operations or activities (*energeiai*) which are self-contained and thus constitute an entelechy (*entelecheia*) or self-per-petuating reality. Like the "thinking on thinking" characteristic of the Unmoved Mover in Aristotle's cosmology, these self-contained immanent operations have no intrinsic limits and thus exercise a type of infinity.

Furthermore, simply as ongoing activities, they are invariably experi-enced as present rather than past or future. There is, in other words, no *before* or *after* in the perception of such activities but only a continuous *now* as long as one remains absorbed in the experience itself. Awareness of past and future enters into consciousness only when the experience of ongoing activity is at least momentarily interrupted and one reflects on what has happened. Finally, as a continuous or an uninterrupted reality in the present, an immanent activity (like seeing or hearing) is paradoxically experienced as permanent and unchanging. In this sense, such an activity can be just as readily described as either a state of being or as a state of becoming. Continuous becoming is a state of being; continuous being is a type of becoming. To generalize from this experience of immanent or self-contained activity within human life, then, one may say that Infinite "Be-ing" and Infinite "Becom-ing" are in the end only nominally distinct from one another. Both seem to imply a universal immanent activity, namely, the activity of existing, which is in itself eternal and continuous and is actual or determinate only in specific beings and various instances of becoming.[12]

Still another link between the notion of infinity and ongoing activity is to be found in reflection on the centuries-old problem of the One and the Many. Is the Infinite to be identified with the One or the Many? As we will see in Chapter 1, Aristotle believes that nothing exists with an infinite number of parts. For, if each of the parts is finite, then their sum must likewise be finite. Hence, the Infinite must somehow be identified with the One. But is the One as a result a transcendent entity or a transcendent activity? If the Infinite be identified with a single, all-encompassing entity, then logically monism results since all plurality is ultimately an illusion (as the Advaita Vedantins claim). On the other hand, if the Infinite is a tran-scendent activity which empowers specific entities to exist in themselves and to be related to one another, then, as already noted, non-dualism results. For the transcendent activity both is and is not the entities in which it is instantiated. Likewise, the entities both are and are not identified with one another since they all originate from this foundational activity and yet are ontologically separate from one another.

These remarks, however, are only intended to introduce the argument of this book, not to settle it. In subsequent chapters I will argue the matter much more closely in terms of classic texts and their possible reinterpretation in the light of my hypothesis. In closing, I would only note that, while this hypothesis is clearly based upon a process-oriented understanding of reality, it is not simply a vindication of Whitehead's philosophy as the hermeneutical tool for understanding the various world religions presented in this book. As already noted above, I am offering an interpretation of the notions of creativity and the extensive continuum within Whitehead's philosophical scheme with which many Whiteheadians would not agree, if only because Whitehead himself cannot be cited in support of it. Hence, what I have done in this book is in line with Neville's methodology for comparative theology: namely, to abstract a pair of categories from one intellectual tradition, free them (as far as possible) from the particularities or constrictions of that same tradition, and then use them as a hermeneutical tool for comparing and contrasting the different understandings of Ultimate Reality within the various world religions.

The results will inevitably be highly tentative and subject to major qualification by experts in the various religions or world views thus analyzed. But dialogue between representatives of those same philosophical and theological traditions may thus be indirectly fostered even as they one and all insist that the interpretive scheme presented in these pages does not quite fit the religion or world view with which they themselves are affiliated or in any case are most familiar. This is, after all, to be expected. Even within a given religious tradition, there are almost as many experiences of the divine as there are worshipers. Yet this does not prevent individuals within each of those traditions from recognizing one another as devotees of the same deity, members of the same sect, in that they all use the same symbols and practice the same rituals. In similar fashion, within contemporary interreligious dialogue much would be gained if individuals could recognize that many of the same basic thought-patterns and/or structures of intelligibility seem to be analogously at work in their respective religious traditions despite obvious specific differences in concrete symbols for the divine and patterns of religious worship. The present book is intended as a preliminary and therefore highly tentative effort to foster conversation in that direction.

time, the divine act of knowing us (and the rest of creation) is constitutive of our finite act of knowing God. One and the same divine act of knowing, accordingly, undergirds both God's knowledge of us and our knowledge of God.[6] From Neo-Platonism, on the other hand, Eckhart derives the doctrine of participation when he affirms that not only to be called but also to be the "Son of God" implies that "we shall be exactly what he is, the same being and the same sensibility and intelligence."[7] But, notes Schürmann, Eckhart here oversteps the traditional understanding of the doctrine of participation since by implication he eliminates the ontological difference between God and human beings. Both the eternal "Son of God" and the human being exist in virtue of one and the same divine act of filiation.[8]

Admittedly, we humans do not realize that we are one and the same being with the "Son of God." This is because our minds are preoccupied with representations of sensible things and their related concepts. But, says Eckhart, there is within the mind "a spark of the intellectual power which is never quenched. This spark is the higher part of the spirit."[9] In virtue of this spark, we attain interior knowledge that "[i]n this life all things are one, they are all together all in all, and all united to all."[10] Just as in this life the various organs of the body in different ways contribute to and share in the life of the total organism, so in the mystical body of Christ in heaven all share in the grace of Mary and the saints as if it were their own. All this happens because in the divine Spirit or "Holy Spirit" the faithful have "the identical being and the identical substance and nature" as the eternal "Son of God" and are thus related to "God the Father" as co-equal "Sons of God."[11]

In the remainder of the sermon, Eckhart exhorts his listeners to shake off attachment to the things of this world, above all, attachment to the self with all its petty concerns and anxieties about self-preservation. On the contrary, one must realize that apart from God one's whole being, indeed, the entire world of creation, is sheer nothingness. One must accept this nothingness of self and the world before God in order "to be transported into the naked being of God, the pure being of the Spirit."[12] Those who are still preoccupied with themselves, still filled with anxiety over the events taking place in this world, have not yet achieved, of course, this spiritual rebirth into the Kingdom of heaven where they will be one being with the "Son of God." But they should take heart because eventually they, too, will achieve full identification with the "Son of God."[13]

In his commentary, Schürmann weaves together citations from this sermon and others related to the same theme in order to reconstruct what seems to be Eckhart's implicit ontology here. He first takes note of the fact that Eckhart distinguishes between the mind with its faculties of knowing and willing and the being or ground of the mind: "'Being,' 'image of God,' 'ground' (*Grunt*), 'abyss' (*Abgrunt*, *Ungrunt*), or 'essence' of the mind': all these words designate the same region of man, eternally at rest, where the mind is closer to God than to the faculties, closer to God than to itself or to

PART I

Eckhart's early period, while focusing on these German sermons which he gives his due. Furthermore, Bernard McGinn, another expert in the mystical theology of Meister Eckhart, comes to many of the same conclusions as Schürmann in his analysis of key texts. McGinn points out, for example, that in German Sermon 6 *iudicium* or *urteil*...

1

Motion and Infinity in the Philosophy of Aristotle

If the question were raised, which is the prior reality, processes or things, most of us would have trouble making up our minds. For, all around us in the world of nature, processes are at work to produce the environment in which we live. Yet we also daily experience that living "things" like ourselves both initiate and terminate processes. As we shall see below, Aristotle, perhaps the first great systematic thinker in the Western philosophical tradition, evidently thought that things are prior to processes. For he sought to explain motion or process in terms of a series of "movers" rather than the series of movers in terms of an underlying motion or process common to them all. From his perspective, whatever is in motion has to be moved by an antecedent cause. Ultimately, that antecedent cause is a transcendent Unmoved Mover which through an elaborate series of intermediaries accounts for all the movement and activity in the world. Furthermore, as we shall see in Chapter 2, this same line of thought was carried forward by Thomas Aquinas in his attempt to provide a philosophical understanding of the God-world relationship. Likewise, with some notable exceptions, philosophers trained in the tradition of Aristotle and Aquinas have accepted unquestioningly the axiom that things are ontologically prior to processes. *Agere sequitur esse.* The activity proper to an entity flows from its antecedent nature or essence, not vice versa.

At the same time, there are indications of the opposite point of view in Aristotle's writings. He declares, for example, that motion in itself (that is, apart from individual entities in motion) is eternal and continuous because motion must be presupposed in moving from a state of rest to a state of movement and vice versa. Likewise, he defines the supreme entity within his metaphysical scheme, namely, the Unmoved Mover, not as a fixed reality but as the subject of an ongoing activity or process, namely, a "thinking on thinking." The presupposition of such an ongoing process, however, raises the question of infinity. Aristotle himself claims that processes are potentially infinite because they are indeterminate, that is, because they can be repeated indefinitely. Entities, on the other hand, are necessarily finite because they are determinate actualities here and now. Yet what is to be said of a process that is by definition eternal and continuous like "thinking on thinking"? Is it still only potentially infinite? Or does it have an actual infinity here and now simply as a process because it has no intrinsic limits, no beginning or end?

These and similar questions will be raised again and again as we undertake this analysis of motion and infinity within Aristotle's philosophy. As I shall make clear in the second part of this chapter, my intention here will be speculative, not historical. That is, I will not try to prove what Aristotle himself had in mind on the subject of motion and infinity but rather to set forth a revisionist understanding of his doctrine through careful reflection on various pertinent texts. In this way, we will be better prepared for a critical evaluation of Aquinas's theology in Chapter 2 since, as noted above, it is heavily based on Aristotle's philosophy.

Ivor Leclerc comments in *The Nature of Physical Existence* that the history of the concept of infinity did not begin with Aristotle, but that he made the first systematic analysis of the concept while taking into account the work of his predecessors.[1] Furthermore, given the extraordinary influence which Aristotle had upon Aquinas and the subsequent history of Western philosophy, it makes good sense to begin our treatment of the subject of infinity with Aristotle's analysis in Book III of the *Physics*. He introduces the notion of infinity within a broader study of the nature of motion. Motion, as he says at the very beginning of Book III, "is supposed to belong to the class of things which are *continuous*; and the *infinite* presents itself first in the continuous—that is how it comes about that 'infinite' is often used in definitions of the continuous ('what is infinitely divisible is continuous')."[2] Thus the infinite for Aristotle is associated from the beginning with what is continuous or, as he says later on, with "a process of coming to be or passing away; definite if you like at each stage, yet always different."[3]

His arguments with his predecessors, moreover, focused precisely on this point: namely, that the infinite is not itself an entity or an attribute of an entity; it is rather a process, a reality which is not yet fully actual. It is not an entity because every entity is determinate whereas the infinite is by definition indeterminate, unbounded.[4] Aristotle, to be sure, is thinking here of the infinite primarily in bodily terms as if it were a physical existent. But it is likewise true of purely spiritual entities like the Unmoved Mover within his cosmology.[5] They, too, as entities are determinate. Nor is the infinite to be understood in terms of extension, since this would imply an infinitely extended material reality which for Aristotle is a contradiction in terms. Everything bodily has boundaries and is thus finite. Even if one were to conceive the infinite as a compound being with an infinite number of parts, questions arise. For, if each of the parts is itself finite, then how can there be an infinite number of parts? In principle, each of the parts is numerable and their aggregate, accordingly, must likewise be finite.[6] Only hypothetical existents such as the non-sensible Void of the Pythagoreans would seem to be indeterminate and therefore infinite. But Aristotle strenuously argues against the existence of a Void separate from the bodies presumed to exist within it.[7]

Aristotle concludes, therefore, that there are no actual infinites but only potential infinites, i.e., processes which can be indefinitely extended.[8] His examples here basically have to do with division or addition of spatial magnitudes. One can always conceive of an increment to any given spatial magnitude, just as one can equally well conceive of a further division of a given spatial magnitude. This does not mean, of course, that a given physical body has an actually infinite number of parts, but only that any physical body by reason of its extension can always be further subdivided or receive a further increment in size. The increments or subdivisions are always finite in number. But the activity or process of adding or dividing can in principle go on indefinitely, *ad infinitum*. At any given moment, the activity or process results in a finite reality, e.g., a given number of parts for a physical body. But the process itself is potentially infinite, since it can be repeated over and over again.

Yet, as noted above, what is to be said about a process or activity which, at least in theory, is ongoing, never ending? Is it potentially infinite or actually infinite? Since it never terminates in a final product but only achieves successive stages of actualization, it would seem to be actually infinite, not indeed as an entity, but simply as a process or form of activity. It has no intrinsic limits but in principle could continue in its mode of existence indefinitely. In Book IX of the *Metaphysics*, for example, Aristotle distinguishes between movements in the strict sense which terminate in some extrinsic end to be achieved (such as a house to be constructed) and activities which contain their own end (such as seeing whose only object or end is the very act of seeing). Such a self-contained activity Aristotle terms an *actuality* in distinction from a *potentiality*.[9] Admittedly, through this choice of words he seems to transfer attention from the activity itself to the subject of the activity (from the act of seeing, for example, to the one who exercises the act of seeing). Furthermore, in thus focusing on the finite entity which exercises the activity, Aristotle never really addresses the question whether a continuous or ongoing activity like seeing is not just potentially but rather actually infinite, without intrinsic limits. For, as already noted, there is no intrinsic reason why seeing as a self-contained activity should not be continued indefinitely. Only the organism's need for sleep at intervals would bring about an interruption in the act of seeing, but this need on the part of the human or animal subject is extrinsic to the act itself of seeing.

In Book VIII of the *Physics*, it is likewise unclear whether Aristotle is talking about entities in motion or the reality of movement, taken by itself. For Aristotle there argues that "motion" must be eternal and continuous because motion would already be presupposed in moving from an antecedent state of rest to a state of motion or from a state of motion to a subsequent state of rest.[10] On the one hand, the way in which he introduces the question at the beginning of Book VIII makes clear that he is trying to formulate an ontological principle with respect to the nature of reality:

> Was there ever a becoming of motion before which it had no being, and is it perishing again so as to leave nothing in motion? Or are we to say that it never had any becoming and is not perishing, but always was and always will be? Is it in fact an immortal never-failing property of things that are, a sort of life as it were to all naturally constituted things?[11]

On the other hand, from a careful reading of Book VIII it is equally clear that his attention is directed, not to the existence of unending motion in itself but to its explanation in terms of a series of movers terminating in an eternal Unmoved Mover.[12] Here too, as in the discussion of the distinction between movements which terminate in a final product and activities which contain their own end, Aristotle seems to direct his attention away from motion itself to the entity that is moved or that moves another. It is as if he antecedently decided to explain motion in terms of a series of movers rather than the series of movers in terms of an underlying motion common to them all. We will deal with this question of the ontological priority of movers to motion (or vice versa) more explicitly in the second half of the chapter. For now, I only wish to point out what seem to be residual ambiguities in Aristotle's analysis of movement and infinity.

In his celebrated definition of motion in Book III of the *Physics*, for example, Aristotle likewise never makes clear whether he is ultimately talking about an entity in motion or the motion of an entity. Motion, he says, is "the fulfilment of what exists potentially, insofar as it exists potentially. . . . When the buildable, insofar as it is just *that*, is fully real, it is *being built*, and this is build*ing*. Similarly, learning, doctoring, rolling, leaping, ripening, ageing."[13] Is Aristotle referring here to the half-built house or to the activity of building? The term "build*ing*" would seem to refer to the process or movement itself, but the term "being built" presumably refers to the entity under construction. Otherwise stated, what is it according to the definition that exists both potentially and actually at the same time? Clearly the half-built house is simply an actuality even in its incomplete state. Only the activity would seem to be the dynamic reality called for by the definition, that is, a process which is passing through successive stages of actualization in which each new actualization immediately serves as the potentiality for the next stage of actualization. Furthermore, it would seem more logical that Aristotle should define motion in terms of an ongoing process rather than in terms of an incomplete entity.[14]

Aristotle, to be sure, seems to urge the opposite point of view in Book VI of the *Physics*: "no process of change is infinite: for every change, whether between contradictories or between contraries, is a change from something to something."[15] But, in thus looking at the terms of the movement, its beginning and end point, has Aristotle effectively spatialized motion and thereby reified it? That is, does he implicitly give more attention to the *potential discontinuity* of motion, namely, its divisibility into discrete units, than to its *actual continuity* here and now? Put another way, the actual experience of motion would seem to be that of a unitary, continuous reality. Yet reflection on or analysis of motion tends to break it up into discrete units, movement from here to there or from there to here.

In one passage, Aristotle even says that one would not be aware of motion except for the obvious change of place of a body which is itself not changing.[16] But here, too, one may ask whether the experience of motion can be reduced to seeing a body now in one place, now in another place. In principle, there may have been no motion there at all but instead the creation and destruction of a body in one place and its replacement in terms of another body looking very much the same in still another place. The actual experience of motion would have to be of something happening between the two points, something, indeed, of a unitary or continuous character which spans the difference between the two points.

Henri Bergson, writing in *Matter and Memory*, may be of assistance here. Noting how a movement from A to B is inwardly experienced as a continuous flow and yet how that same movement can be mentally divided into a juxtaposition of successive points, he concludes:

> [B]y the very fact that you represent the movement to yourself successively in these different points, you necessarily arrest it in each of them; your successive positions are, at bottom, only so many imaginary halts. You substitute the path for the journey, and because the journey is subtended by the path you think that the two coincide. But how should a *progress* coincide with a *thing*, a movement with an immobility.[17]

Bergson, accordingly, distinguishes between *intelligence* and *intuition* as two related but nevertheless distinct ways of knowing: "Intelligence starts ordinarily from the immobile, and reconstructs movement as best it can with immobilities in juxtaposition. Intuition starts from movement, posits it, or rather perceives it as reality itself, and sees in immobility only an abstract moment, a snapshot taken by our mind, of a mobility."[18]

With his description of motion in largely spatial terms as the passage from one point to another and with his focus on the entity in motion rather than on the motion itself, Aristotle seems to be using intelligence rather than intuition for the analysis of motion. Yet intuition may also be present in his definition of motion as the fulfilment or actuality of what exists potentially, insofar as it exists potentially, provided that one thinks of it as the description of a process rather than as the description of an incomplete entity.

Furthermore, Aristotle encounters the same ambivalence of perspective in his analysis of time, above all, of the present moment. "But we apprehend time only when we have marked motion, marking it by 'before' and 'after'; and it is only when we have perceived 'before' and 'after' in motion that we say that time has elapsed."[19] Thus time, like motion of which it is the measure, is initially experienced as a continuous, unbroken reality. But, when one reflects on time, becomes aware of its passage, then it is divisible into quantitatively discrete units, into a succession of indivisible "nows" which are different from one another. Time as continuous, then, would seem to be the intermediate or "substratum" between the two discrete moments or "nows." But, one may ask, what is experienced within the "now"? Certainly, one cannot experience motion in terms of *before* and *after* within the "now." For, this would break up the original "now" into two "sub-nows" and these, in turn, into still further "sub-nows" *ad infinitum*. Logically, therefore, within each "now," as well as between separate "nows," one should experience continuity, motion which is not distinguished by *before* and *after* but which is present to the observer as a unitary reality.

Aristotle's subsequent discussion of the "present" or the "moment" in Book VI of the *Physics* would seem to throw some light on this issue. As he comments, "the present is something that is an extremity of the past (no part of the future being on this side of it) and also of the future (no part of the past being on the other side of it): it is, as we have said, a limit of both."[20] The present is continuous with both the past and the future; it is their common boundary. But what is it in itself, if not motion before the division into *before* and *after*? It cannot be something static since it is an integral part of the motion from the past into the future. It must be something dynamic but without parts or a division into *before* and *after*. It is the purest experience of motion, namely, as infinite or unlimited in terms of boundaries, without beginning or end. Some might argue that this is an experience of eternity, not time. But perhaps the experience of eternity, at least in this life, is nothing more than the experience of the unending flow of time in the present, before the reflective awareness of *before* and *after*. Or, otherwise stated, the human experience of eternity is the experience of activity without a feeling of locomotion, transition from here to there; it is a sense of being passive (or at rest) and active (or in motion) at the same time.[21]

In Book VIII of the *Physics*, Aristotle notes that "of the three kinds of motion that there are—motion in respect of magnitude, motion in respect of affection, and motion in respect of place—it is this last, which we call locomotion, that must be primary."[22] Yet in that same discourse he also claims that the perfect form of locomotion is circular motion, since it alone is continuous and eternal.[23] Ongoing circular motion, however, is likewise an example of what I have just referred to as an activity which is simultaneously in motion and at rest; it is, therefore, at the same time both a state of being and a form of becoming. Since it never deviates from its predetermined orbit, circular motion is a state of being; it has achieved its complete reality (*entelecheia*) or actuality (*energeia*) as a circle.[24] Yet it is never in the same place in successive moments; hence, it is also a form of becoming or progressive self-actualization.

Furthermore, if we now attend to Aristotle's doctrine of the Unmoved Mover, that which through final causality produces this circular motion of the outermost celestial sphere, we note the same ambiguity in Aristotle's understanding of a self-contained activity (*entelecheia*) or actuality (*energeia*) as above. On the one hand, Aristotle claims that the activity of the Unmoved Mover, namely, a "thinking on thinking," is unchanging since "change would be change for the worse, and this would already be a movement."[25] In Aristotle's mind, accordingly, change or movement from potentiality to actuality is to be avoided because it implies the possibility of a cessation or at least an alteration of that same activity. But, on the other hand, if a self-contained activity like "thinking on thinking" is to remain an activity and not become an entity or fixed reality (in this case, an idea or thought), then, as I see it, it must be continually self-actualizing. That is, it must be continually moving from potentiality to actuality in the exercise of its predetermined form of activity. Similarly, the Unmoved Mover, as the subject of such an ongoing act of self-reflection, is less an actuality in the sense of a fixed reality than an hypostatized activity; that is, its being or *ousia* is pure self-actualizing activity.

John Herman Randall argues that being (*ousia*), insofar as it is the outcome or product of prior activity, is ultimately secondary in Aristotle's mind to being as itself a form of activity. But this would seem to imply that individual beings are best understood as subsistent forms of activity.[26] Their "being-ness," in other words, consists not so much in being fixed or static realities but rather in being subjects of ongoing activities and thus dynamic realities. In that case, however, one may suitably ask two questions. First of all, should Ultimate Reality for Aristotle be an entity, namely, the Unmoved Mover on whom all else depends for its movement or activity? Or should it rather be a universal underlying activity on whom all entities, even the Unmoved Mover, depend for their individual existence and activity? Secondly, if this be admitted as possible, should Aristotle not have allowed for an actual Infinite within his philosophy, namely, the infinity of that same universal underlying activity on whom all entities, all determinate realities (including the Unmoved Mover), ultimately depend?

In this second part of the chapter, I will try to answer these two questions. My argument, as noted above, will be speculative rather than historical. That is, I will not be seeking to prove that Aristotle himself implicitly espoused the hypothesis which I will set forward. Rather, I will simply try to establish that this revisionist approach to Aristotle's metaphysics clears up some of the ambiguities in his analysis of motion and infinity in the *Physics* and *Metaphysics*. I will begin with Aristotle's discussion of the first principles of nature in Book I of the *Physics*.

He argues that change or becoming is invariably a passage between contraries in virtue of a common substrate.[27] That is, the principles of becoming are not simply matter and form, since matter and form are, strictly speaking, not contraries. Rather, formless matter or matter without form is opposed to matter as shaped by some intelligible form. Thus matter is the common substrate for the passage from potentiality, a state of privation of form, to full actuality, the state of being already formed. But what is matter itself, the common substrate? Aristotle is not very clear on this point. Matter is not one of the four primitive "elements" (earth, air, fire, and water) nor a combination thereof. Likewise, it is not one of the contrarieties (e.g., hot and cold).[28] Elsewhere he defines matter as "the primary substratum of each thing, from which it comes to be without qualification, and which persists in the result."[29] It is that which in some sense exists before the particular entity comes into being and that which persists after it ceases to be.

But, if that is the case, one may conjecture that the most suitable candidate for the reality of "matter" within Aristotle's system of categories is motion itself. For, as already noted, Aristotle himself claims that motion is eternal and continuous: "there never was a time when there was not motion, and never will be a time when there will not be motion."[30] Admittedly, as noted above, Aristotle was specifically thinking here of the movement of the outermost celestial sphere. But, as Randall comments, what Aristotle is trying to establish on the level of ontological principle is that "[m]otion has no efficient cause. Nothing 'makes' motion in general take place. Motion in general is uncaused and eternal."[31] Furthermore, if motion in general is not just an abstract concept but a universal underlying reality, and if it is in itself formless or without determination, then it would seem to bear a close resemblance to what Aristotle means by prime matter.

At least two objections to this hypothesis immediately come to mind. First of all, from his own examples in discussing the four causes, Aristotle clearly has in mind with the notion of matter some material reality (e.g., "the bronze of the statue, the silver of the bowl"[32]) out of which an artifact is produced through the activity of a craftsman. The material reality is thus inert and passive, that which receives a form through the action of an external cause. Yet, as Aristotle himself concedes, the notion of matter has to be broader than simply the "stuff" out of which things are made. It must also serve as the substrate for the other types of change in nature such as the generation and corruption of living beings. Hence, in its broadest description matter is simply "an underlying something, namely that which becomes," and which, "though always one numerically, in form at least is not one."[33] Motion, however, meets this broader definition of matter quite well. It does indeed "become" in the sense that it undergoes successive stages of actualization. Likewise, it is numerically one, even though it always appears under different forms, depending upon the entity in which it is embodied.

Yet one may further object that for Aristotle motion is much more properly associated with form than with matter. Form is, to be sure, in Aristotle's mind closely associated with motion. But it is associated with motion as that which gives a particular pattern or shape to motion: "what we seek is the cause, i.e., the form, by reason of which the matter [i.e., motion] is some definite thing."[34] Moreover, form is not itself the source of motion since motion by definition has no beginning or end; it is simply an empirical given. Thus motion (as "matter") is in itself formless. It is that which is given shape or structure by form.

There is, of course, never a state in which there is simply motion without form. All motion is motion of an entity which already has some form but which is in process of gaining a new form or further actualizing the form which it already has. Yet here, too, we must ask which is ontologically prior: the entity or the motion. In individual cases, it is obvious that the entity first exists and then engages in some form of activity. But, if Aristotle is correct in affirming that motion in general is eternal and continuous, then motion is ontologically prior to the entities in which it exists. Entities, after all, come into existence and cease to be; motion by definition endures forever. Motion, therefore, is the principle or cause for the existence of entities, not vice versa. Yet, as noted above, motion never exists in itself apart from entities. It is the cause of entities in that it is the internal principle for the existence and activity of those same entities. If it existed apart from entities as their external cause, then it would be itself another kind of entity and one would have to ask what causes it to exist. The search for an ultimate first cause only comes to an end when one locates that first cause in an immanent principle of activity within all entities rather than in some transcendent entity, as we shall see more in detail in the next two chapters.

In brief, then, while motion always exists in terms of persons who act and things that are moved, those same persons and things are the end point or result of antecedent activities and the starting point or origin of subsequent activities. Thus motion in some form or other is eternal and continuous, while persons and things are inevitably time bound and discontinuous. Even those persons and things which seem to be relatively unchanging and continuous through space and time are still experiencing motion all the time in one of the ways described by Aristotle: i.e., in terms of locomotion, qualitative change or quantitative change. They are continuously the end point of antecedent activities and the starting point of subsequent activities which together constitute a continuum or unitary reality. Only change in the strict sense, that is, the corruption of one substance and the generation of another, involves a break in continuity. But, even here, the activities which resulted in the corruption of the one substance merge with the activities which result in the generation of the subsequent entity or entities. Thus continuity is assured even in the midst of discontinuity because of the common substrate which, as I see it, is motion as such.

Hence, contrary to what might be an initial negative impression, motion could well be seen as "the underlying something" or "matter" within Aristotle's metaphysical scheme. This is not to say, of course, that Aristotle himself implicitly had motion in mind when setting forth his notion of matter. In all likelihood, he had nothing specific in mind on that topic; he only knew that logically there had to be an "underlying something" in terms of which entities could change form or in some other way undergo change. As a matter of fact, it was probably his bias in favor of entities as the principles of explanation for change that prevented him from accepting the implications of his own dictum that motion is eternal or continuous. That is, because he tended to explain change in terms of a series of Movers which move entities but are themselves moved by still other entities, he missed the more obvious conclusion that all these entities in their activity presuppose that which they are supposed to explain, namely, motion itself as an empirical given.

To establish this point, let us now look briefly at Aristotle's proofs for the eternity of motion and for the existence of an eternal Unmoved Mover in Book VIII of the *Physics*. In Chapter 1, he argues that motion must be eternal and continuous because motion would already be presupposed in moving from an antecedent state of rest to a state of motion or from a state of motion to a subsequent state of rest.[35] Then, having disposed of various objections to this hypothesis in Chapter 2, Aristotle shifts his attention in Chapter 3 and following chapters to the fact of motion in individual entities and asks himself what causes a particular motion in this or that entity. Since it is axiomatic with him that whatever is in motion requires an explanation for its movement,[36] he cannot simply say that one thing moved another through physical contact; he has to question further what caused the initial mover itself to be moved so as to move the other entity. This line of thinking inevitably leads him to establish an ontological hierarchy of moved movers, terminating in the postulate of an eternal Unmoved Mover which moves other entities without itself being moved.[37]

Thus, in pursuing an explanation of motion in terms of its entitative causes, that is, in terms of movers and things moved, Aristotle distances himself psychologically from his own dictum that motion is a self-perpetuating or ongoing reality. That is, motion should be its own explanation in that it is eternal and continuous. Nothing brings it into being and nothing can cause it to cease to be. All that requires explanation is the particular form of movement, and this is accounted for in terms of the way that entities by their interaction with one another either perpetuate an already existing form of activity or generate a new form (or forms) of activity.

Further examination of Aristotle's doctrine of the eternal Unmoved Mover makes clear the difference between these two rival explanations of the fact of change. Aristotle argues in the *Physics* that even things that move themselves, such as living organisms, do not move themselves as a whole, since the whole organism would thus simultaneously both undergo and cause a given movement. Rather, "when a thing moves itself it is one part of it that is the movent and another part that is moved."[38] But, since every temporal "movent" is itself moved in moving something else,[39] there must be a primary eternal "movent" which remains unmoved even as it moves directly the outermost celestial sphere and indirectly everything else. What is critical for Aristotle's argument here is that an entity, the eternal Unmoved Mover, is needed to account for the fact of eternal and continuous motion in the world around us.

Using the opposite starting point, however, namely, that motion is self-explanatory and that entities are to be explained in terms of their participation in the reality of motion, then, one could just as well argue that the eternal Unmoved Mover is both the primordial instance of the fact of motion and the concrete exemplar or ideal for every other form of motion in the world.[40] Prima facie, of course, this would seem to be contradictory; the eternal Unmoved Mover cannot be itself an instance of motion. But this fails to account for what Aristotle says about the reality of the Unmoved Mover in the *Metaphysics*. The eternal Unmoved Mover is there described as a "thinking on thinking."[41] As noted above, "thinking on thinking" is an immanent or strictly self-contained activity (*entelecheia*) or actuality (*energeia*). The Unmoved Mover, accordingly, is to be understood as the ongoing subject of the never-ending activity of self-reflection.

Which, however, is the prior reality: the activity of self-reflection or the Unmoved Mover as the ongoing subject of that activity? Evidently, they cannot be separated. But, insofar as the total being of the Unmoved Mover is a "thinking on thinking," one must say that the activity of self-reflection is the prior reality; for it is the ontological ground or vital source for the existence of the Unmoved Mover as the subject of that activity. In Chapter 3, I will make clear how this notion of ground or vital source is different from the concept of cause. Entities stand in causal relationship to one another and as such are ontologically distinct from one another. But the ground or vital source of an entity is its nature or interior principle of existence and activity. As such, it cannot be separated from the entity which it thereby empowers to exist. Yet as its dynamic principle of existence and activity the ground or vital source is ontologically prior to the entity as an existent. From that perspective, the Unmoved Mover, while uncaused by another entity, is nevertheless an instance of motion or activity. It exists in virtue of the ongoing activity of self-reflection.

In comparing these two quite different explanations of the fact of change or process, one is forcefully reminded of Martin Heidegger's claim that the history of Western metaphysics is the history of the forgetfulness of the distinction between being and beings.[42] For, Aristotle appears to be explaining being or activity in terms of beings, that is, already existing things. That is, he explains activity or movement in terms of a series of movers and things moved which culminates in the postulate of an eternal Unmoved Mover. It is the eternal Unmoved Mover which by its existence ultimately accounts for the reality of motion in all other things. My alternative explanation of the dynamic character of reality, on the other hand, explains beings, including the primordial being, the Unmoved Mover, in terms of being itself (understood as universal process or activity). Being as process is thus primary, not beings, not even the Supreme Being.

Is there, then, no God in Aristotle's philosophy? Is it in effect an atheistic system of thought? First of all, one should realize, as W. D. Ross points out, that Aristotle's eternal Unmoved Mover bears little resemblance to the God of the Hebrew and Christian Bible. "God, as conceived by Aristotle, has a knowledge which is not knowledge of the universe, and an influence on the universe which does not flow from His knowledge; an influence which can hardly be called an activity since it is the sort of influence that one person may unconsciously have on another, or that even a statue or a picture may have on its admirer."[43] Since the eternal Unmoved Mover is simply a "thinking on thinking," it only knows itself and, unlike the God of the Hebrew and Christian Bible, has no knowledge of events taking place in this world. Nor does it exercise any providence over any of the creatures of this world since it moves other things only by being the fixed object of thought and desire, first, for the intelligence governing the outermost celestial sphere and then indirectly for all other beings as well.[44]

The absence of such a "God" from one's system of thought, accordingly, would be no great loss for one trained in the Christian tradition. The far more serious question is whether and how this alleged priority of being (understood as motion or ongoing activity) over beings (understood as the results of that activity) would likewise affect one's understanding of God as Subsistent Being in the theology of Thomas Aquinas and other specifically Christian thinkers in the Middle Ages. But this is a matter for the next two chapters. For the moment, I only wish to summarize the results of my speculative reconstruction of Aristotle's doctrine of motion and infinity in the *Physics* and add one final conclusion.

I began by taking note of the fact that for Aristotle motion belongs to the class of things which are continuous, and the infinite presents itself first as something continuous. There is, then, a linkage between motion and infinity in virtue of the common association with the continuous. Entities, on the other hand, are invariably finite and discontinuous, that is, separate from one another. Motion is what links these separate entities or separate states of the same entity together. Thus, in contrast to entities which are always finite and determinate, motion is infinite and indeterminate since it is not limited to any one entity or to any one state of the same entity. In principle, it must transcend whatever stage of actualization it has already achieved in order to remain itself as a dynamic reality rather than become an entity with a fixed reality. As Aristotle comments, it is the fulfilment or actuality of the potential insofar as it is potential, not yet fully realized.

Aristotle, to be sure, describes motion or process as potentially infinite, not actually infinite. But this is because for him the notion of an actually infinite reality appears contradictory. Any *entity* which is actual is automatically finite because its very actuality makes it finite or determinate. Motion, however, as a *process* or activity is indeed infinite, but only because it can be repeated indefinitely. Yet, in thus focusing on the discrete intermediate stages of the process, Aristotle appears to lose the dynamic reality of the process itself. As we noted above in connection with the philosophy of Henri Bergson, it is easy to miss the difference between the journey and the path. The path can be divided into a series of intermediate steps; but the journey is necessarily a continuous reality or it ceases to be motion and becomes a resting place along the way.

Hence, contrary to what Aristotle explicitly affirms, I would argue that motion not only is actual in terms of its instantiations, namely, entities in motion, but possesses its own actuality simply as a process. Furthermore, this actuality of motion, whenever it is self-contained rather than ordered to some extrinsic end, would seem to be infinite since it is in principle unbounded or continuous, without intrinsic limits. Be-ing, for example, as the self-contained activity of existing is in itself unlimited; it is limited only by the beings (entities) in which it is instantiated. As specific entities, they are necessarily finite and determinate; but the activity itself transcends all its instantiations and thus achieves an infinity here and now which is not merely potential but likewise actual. It is, however, not the fully determinate actuality of an entity but the inevitably indeterminate actuality of a process or ongoing activity (as Aristotle himself recognizes in his definition of motion as the fulfilment of a potentiality insofar as it remains a potentiality, something yet to be fully achieved). Only thus can an activity or process in contrast to an entity be both actual and infinite.[45]

Here one might object that I have thereby reified or hypostasized what is only a logical abstraction. In the end, only entities exist. One may indeed refer to their common activities (e.g., the act of existing), but this is only an empirical generalization drawn from specific instances of actual persons/things that perform certain activities. Against this objection, I would urge that this is contrary to the whole thrust of Aristotle's argument in the *Physics* and *Metaphysics*. That is, on every page of these works he is prepared to admit the existence of suprasensible principles as transcendent causes of sensible things. *Matter* and *form*, for example, evidently enjoy ontological reality within Aristotle's categoreal scheme even though they too are not entities but principles of existence and activity. Hence, if these categories are not simply logical generalizations but ontological realities within entities, why should not motion as a universal phenomenon within this world of entities likewise be accorded metaphysical status?

Furthermore, as I pointed out above, motion would seem to be functionally equivalent to what Aristotle means by *prime matter*. But, if that be the case, then motion is "the primary substratum of each thing, from which it comes to be without qualification, and which persists in the result." Hence, it is just as real as the finite entities in which it is embodied, perhaps even more real since it survives their gradual change and ultimate dissolution so as to be the primary substratum for still other finite entities. Yet, like prime matter in Aristotle's conception, it is not itself an entity but rather the dynamic source or ontological principle for the existence of entities perceptible to the senses.

Admittedly, one is dealing here with fundamental assumptions about the nature of reality, in the light of which one constructs a theoretical scheme for the interpretation of reality. One cannot, in other words, prove one's basic assumptions without becoming involved in a *petitio principii*, using one's basic assumptions to prove their antecedent existence and validity. Hence, I conclude this first chapter by noting that the assumption of motion as a universal activity which underlies the existence and activity of all determinate entities in this world will be axiomatic for me in dealing with the problem of the Infinite or Ultimate Reality in the rest of the book. At the same time, I hope to have established that this assumption takes its rise from reflection on Aristotle's own somewhat paradoxical remarks on the nature of motion and infinity in the *Physics* and *Metaphysics*.

Aristotle, for example, complained in the *Physics* that the concept of motion is hard to grasp because it does not fit readily into the categories designed for things.[46] Likewise, in another place, he complains that the Infinite is hard to comprehend because its being is not that of a substance but rather of a process of coming to be or passing away.[47] Finally, in still a third place, he argues that in the act of motion both the mover and the thing moved possess the same actuality; equivalently, then, both of these finite entities are absorbed into the overarching actuality of motion itself at that moment.[48] Perhaps if he had compared these three statements with one another more carefully, Aristotle might have avoided the postulate of an eternal Unmoved Mover to account for the reality of unending motion in the world. He might have recognized, in other words, that the true Absolute or the Infinite in his philosophical system was motion itself simply as an empirical given. Yet Aristotle may have postulated the existence of an Unmoved Mover, at least in part, because he wanted to ground the reality of this world in something Transcendent or Divine, however dimly understood. In the next two chapters, we will see how a number of Christian thinkers relying upon the insights of Aristotle into the reality of motion have addressed this same problem.

2

Being and Relations in the Theology of Thomas Aquinas

Roughly 1500 years separate the lifetimes of Aristotle and the medieval theologian Thomas Aquinas. In that interval, the contours of what has subsequently come to be known as Western civilization changed dramatically. Geographically, Aquinas lived in a much bigger world than Aristotle, for he lived and worked not only in the south of Europe but also north of the Alps in what is today Germany. Likewise culturally, Aquinas inhabited a different world. As Ivor Leclerc points out, with the passing of the era of classical Greek humanism, a new interest in the divine as utterly transcendent gripped the ancient mind.[1] Part of this interest, to be sure, was Greek in its origins. E. R. Dodds points out the striking similarities in overall world view between Christians and pagans in what he calls "the age of anxiety" in late antiquity. Both pagans and Christians, for example, expressed disdain for the body and, indeed, for life in this world as a whole.[2] Likewise, both pagans and Christians in large numbers tried to escape from the trials of this earthly life through various forms of mystical experience.[3]

Within intellectual circles, moreover, new efforts were being made to understand the relation between the transcendent divine principle and the material universe. The *Enneads* of Plotinus, for example, set forth the theory of the emanation of the material world from the immaterial One via the hypostases of the Divine Mind and the World Soul.[4] Likewise, first in Jewish and then in early Christian circles, the relation of the God of the Bible to the world of nature was philosophically analyzed. The Jewish philosopher Philo proposed that Jahweh alone is eternal and unchanging and that the mutable world of nature is, accordingly, dependent for its very existence upon the sovereign will of Jahweh.[5] Likewise, Christian thinkers like Origen and Augustine began to ponder the philosophical implications of belief in a Creator God. Origen suggested that if God is by nature a Creator God, there never was a time when God was not creative. Thus our finite world must be only one in a series of worlds created by God.[6] Augustine, on the other hand, proposed that time itself came into being with the creation of this world.[7]

Aquinas, living many centuries later, was the clear beneficiary of all this philosophical reflection on the God-world relationship at the close of the Graeco-Roman era of Western civilization. From his predecessors, he inherited unquestioning belief in God as infinite.[8] In addition, he accepted without question belief in God as Creator of heaven and earth; by that phrase he meant, of course, calling finite reality into existence out of nothing.[9] On both these counts, Aquinas differed sharply from Aristotle, who maintained, first, that all entities, even immaterial entities like the Unmoved Mover, are (in a technical sense) finite or determined in their nature and, secondly, that creation out of nothing is impossible. All coming to be and passing away presuppose an enduring substrate (namely, "prime matter") which, to be sure, does not exist in itself but is an indispensable condition for all substantial change.

In the following paragraphs, I will first set forth in greater detail Aquinas's position on the God-world relationship, above all, in terms of his key structural insight into the relationship between essence and existence both in God and in creatures. Then I will make clear what presumably would be Aristotle's objections to the introduction of this new category of existence (over and above essence) into a philosophical system otherwise remarkably similar to his own. Afterwards, in the second half of this essay, I will attempt a reconciliation of the thought of Aristotle and of Aquinas on the nature of Ultimate Reality, using my reconstruction of Aristotle's insights into the infinity of motion developed in the preceding chapter. At the same time, I will also develop a new interpretation of Aquinas's doctrine on the Trinity, in particular, his proposal that the three divine persons are, ontologically speaking, subsistent relations. In brief, I will argue that the divine persons/subsistent relations are best understood as interrelated subjects of one and the same activity, namely, the act of being understood as an ongoing conversion of potentiality into actuality.

As noted above, Aquinas took for granted that God is eternal and unchanging being and that God is Creator of heaven and earth, i.e., of everything other than God. Philosophically speaking, he expressed these convictions arising out of his Christian faith in the following manner. First, God is the only being whose essence is existence itself.[10] That is, since God is immaterial and thus not composed of matter and form, God is identical with the divine form or essence. But the divine essence is itself identical with being or the act of existence. Earlier in his exposition of this issue in the *Summa Theologica*, Aquinas had established that God is the first efficient cause of all else that exists.[11] Therefore, since no being other than God brings God into existence and since no being can bring itself into existence simply in terms of its own innate powers,[12] God's essence must be identical with existence itself. God, in a word, is uncaused being, identical with existence itself as that which is.

In effect, then, form or essence is not what is ultimately real as in the philosophy of Aristotle. Rather, form, while fully actual on the level of essence, represents potentiality on the higher level of existence. For, to be this or that form or mode of being is ultimately contingent upon a proportionate act of existence in order simply to be. Since in God there is no potentiality of any kind, it follows that God's essence is itself the fullness of the act of existence. Being in God is not limited by any essence or finite principle of determination. God is being itself and, therefore, by implication the first efficient cause of the being of all finite entities.

This brings us to Aquinas's philosophical justification of his second conviction based on the Christian world view, namely, that God is Creator of heaven and earth. He argues that, since in God alone essence and existence are identical, all other beings participate in the act of existence through the creative action of God. God, in other words, communicates to all finite beings a share in the divine being proportionate to their finite essence. Their act of existence, accordingly, is their own even as it participates in the unlimited act of existence proper to God.[13] Even "prime matter" as an essential principle of material beings is created by God in the communication of the act of being: "whatever is the cause of things considered as beings, must be the cause of things, not only according as they are *such* by accidental forms, nor according as they are *these* by substantial forms, but also according to all that belongs to their being at all in any way."[14] Contrary to Aristotle, therefore, Aquinas believes that creation is a passage from non-being (in the sense of absolute nothingness) to being as such rather than from non-being (in the sense of an underlying substrate) to being some determinate reality.[15]

In *The Spirit of Mediaeval Philosophy*, Etienne Gilson extolls the superiority of Aquinas's metaphysical scheme based on the distinction between essence and existence over the metaphysical schemes of Plato and Aristotle based on the actuality of forms or essences.[16] Because they did not have the benefit of divine revelation as given in the Hebrew and Christian Bible, of course, one would not expect them to penetrate so deeply into the reality of God and the nature of the God-world relationship. But clearly, while Plato grasped the contingency of material reality with respect to the world of Forms, and while Aristotle recognized the contingency of all finite beings that are moved vis-à-vis the eternal Unmoved Mover, neither of them grasped the most fundamental contingency of all, namely, contingency in the act of being or existence. As a result, Plato and Aristotle were limited to explaining why things are the way they are; neither was in a position to explain why things exist in the first place, why there is something rather than nothing.[17]

Aristotle, to be sure, is no longer available for comment on Aquinas's innovative adaptation of Aristotle's own metaphysics of act and potency to the data of Jewish and Christian revelation. But what might he say in defense of his own position? Presumably he would question Aquinas's foundational distinction between essence and existence, and that on at least two grounds. First of all, he would argue that existence cannot be compared to essence as actuality to potentiality. For, an actuality, even the actuality of the Unmoved Mover, is always something definite, something determinate. Existence, on the other hand, is by definition something indeterminate, that which can be predicated of everything that exists simply by reason of the fact that it is there. Existence, accordingly, cannot be said to be the essence of any being, even the Supreme Being, since it says nothing about the nature or basic intelligibility of the being in question. Secondly, Aristotle would probably contend that to make God co-terminous with being is implicitly to be guilty of either nominalism or pantheism. For, in the one case, "God" becomes simply the name for the collectivity of things that currently exist; God has no separate existence apart from the world of things. In the other case, if Aquinas insists that God is a separate being, then he is guilty of pantheism. For, the finite beings of this world can participate in the act of existence proper to God as a separate entity only if they are reduced to accidental modifications of the divine being.

A disciple of Aquinas, of course, will counter-argue that every finite being has its own act of existence proportionate to its distinctive essence. But Aristotle or one of his disciples would surely reply by raising the issue of nominalism once again. If every finite being has its own act of existence, then every being is different from every other being on the level of existence. Thus "existence" is an empty category without meaning or significance for the intelligibility of being, and "God" is simply the name for the collectivity of currently existing finite beings.

Naturally, these arguments between the adherents of rival schools of thought about their respective strengths and weaknesses are never conclusive. Further arguments can always be adduced from both sides either to bolster one's own position or to expose the weakness of the other side. Followers of Aquinas, however, should be aware that they cannot use texts from the Hebrew or Christian Bible to prove the identity of God and being in the same literal way that the master himself obviously did. In particular, they cannot use Exodus 3:14—God saying to Moses, "I am who am"— as God's self-revelation of the nature of the divine being. Modern Scripture scholarship tends to interpret that statement more as a promise of God's covenantal fidelity to Moses and the Jewish people during the time of trial still before them.[18] Likewise, those same students of Aquinas might well ponder the words of Heidegger in the introduction to *Being and Time*: "Basically, all ontology, no matter how rich and firmly compacted a system of categories it has at its disposal, remains blind and perverted from its ownmost aim, if it has not first adequately clarified the meaning of Being, and conceived this clarification as its fundamental task."[19] Is it possible that, in identifying being with God and vice versa, Aquinas failed to probe the deeper meaning of being in working out his own distinctive system of metaphysics?

In the remainder of this chapter, I plan to explore that possibility. My governing presupposition will be that Aquinas was not wrong in identifying God in a qualified sense with being. But one must further inquire what being is and how the proper understanding of being impacts upon the traditional Christian understanding of God. In line with the thought of the preceding chapter, I propose that being is properly speaking an activity rather than an entity although it never exists except as instantiated in an entity as the subject of that activity. Thus God is Subsistent Being (or Subsistent Activity) in that God is the primordial subject of the activity of existing. Being, when understood as the act of existence, therefore, is the nature of God. God as the Supreme Being, in other words, is grounded in the divine nature, the activity of existing. Furthermore, as will be explained at greater length in the next chapter, when humans and other created beings are said to share in the divine being, this means that they too participate in the ground of being, that is, in the underlying nature of God or the activity of existing. But they do not share in the entitative reality of God. For they are not God but remain themselves as independent finite realities, even though they draw their existence from the ground of being, the divine nature or the divine act of being.

Unfortunately, Aquinas did not make these distinctions between being as the underlying nature of God and the entitative reality of God as the Supreme Being. As a result, when he speaks of the *essential* perfections of God in Part One of the *Summa Theologica*, he is implicitly referring more to the underlying nature of God than to God as the Supreme Being. For, in point of fact, God is not one person but three persons, that is, three interrelated subjects of the divine act of existing. Hence, when Aquinas in these early questions refers to God in the singular, he is not referring to any one of the divine persons in particular, but simply to God as the indeterminate subject of the divine act of existence. God as the Supreme Being is thus unconsciously confused in Aquinas's mind with being as the act of existence or the underlying nature of God.

Moreover, because he thus implicitly identifies God as the Supreme Being with being as the underlying nature of God, Aquinas presupposes that God is infinite. Being is infinite; therefore, God as the Supreme Being is infinite. But if being is an activity, then the infinity of being, as I made clear in the preceding chapter on Aristotle, is dynamic, not fixed. That is, as an activity, being is a processive reality, a never-ending conversion of potentiality into actuality. Accordingly, God as the Supreme Being is likewise infinite in a dynamic, not a fixed sense. That is, as the subject of the ongoing act of existence, God experiences successive stages of actualization. Each stage of actualization is fully determinate; God is all that God can be at this moment in the divine existence. Yet in the next moment God can acquire a new determination so that God is in some sense other than (though not better than) what God is here and now. In both cases, God is the fullness of the act of being; but what it concretely means to be the fullness of being can and does change with successive moments in the divine existence.[20]

Perhaps at this point it would be best to examine more carefully Aquinas's discussion of the essential attributes of God in the early Questions of Part One of the *Summa Theologica*. For in this way I will be able to make clear both my own position as stated above and what I consider to be the ambiguity of Aquinas's thinking on the relationship between God and being, that is, between the supreme subject of the activity of existing and the activity itself as the underlying divine nature. In Question 3, for example, Aquinas analyzes the simplicity of God and inquires whether God has a body. Since God is simple, that is, without parts, God does not have a body. Rather, God is an immaterial entity which exists in virtue of its form or essence alone, apart from the conditions of matter.[21] Angels, to be sure, are likewise immaterial entities, but God's form or essence is the act of existence itself.[22]

Yet, if God's essence is existence itself, then God is always active as the subject of the ongoing act of existence. Thus one may just as readily say that God is Subsistent Activity, that is, the ongoing subject of the activity of existing, as say that God is Subsistent Being in the sense of the First Cause or Supreme Being. The only difference between the two terms is that in the first the nature of God as the activity of existing is in the foreground and the entitative reality of God as the ongoing subject of that act of existence is in the background; whereas in the second term, namely, that of God as the Supreme Being or the transcendent First Cause, precisely the opposite situation prevails. That is, the entitative reality of God as the Supreme Being is in the foreground and the underlying nature of God as the ongoing act of existence is virtually ignored.

But how does this affect God's relationship to creatures? Here perhaps is the deeper reason why in these early Questions of the *Summa Theologica* Aquinas prefers to think of God (in the singular) as an immutable entity rather than as the subject of an ongoing activity. His understanding of causality requires that God as Supreme Being bring into existence creatures as the effects of the divine causality. Thus, if creatures are beings, then God as their first efficient cause must likewise be a being. But, if one were further to presuppose that creatures are likewise subjects of the act of existence, albeit in a more limited way, would the foregoing objection disappear? Can God as the transcendent subject of the act of existence be the first efficient cause of more limited subjects of the act of existence? For that matter, does it not make even better sense to think of God's interaction with creatures in terms of God sharing the act of being in all its manifold forms with creatures?

Admittedly, this is a difficult question to answer since, as already noted in Chapter 1, we habitually think of entities as somehow prior to activities. Entities first exist and then act, not vice versa. Yet there are latent problems in taking this approach to causality. How, for example, does one entity effect a change in another entity? Aquinas says that it does so in virtue of its own form or essence which is specifically but not numerically the same as the form produced in the effect.[23] But this paradoxically seems to make the opposite point since the form or essence is the principle of activity for the entity which is the causal agent and likewise the principle of activity for the entity which undergoes the change. Thus, even in Aquinas's metaphysical scheme, an activity resident in one entity seems to produce its likeness in another entity. Hence, causality is more a matter of separate subjects sharing the same activity (e.g., God sharing the act of being with creatures) than one entity externally affecting another entity (e.g., one billiard ball striking another and thus causing it to move or change direction if already moving).

Leaving this question aside for the moment, however, I turn now to an analysis of some of the other essential attributes of God as described by Aquinas in the *Summa Theologica*. Here, too, we note that it is difficult to decide whether Aquinas is talking about God as a fixed reality, namely, the Supreme Being, or about God as the ongoing subject of the activity of existing. With reference to the perfection of God, for example, Aquinas says that "a thing is perfect in proportion to its state of actuality, because we call that perfect which lacks nothing of the mode of its perfection."[24] This would seem quite well to describe God as the Subsistent Activity of existing. For, as noted above, at every moment God is the fullness of the act of being. Yet an objection may be raised. If activity necessarily involves an ongoing transit from potentiality to actuality, then, is God understood as Subsistent Activity truly compatible with the perfection or, for that matter, the immutability of God?

To answer this question, I will first summarize my discussion of Aristotle's notion of the continuous in the preceding chapter. Two "things" are continuous if their extremities overlap.[25] Applied to immanent or self-contained activities, this would mean that there can be distinct stages within an ongoing activity provided that these stages overlap, flow into one another in a unilateral direction. Thus the actuality of one stage becomes ipso facto the potentiality of the next stage and the continuity of the activity is sustained even as the separate stages succeed one another. To be more specific, the act of seeing is then not one continuous act but a series of separate acts which flow into one another and thus give the impression of a single unbroken act. For, only in this case, is Aristotle's definition of motion as the actuality of the moveable (what is potential) insofar as it is still moveable (still in potency) truly verified. That is, if seeing is a single act, then there is no potentiality present but only actuality. Only if there are separate acts of seeing flowing into one another with each act serving as the potentiality for its successor, is there a combination of potentiality and actuality within the same process as demanded by Aristotle's definition.

Yet, if the divine life be thus understood as an ongoing series of separate acts of existence with each individual act serving as the potentiality for its successor, is this compatible with the notion of divine perfection? Provided that at each moment the divine act of existence is complete and without defect, this would seem to be a legitimate interpretation of the perfection of the divine being. In fact, it would seem to be preferable to the opposite alternative, namely, that the perfection of the divine being is pure actuality without any admixture of potentiality, because it makes eminently clear that the divine being is also divine life. Life, in other words, seems to involve potentiality or growth, transit from one stage of existence to another. The divine being understood as pure actuality contains no hint of life since there is no movement possible within the divine act of existence.[26] Only with the presupposition of an ongoing transit from potentiality to actuality within the divine being can one speak of God as possessing life as well as mere existence.

Aquinas, to be sure, expressly rules out the possibility that in God there is anything like a conversion of potentiality to actuality. For, if God is the Supreme Being, then God must be pure actuality since only what is itself in act can move something else from potency into act.[27] Here Aquinas is following Aristotle's presupposition of an Unmoved Mover, that entity which directly or indirectly moves everything else but is itself pure actuality and thus unmoved. Even organic substances which possess a "soul" and thus may be said to move themselves possess a "part" that moves and a "part" that is moved. Moreover, the "part" that moves is itself ultimately moved by the Unmoved Mover.[28] And yet, as noted in Chapter 1, there is a certain inconsistency in Aristotle's thinking here. For, if, as Aristotle says in the *Metaphysics*, the reality of the Unmoved Mover is "a thinking on thinking,"[29] then this *thinking* is itself an activity which is ongoing and thus here and now incomplete. It cannot be complete without ceasing to be an activity and in effect becoming an entity (namely, a thought) with a fixed or static reality. There is necessarily, in other words, even within the Unmoved Mover a continuous conversion from potentiality to actuality, but in such a way that there is no danger of a cessation of this activity or its conversion into still another type of activity. For, "thinking on thinking" as an entelechy (*entelecheia*) or self-contained activity has already achieved its essential perfection or form even as it continues to exercise that perfection in successive stages of actualization.

Similarly, I would argue that Aquinas's notion of God, if reinterpreted as Subsistent Activity, demands a continuous conversion from potentiality to actuality. For, understood as Subsistent Activity, the divine being requires no extrinsic "mover" but rather moves itself from potency to actuality in virtue of its own intrinsic dynamism. I presuppose here the distinction between *cause* and *ground* (or *vital source*) already mentioned in Chapter 1. That is, *cause* and *effect* are ontologically separate categories of being so that no entity (not even God) can, strictly speaking, be the cause of its own existence. On the other hand, if God be thought of as Subsistent Activity, then God's existence is grounded in the act of being, the activity of existing. The act of being, in other words, is the *ground* of the divine being; it is that principle of existence and activity which enables God to be God. Yet the ground of the divine being and God as an existent are not thereby distinct from one another as cause and effect. Rather, they are interrelated dimensions of one and the same entitative reality of God. Furthermore, as I shall make clear in the next chapter, the ground of the divine being, when understood as the act of being, is likewise the ontological ground for the existence of all creatures. For the moment, however, it is sufficient to note that God as Subsistent Activity is always in act. But God is in act as the subject of an ongoing activity, not as a fixed reality; hence, by nature God is in continuous passage from potency to act.[30]

What is to be said, however, about divine infinity? Aquinas argues that the infinity of God is based on the fact that God's essence is existence itself.[31] Because the act of existence is in principle unlimited, then God whose essence is existence is likewise in principle unlimited. What Aquinas seems to overlook, however, is that at any given moment the act of being is limited in terms of the entities which de facto exist. Furthermore, in the next moment new entities will come into existence and the act of existence will thus acquire new determinations. Being or the act of existence, accordingly, is both determinate and indeterminate. It is determinate with respect to what already is and indeterminate with respect to what can be. Only non-being or the principle of potentiality (i.e., prime matter) is purely indeterminate and thus unlimited in an absolute sense.

Aquinas, to be sure, did not think of the act of existence in these terms. He evidently conceived it in abstraction from its finite instantiations and then identified it as such with the divine act of being. In this way, he was able to claim that the act of existence is both actual and infinite or unlimited at the same time within God. The key question, however, is whether this coupling of actuality and infinity is really possible even within God. For, if God is a determinate reality, albeit a determinate reality which "infinitely" exceeds the capacity of the human mind to comprehend, then God is not completely unlimited. Creatures limit God in that they too subjectively exercise the act of being, albeit in an imperfect way. God, to be sure, may *objectively* possess the perfection of human nature or any other created act of being within the divine being, but God cannot *subjectively* exercise that created act of being without becoming the creature and thus undermining its independence from God. In brief, then, if God is strictly unlimited in the exercise of the act of being, then only God exists. If God somehow shares the act of being with creatures, then the latter limit God in virtue of their own subjective exercise of the act of being. As noted above, only pure potentiality or prime matter is completely unlimited, but this is because it is not an entity but simply a principle of being common to all finite entities.

On the other hand, if the act of existence be understood not as a fixed perfection but as an ongoing activity, then God as the enduring subject of that activity can be considered infinite in the same way that this activity is infinite. That is, as Aristotle noted, motion is the fulfilment here and now of what continues to exist in a state of potentiality. God as the primordial subject of the never-ending act of existence is, therefore, a determinate reality here and now but with the unlimited capacity to acquire further determinations in later moments of the divine existence. Furthermore, as already mentioned, God experiences no limits in the exercise of the divine act of existence. God is all that God can be right now. Nothing is lacking to God's perfection or actuality at the present moment. Thus God is infinite within the limits of God's own being at the present moment.

Likewise, in the next moment, God will be *essentially* what God already is right now, namely, the subsistent act of existence. Whatever further determinations which may accrue to God, for example, as a result of interaction with creatures, will not alter what God always has been and always will be, namely, the primordial subject of the act of existence. Hence, the future will involve no fundamental change for God in the sense of a reverse movement from the more perfect to the less perfect. Rather, the future will be for God basically the unbroken continuation of the divine act of existence without any sense of *before* and *after*; it will be simply the experience of continuous divine activity in the present.

This brings us to a discussion of God's eternality and immutability. Aquinas defines eternity as "the total, simultaneous and perfect possession of unending life" and declares God to be eternal in virtue of the divine immutability.[32] At first glance, therefore, God can in no way be eternal or immutable within the scheme which I am proposing here. Yet, once again I resort to Aristotle, here his analysis of time and the "present" in the *Physics*. As already noted in the preceding chapter, he remarks about time: "we apprehend time only when we have marked motion, marking it by 'before' and 'after'; and it is only when we have perceived 'before' and 'after' in motion that we say that time has elapsed."[33] The "present," on the other hand, he describes as the "extremity" of the past and of the future, in a word, their common boundary.[34] If the divine acts of existence, as noted above, successively flow into one another so that there is no sense of "before" and "after" as separate moments but only an experience of ongoing activity in a "present" without beginning or end, then one can say that God, understood as Subsistent Activity, is both eternal and immutable. For God, eternity is a continuous "now" which in its essential structure never changes. That is, it is a never-ending conversion of divine potentiality into actuality; and as such it can be aptly described as "the total, simultaneous and perfect possession of unending life."[35]

Within this scheme, to be sure, the future enters into the present for God only by way of anticipation, not as an already fixed actuality. Even God cannot know as actual what only exists here and now as a potentiality. Yet, as already noted, God will be in the future what God already is right now, namely, the subsistent act of existence. Hence, apart from God's relationship to creation, there is presumably no change at all in the divine nature as the ongoing act of existence. Furthermore, even allowing for change in God's relationship to creatures as time goes on, one may still say that the *essential* structure of the divine being and of the divine relationship to creatures remains unchanged since it is rooted in the unchanging character of the act of existence. In this sense, then, one may still attribute to God, understood as Subsistent Activity or the primordial subject of the ongoing act of existence, both eternity and immutability.

At this point, we may turn to a consideration of the operations of knowing and willing in God. These attributes of the divine being, to be sure, seem to apply less to the divine nature than to God in an entitative sense, namely, as a personal being. Yet, upon closer examination, we find that Aquinas equates the divine intellect and the divine will (or, more properly, the divine *activities* of knowing and willing) with the divine being or divine act of existence. There is, after all, no multiplicity in God. The proper object of the divine activities of knowing and loving is the divine nature, and the divine nature or essence is co-terminous with the divine act of existence.[36] Hence, contrary to what might be at first supposed, the activities of knowing and willing in God pertain more to the divine nature than to God as an entitative reality. They represent, so to speak, further specifications of the divine act of existence. God exists as subsistent knowing and willing: first, knowing and willing the divine being itself and then knowing and willing all finite entities in and through the divine being.[37]

Yet God is a personal or, more precisely, a tripersonal being: "Father," "Son" and "Holy Spirit."[38] Hence, these activities of knowing and willing pertain not only to the divine nature but likewise to each of the persons. For that matter, all the other essential attributes of God pertain not only to the divine nature but to each of the persons. Each of the persons possesses the attributes of simplicity, perfection, infinity, immutability, etc. For, as Aquinas notes, the concepts *person* and *nature* are only rationally distinct within the divine being.[39] Each of the persons is the divine nature and the divine nature subsists only in the persons. Thus, before bringing this chapter to a close, we must consider how God precisely as tripersonal is the ongoing subject of the divine act of existence.

First of all, it should be noted that the reality of God as simultaneously "Father," "Son" and "Holy Spirit" indirectly confirms the fact that the divine act of existence is exercised in three quite different ways. For, the reality of God as "Father" is other than the reality of God as "Son" or "Holy Spirit"; the reality of the "Son" is different from the reality of the "Father" or the "Holy Spirit"; the reality of the "Spirit" is different from the reality of the "Father" or the "Son." Thus, even though they each are fully God, subjects of the divine act of existence, they define or limit one another in the exercise of that same act. They cannot be themselves as individual persons, unique subjects of the divine act of existence, and still be the complete reality of the other two persons. The "Father," for example, may *objectively* know what it means to be the "Son," but the "Father" cannot *subjectively* be the "Son" without simultaneously ceasing to be the "Father." The three divine persons, accordingly, existing in ongoing relation to one another, inevitably determine what it means to be God in terms of three quite different subjectivities, namely, "Father," "Son" and "Holy Spirit."[40]

Secondly, as I have explained elsewhere in greater detail,[41] the reality of the three divine persons as interrelated subjects of the ongoing divine act of existence is perhaps best understood in terms of the relation between the terms *actual occasion* and *personally ordered society* within the philosophy of Alfred North Whitehead. For Whitehead, an actual occasion is a momentary subject of experience which exists as an actuality only as long as its process of self-constitution continues.[42] It describes accordingly quite well the reality of each of the divine persons at any given moment within the scheme outlined above. That is, at any given moment, each of the divine persons is a specific actualization of the divine act of existence for that moment. The "Father" is "Father" in a specific way for just that moment; the "Son" and the "Spirit" are likewise "Son" and "Spirit" in a specific way for just that moment.

But each of them is likewise an enduring subject of the divine act of existence. They exist as "Father," "Son" and "Holy Spirit" not just for the moment but for all time. Hence, the full reality of the divine persons is that each of them is in Whitehead's terms a personally ordered society of living actual occasions.[43] That is, each of them is a series of such actual occasions, such momentary actualizations of the divine act of existence, which flow into one another successively in a unilateral direction so as to constitute an ongoing personalized subject of the divine act of existence. A Whiteheadian personally ordered society of living occasions, in other words, corresponds to the reality of each of the divine persons insofar as they each pass through innumerable stages of actualization and yet preserve at the same time a unique identity as "Father," "Son" and "Holy Spirit."

Finally, as I have also indicated elsewhere, their unity as one God is the unity of a Whiteheadian *structured society* or society of subsocieties.[44] That is, each of the divine persons is, as noted above, a personally ordered society of living actual occasions, and together they form a more complex society or community which is then the corporate subject of the divine act of existence. Hence, "God" is not the name of an individual entity but rather the name for the divine community in which "Father," "Son" and "Holy Spirit" play constitutive roles. The divine community, in other words, cannot exist without the interrelated activity of all three persons vis-à-vis one another. But the individual persons cannot be themselves, namely, "Father," "Son" and "Holy Spirit," except as members of this unique community in which they each play such specific roles.

Further details of this Whiteheadian (or, more precisely, neo-Whiteheadian) scheme for the understanding of the traditional doctrine of the Trinity will be elaborated in Chapter 4 of this book. For the moment, however, it is only important to note that the scheme as thus far presented confirms the principal hypothesis of this chapter and this book: namely, that being is an activity rather than an entity and that the entities which are the subjects of this activity are necessarily involved in an ongoing transit from potentiality to actuality. Thus the three divine persons in the exercise of the act of existence are involved in an ongoing transit from potentiality to actuality. The Whiteheadian notions of *actual occasion* and *personally ordered society* aptly explain, in my judgment, how they still preserve continuous self-identity as "Father," "Son" and "Holy Spirit" even with the further postulate of discrete stages of actualization. Naturally, if this is true of the divine persons, it must likewise be true of all their creatures. But an explanation of how *actual occasion* and *personally ordered society* apply like-wise to the world of creation and, even more importantly, how all created beings become part of the communitarian life of God will have to wait until later.

To summarize the results of this and the preceding chapter, then, I would claim that I have combined the insights of Aristotle and Aquinas in a way that perhaps neither could have strictly speaking anticipated. From Aristotle I borrowed the idea that entities are always determinate, but that self-contained activities are indeterminate or infinite since they have in principle no beginning or end. From Aquinas, I borrowed the idea that existence does represent a higher level of perfection or actuality than essence and that existence is somehow synonymous with the reality of God. My synthesis of these insights was to the effect that being or the act of existence is the underlying nature of God, the ontological ground out of which the three divine persons are continually passing from potentiality to actuality both as individuals and as members of an ongoing community. Thus the three divine persons at any given moment are fully determinate (and thus, in a qualified sense, "finite") both in terms of their individual existence and in terms of their ongoing relations to one another. But, insofar as they are Subsistent Activities, that is, enduring subjects of the divine act of existence (albeit in different ways), they share in the indeterminacy or infinity of the divine act of existence. Essentially, however, they will always be what they already are at present, namely, interrelated subjects of the self-perpetuating act of divine existence.

3

The Ground of Subjectivity in Eckhart, Schelling, and Heidegger

Less than fifty years separate the lifetimes of Thomas Aquinas and Meister Eckhart. Both were Dominican friars, trained at the University of Paris, who taught theology to younger members of their community. Eckhart, to be sure, was more of a public figure because of the vast amount of preaching and spiritual direction which he undertook in addition to his teaching responsibilities. But he, like Aquinas before him, was quite at home in the world of scholastic philosophy and theology.[1] Yet his writings, above all, his published sermons, reflect a different spirit. In brief, he seems to be more concerned with the subjective experience of God than with an objective understanding of the nature of God and the causal relations between God and the world of creation. As a result, without explicitly using the term, Eckhart was involved with the issue of subjectivity, both human and divine.

Moreover, in probing into the *ground* or foundation of human and divine subjectivity, he found himself using language more metaphorically, in a manner quite different from the conceptually precise terminology of scholastic metaphysics. In the short run, this resulted in an official condemnation of some of his teachings by church authorities shortly after his death. But in the long run, Eckhart's more experiential reflections on the soul's relationship to God in prayer have had considerable influence on post-Kantian thinkers preoccupied with the nature of subjectivity, either human or divine. One of these, surely, was the German Idealist Friedrich Schelling who startled the German academic world with a heavily anthropomorphic description of the divine being or divine subjectivity in his *Essay on Human Freedom* in 1809. Similarly, Martin Heidegger admitted on more than one occasion his debt to Meister Eckhart in thinking out his own controversial understanding of the nature of being and the ground of human subjectivity.[2] Likewise, in 1936 Heidegger delivered a series of lectures on Schelling's *Essay on Human Freedom* in which he probed into the latter's distinction between ground and existence within divine and human subjectivity.

In any event, within this chapter I will continue the investigation of the philosophical notion of infinity begun in the preceding two chapters. My principal focus will be on Meister Eckhart and his notion of the Godhead as the ontological ground for both divine and human subjectivity. But I will also offer some reflections on the *Urgrund* or primal ground of being within Schelling's philosophy and indicate why Heidegger resists the idea of an *Urgrund* even as he enthusiastically endorses the distinction between ground and existence within human subjectivity. In this way, my earlier contention that the Infinite is an activity rather than a being as such should be brought more clearly into focus. For, as I see it, only as an activity can the Infinite be the ontological ground of divine and human subjectivity.

As mentioned above, Eckhart was certainly familiar with the terminology of thirteenth-century scholastic metaphysics, but he employed these terms in new ways that reflected his own and presumably others' experience of God in prayer. As a result, one might erroneously conclude that Eckhart was simply a popularizer of the more rigorously systematic thought of Aquinas and other scholastic thinkers. Quite the contrary, in my judgment Eckhart was an equally systematic thinker. But the system of thought which he was elaborating was strikingly different from that of most of his contemporaries. In effect, he was thinking in terms of at least an implicit event- or process-oriented ontology which stood in sharp contrast to the more static substance-oriented ontology of Aquinas and other scholastics of the day.[3] Admittedly, he himself probably did not think out the full implications of this new approach to the God-world relationship. But the confrontation with church authorities toward the end of his life must have sharpened his own sense of the novelty of his views even as he felt constrained to try to justify them in terms of the older system of ideas.

Some years ago Reiner Schürmann translated into English a number of Eckhart's vernacular sermons in Middle High German; at the same time, he did a careful text-analysis of several of them and added a commentary on their philosophical implications. As the basis for my own investigation into Eckhart's embryonic process-oriented ontology, I have chosen one of those sermons, namely, "See What Love" [*Videte qualem caritatem dedit nobis pater, ut filii dei nominemur et simus,* I John 3:1], together with Schürmann's analysis and commentary.[4]

As the Latin title itself makes clear, the sermon represents Eckhart's reflections on how human beings under the inspiration of divine grace can equivalently be divinized, i.e., become one being with the eternal Son of God. Schürmann notes that Eckhart begins the sermon by making passing reference to key principles of both Aristotelian and Neo-Platonic metaphysics. From Aristotle he derives the notion that, in the act of knowing, the knower and the object known are one.[5] Thus we can know God only because God concomitantly knows us. Without our fully realizing it at the time, the divine act of knowing us (and the rest of creation) is constitutive of our finite act of knowing God. One and the same divine act of knowing, accordingly, undergirds both God's knowledge of us and our knowledge of God.[6] From Neo-Platonism, on the other hand, Eckhart derives the doctrine of participation when he affirms that not only to be called but also to be the "Son of God" implies that "we shall be exactly what he is, the same being and the same sensibility and intelligence."[7] But, notes Schürmann, Eckhart here oversteps the traditional understanding of the doctrine of participation since by implication he eliminates the ontological difference between God and human beings. Both the eternal "Son of God" and the human being exist in virtue of one and the same divine act of filiation.[8]

Admittedly, we humans do not realize that we are one and the same being with the "Son of God." This is because our minds are preoccupied with representations of sensible things and their related concepts. But, says Eckhart, there is within the mind "a spark of the intellectual power which is never quenched. This spark is the higher part of the spirit."[9] In virtue of this spark, we attain interior knowledge that "[i]n this life all things are one, they are all together all in all, and all united to all."[10] Just as in this life the various organs of the body in different ways contribute to and share in the life of the total organism, so in the mystical body of Christ in heaven all share in the grace of Mary and the saints as if it were their own. All this happens because in the divine Spirit or "Holy Spirit" the faithful have "the identical being and the identical substance and nature" as the eternal "Son of God" and are thus related to "God the Father" as co-equal "Sons of God."[11]

In the remainder of the sermon, Eckhart exhorts his listeners to shake off attachment to the things of this world, above all, attachment to the self with all its petty concerns and anxieties about self-preservation. On the contrary, one must realize that apart from God one's whole being, indeed, the entire world of creation, is sheer nothingness. One must accept this nothingness of self and the world before God in order "to be transported into the naked being of God, the pure being of the Spirit."[12] Those who are still preoccupied with themselves, still filled with anxiety over the events taking place in this world, have not yet achieved, of course, this spiritual rebirth into the Kingdom of heaven where they will be one being with the "Son of God." But they should take heart because eventually they, too, will achieve full identification with the "Son of God."[13]

In his commentary, Schürmann weaves together citations from this sermon and others related to the same theme in order to reconstruct what seems to be Eckhart's implicit ontology here. He first takes note of the fact that Eckhart distinguishes between the mind with its faculties of knowing and willing and the being or ground of the mind: "'Being,' 'image of God,' 'ground' (*Grunt*), 'abyss' (*Abgrunt, Ungrunt*), or 'essence of the mind': all these words designate the same region of man, eternally at rest, where the mind is closer to God than to the faculties, closer to God than to itself or to the world."[14] Here the mind in terms of its own activities of knowing and willing is passive. For, God alone is operative here, and the effect of the divine operation is to engender the "Son" in the mind and thereby to transform the mind into the "Son."[15]

The second point made by Schürmann is that the identity thus achieved between the human mind and God is not a union of separate substances but the unity of one and the same activity operative both in God and in the human mind. Equivalently, it is the Godhead or the divine nature which is operative both within the divine being to effect the distinction between the divine persons and within the human mind to produce the reality of the "Son."[16] Only thus can the mind both give birth to the "Son" and be itself transformed into the "Son" at the same time. But this gives rise to a practical question. Is the goal of the spiritual life identity with the "Son" or identity with the Godhead, the underlying activity which grounds the existence of the "Son" both within the Trinity and within the human mind? To answer this question, Schürmann points to Eckhart's own example in the sermon under consideration.

In the act of learning, teacher and pupil are one and what is born of their joint effort is wisdom or knowledge shared by both parties.[17] In effect, then, only the event of the "word" or the process of the birth of knowledge "is"; teacher and pupil as separate substances "are" no longer. "The word initiates the energetic identity of being."[18] By "energetic identity of being," Schürmann has in mind an operational identity of kindred activities rather than a traditional ontological identity of substances. Applied to the birth of the "Son" in the ground of the human mind, this would mean that the act of self-appropriation whereby the human mind both gives birth to and itself becomes the "Son" is ultimately identical with the act of self-appropriation whereby God is differentiated into "Father" and "Son" within the Trinity.

In answer to the question whether the goal of the spiritual life is identity with the "Son" or with the Godhead, then, Schürmann's third point is that in either case being enacts itself as an event, the event of self-appropriation, but that the event of a "breakthrough" to the nothingness of the Godhead would seem to be more fundamental or foundational than the event of the birth of the "Son" in the being of the mind. "The birth of the Son and the breakthrough beyond God are neither opposed nor added one upon the other. But 'breakthrough' says more than 'birth,' as it carries the understanding of being as a process to the destruction of all conceivable contents."[19] He then adds that, since the mind has to recognize its nothingness before God in order to become one with the "naked being of God," it is logical that it has to divest itself even of its personal identity with the "Son" in order to enter into the nakedness of the divine being contained in the Godhead.[20]

One might possibly question whether Schürmann's interpretation of Eckhart here is sound because it is based so heavily on just a few sermons. Yet, as noted above, Schürmann makes liberal reference to the rest of

Eckhart's published works while focusing on those German sermons which set forth his implicit ontology. Furthermore, Bernard McGinn, another expert in the mystical theology of Meister Eckhart, comes to many of the same conclusions as Schürmann in his analysis of key texts. McGinn points out, for example, that in German Sermon 6 (*Justi vivent in aeternum* [Wis. 5:16]) Eckhart says:

> The Father gives birth to His Son without ceasing; and I say more: He gives birth not only to me, his Son, but he gives birth to me as himself and himself as me and to me as his being and nature. In the innermost source, there I spring out in the Holy Spirit, where there is one life and one being and one work.[21]

Thus, in its ground or being, the mind is identical not only with the "Son" and the "Father" but also with the "Holy Spirit." Furthermore, "if the identity of ground between God and the soul shows how the latter partakes of the inner-Trinitarian *bullitio* [literally, "boiling," i.e., the divine life], the same is true of the divine creative activity, or *ebullitio* [literally, "boiling over"]. This is why Sermon 52 can speak of the soul as its own creator: 'For in the same being of God where God is above being and above distinction, there I myself was, there I willed myself and committed myself to create this man [i.e., me].' "[22]

The question, then, is not whether Eckhart made these extraordinary statements about the ultimate identity of the mind in its ground or being with the ground or being of God, i.e., the Godhead, and through the Godhead with the divine persons themselves. Rather, it is a question of how to interpret these statements. Schürmann proposes that Eckhart was at least implicitly working with an event- or process-oriented ontology in which the divine persons and the human mind "disappear" as separate substances and only their joint process of becoming "is."[23] At the same time, beyond showing that the traditional scholastic analogy of being will not work to explain Eckhart's understanding of being (or becoming), he does not offer much by way of an explanation for this new event- or process-oriented ontology. He does indicate, to be sure, the affinity of Eckhart's thought with that of Martin Heidegger, a theme to which I will return later in the chapter. But even here there are only hints of what might be a systematic understanding of being as process or event. Hence, in the following paragraphs, I will continue my discussion of the notion of infinity begun in the preceding two chapters and try to show how Eckhart's thought likewise verifies my proposal that the Infinite is, properly speaking, not an entity, not even God as the divine entity, but an all-comprehensive activity.

To review briefly the points already made, in Chapter 1, I studied carefully Aristotle's definition of motion as the actuality of the potential insofar as it is potential; I concluded that self-contained activities or entelechies (*entelecheiai*) are not only potentially infinite, as Aristotle himself maintained, but rather actually infinite since in principle they have no beginning or end. Aristotle claimed that motion is eternal and continuous since motion would be needed either to pass from a state of rest to a state of movement or from a state of movement to a state of rest. While this dictum is usually seen as applicable to the movement of the outermost celestial sphere within Aristotle's cosmology, in my judgment it applies equally well to various immanent activities such as the "thinking on thinking" characteristic of the Unmoved Mover. For, unlike "transient" activities which are ordered to a goal or product extrinsic to the activity itself, immanent activities are self-perpetuating, once activated, and thus enjoy a type of actual infinity precisely as an ongoing activity.

Then in Chapter 2, I reviewed Aquinas's understanding of God as *Ipsum Esse Subsistens* and came to the conclusion that the term really describes the underlying nature of God rather than God as the Supreme Being or Highest Entity. For, most of the attributes of God such as simplicity, infinity, immutability, etc., apply more properly to the nature of God than to the divine persons. Even those perfections of God which seem to describe God as a personal being, such as the divine justice, mercy, goodness, etc., are in the end convertible with the divine act of being or the divine nature. For, knowing and willing in God are only rationally distinct both from one another and from the divine act of existence.

The divine persons, to be sure, exist as ongoing interrelated entities within the unity of the divine life. But they are thus interrelated only because they specify in different ways the divine act of being. That is, the "Father" represents the principle of potentiality within the divine life; the "Son" represents the principle of concretion or provisional actuality here and now within that same act of being; the "Holy Spirit," finally, represents the goal or principle of ultimate actuality within the divine life. All this will be explained more fully in Chapter 4. For now, it is sufficient to note that the three divine persons are indeed distinct entities, but entities whose very being is to be in different ways the subject of the divine act of being. Hence, they are fittingly called by Aquinas *subsistent relations*.[21] As *subsistent*, they are entities. But, as *relations*, they are interdependent subjects of one and the same divine act of existence.

Within this context, the dramatic statements by Eckhart on the operative identity between the human mind in its ground and the divine persons in their common ground are not so startling as might seem at first reading. Since his focus was primarily on the *experience* of God in prayer rather than on the *conceptual understanding* of God derived from rational reflection, it is quite understandable that Eckhart found himself at least implicitly thinking in process-oriented rather than in substantialist terms. That is, for Eckhart, ground (both in the divine being and in human beings) is not so much extrinsic cause as rather vital source for the existent which emerges out of the ground. Furthermore, the existent in each case is not so much an object of thought as rather a subject of experience which is empowered to become this rather than that in virtue of its ground or dynamic source of activity.

Thus the divine persons and all their creatures can share a common ground or source of activity and yet be distinct from one another as separate entities or existents.

In this way, the logically opposed requirements of divine transcendence of and immanence to creation are unexpectedly fulfilled. For, not only the divine persons, but likewise all finite entities, transcend one another as separate existents and yet are immanent to one another in terms of their common ground or source of activity. Finally, since this common ground is not itself an entity but the source or principle for the existence of entities, it can be suitably described as "no-thingness," that which is operative in all entities but never exists in its own right.

To verify this interpretation of Eckhart's mystical theology, I will now take up some of his key statements cited above and indicate how they can be quite readily understood within this conceptual framework. The main point of Eckhart's sermon "See What Love," for example, is that through the action of grace Christians possess the same being, substance and nature as the eternal "Son of God."[25] But then the clear inference of Eckhart's statement is that the divine nature or ground of the divine being is likewise the ground or vital source of my being. I exist in virtue of the same divine power or activity by which the "Son of God" exists. In this sense, I am the "Son of God." This is not to say that I am numerically one and the same person with the "Son of God." Other statements by Eckhart in the same essay indicate that he distinguishes between the personhood of the human being and the personhood of the divine "Son." After noting that Christians possess the same being as the "Son of God," for example, he says: "It is the possession of this identical being that likens us to him and makes us see him in his divinity."[26] Thus the Christian is like Christ and is divinized through seeing him in his divinity, but the Christian is not one person with Christ. Rather, the Christian shares the same nature or ground of being with Christ.

Similarly, in German Sermon 6 "Justi vivent in aeternum," cited by Bernard McGinn, Eckhart's statement that God the Father "gives birth not only to me, his Son, but he gives birth to me as himself and himself as me, and to me as his being and nature"[27] is intelligible only if one recognizes that he is talking about a unity within the divine nature, not about a union of persons as such. One cannot be one and the same person with both the "Father" and the "Son" simultaneously. But one can be united with both of them in what makes them to be divine persons and oneself to be a human person, namely, in the divine nature or vital principle of activity for everything that is. Eckhart himself seems to be saying the same thing when he adds: "In the innermost source, there I spring out in the Holy Spirit, where there is one life and one being and one work."[28] Here there is reference to the Spirit as well as to the "Father" and the "Son," but Eckhart is careful to say that the unity in question is in the nature or "innermost source," not in one of the divine persons as such. One is in a qualified sense all three divine persons, but only because one shares with them their underlying nature or principle of activity.

Finally, in German Sermon 52 "Beati pauperes spiritu," likewise cited by McGinn, where Eckhart claims to be with God above being and in that state to will his own existence in the temporal order,[29] there seems to be no logical explanation beyond what I have indicated above, namely, that Eckhart is implicitly referring to the underlying nature of God which the three divine persons share with their creatures in and through the act of creation. The celebrated "breakthrough" (*Durchbruch*) which Eckhart claims is necessary for full union with God is a breakthrough into the Godhead, that is, into the vital source of existence and activity for the divine persons themselves. For, only as one with this eternal divine principle of activity can Eckhart will from all eternity his own existence in the temporal order. As he says in the same passage, "I am the cause of myself in the order of my being, which is eternal, and not in the order of my becoming, which is temporal. And therefore I am unborn, and in the manner in which I am unborn I can never die. In my unborn manner I have been eternally, and am now, and shall eternally remain."[30]

For Eckhart, then, the deepest union with God is not with one of the divine persons, nor even with all three of them together, but with the divine nature as their common source of existence and activity. For this reason, here as elsewhere in his German sermons, Eckhart prays to be free of God, if by "God" is meant one or other of the divine persons in relation to creation.[31] Likewise, he here claims to be the cause of "God" in virtue of his own existence as a creature.[32] On the one hand, this latter statement is a recognition that God is logically not "God" to God's own self, that is, to the three divine persons. God is "God" only to creatures who thus paradoxically make God to be "God" by their very existence as creatures. But, on a deeper level, as Richard Woods comments, "such 'God-riddance' also signifies the overcoming of the cognitive distance between 'I' and 'God' in human consciousness through the re-cognition or dis-covery of the soul's profound and persistent unity with God in its own ground, the 'abyss.' "[33] This "abyss," moreover, is in my judgment simultaneously the ground or abyss of the divine being.

I turn now to a brief consideration of the use of the term *ground* in the philosophy of the German Idealist, Friedrich Schelling, above all in the middle period of his life, when he wrote the *Essay on Human Freedom* and the never-completed *Ages of the World*. It is generally recognized that Schelling was heavily influenced in the use of this term, not so much by Meister Eckhart, but rather by a seventeenth-century German mystic, Jacob Boehme, who was himself familiar with the writings of Eckhart and other medieval mystics.[34] Unlike Meister Eckhart and the medieval mystics, however, Boehme was less interested in the soul's union with the divine ground of being and much more interested in the intradivine process whereby the one personal God comes to full self-consciousness in and through the creation of the world.35 Schelling followed Boehme on this point, investigating the divine ground of being, not as the end-point of the soul's ascent to God, but as the starting-point for the process of divine self-realization through creation. Moreover, in thus sketching how God comes to personhood and full self-realization in and through creation, Schelling was also indirectly setting forth his psychology of human personhood and self-realization. For, since God achieves full self-realization only in and through the self-conscious human being, the two processes of self-realization are mirror images of one another with the qualification that what infallibly goes forward within the divine consciousness is subject to distortion and sinful aberration within human consciousness.

A brief summary of the divine process of self-realization as given in the *Essay on Human Freedom* would run as follows. In the beginning, God was the "Absolute Indifference" of being and existence, possessing neither a nature nor a concrete existence.36 Out of this Absolute Indifference or *Ungrund*, however, came forward two eternal beginnings (*Anfänge*) in dialectical opposition to one another: one is the ground or the eternal nature of God, the other is God as a concrete existent.37 The ground is the subjective vital principle within the divine being which simultaneously resists the process of divine self-development and yet is the source or potentiality for all that is to follow.38 The other is the objective rational principle of the divine self-development, that which overcomes the resistance of the subjective principle to self-expression and yet at the same time constrains it to be just one determinate reality at a time. The goal of the process of divine self-realization is, as noted above, that all that is potential within the divine nature be brought into the light and subordinated to the objective rational principle within the divine being. In this way, God becomes self-conscious Spirit in and through creation; God is the Absolute Identity of the vital and the rational principles both within the divine being and within creation.39

As noted above, the human being in Schelling's scheme stands at the apex of creation; as the full self-realization of God in creation, the human person is created spirit, the dynamic unity of the vital and rational principles in creation.40 But, since the human being like God is free by nature, he or she can reverse the subordination of the vital principle to the rational principle within his or her consciousness and thus become an evil rather than a good spirit, a creature in rebellion against the order of nature rather than the image of God in creation. As Schelling sees it, this fateful decision (or *Abfall*) was accomplished initially by the first human being, and all subsequent human beings are at least strongly tempted to follow suit. Furthermore, this decision to subordinate the rational principle to the vital principle in one's consciousness seems to be purely spontaneous, the result of a decision made before all time at the beginning of creation.41 Hence, through the collective decisions of human beings over the centuries, creation as a whole is now in the grip of the non-rational vital principle emanating from the divine being. Only at the end of the process of creation, as noted above, will the rational ordering principle within the process of creation definitively subordinate the vital principle to itself and allow for God as divine Spirit to be fully manifest in creation.

There is, accordingly, a double reference for the term *ground* in Schelling's philosophy. There is, first, the *Urgrund* or cosmic ground of being from which God as an existent and all creatures ultimately proceed.[42] Then there is the dialectical principle of the ground which is operative within God and all creatures in opposition to another dialectical principle, that of existence. Either as the cosmic ground of being or as a dialectical principle, however, ground has to do with a principle of subjectivity or potentiality which does not exist in itself but rather serves as the vital source or principle of activity for God or some creature. Thus, despite the verbal ambiguity here, on a deeper level Schelling is quite consistent in always thinking of ground not as an extrinsic cause but as an intrinsic principle of activity for a given entity.

I emphasize this fact because, as I see it, this is where Schelling's notion of the divine *Urgrund* overlaps with Eckhart's understanding of the Godhead. In neither case are we dealing with God as an existent, but with the underlying nature of God, that which makes God as an existent to be God. Again, like the Godhead in Eckhart's scheme, the divine *Urgrund* for Schelling is really not the cause of God's existence since it itself is part of the divine being. Rather, it is the ongoing vital source or principle of activity for God as an existent, the underlying nature as opposed to the personhood of God. Here one might object that this is the role which the dialectical principle of the ground plays with reference to the other dialectical principle of *existence* within Schelling's scheme for the divine nature. The difference, however, is that the dialectical principle of the ground is already something; it is an incipient subject of existence which is being stirred into activity by the rival dialectical principle of existence. The *Urgrund*, on the other hand, is not even a subject of existence with a potentiality for actual existence. Rather, it is simply a power or principle of activity which first gives rise to the opposition of dialectical principles within the divine nature and then makes possible the free choice which allows God to be an actual existent as divine Spirit, the conscious synthesis of potentiality and actuality, subjectivity and objectivity.

One further point should be made before concluding this discussion of the divine *Urgrund* within Schelling's philosophy. As noted above, the *Urgrund* is the source for the operation of the dialectical principles not only within the divine being but likewise within creation. All finite entities, accordingly, have the ground of their being within the divine *Urgrund*.[43] Likewise, human beings are constituted by dialectical principles having their source in the divine nature. Even the free choice which human beings make to establish the priority of the rational over the vital principle within consciousness or vice versa arises out of the divine *Urgrund* even as it remains the decision of each individual. God, in other words, communicates the divine power of decision making to human beings as the counter-part of God in creation. What human beings do with that power is their own responsibility; but the power itself comes from God or, more precisely, from the divine *Urgrund*, its source in God.[44] Thus the divine *Urgrund* is the source of human freedom as well as divine freedom.

Bearing this in mind, we may now turn to a consideration of Martin Heidegger's use of the term *Grund* in his philosophy. As Michael Vater comments, it is interesting to speculate how much Schelling's *Essay on Human Freedom* may have influenced Heidegger's thinking in this regard.[45] For, Heidegger gave his lectures on this text for the first time in the winter semester of 1927-1928 at the University of Freiburg in Breisgau; *Vom Wesen des Grundes* which sets forth Heidegger's own reflections on the notion of *Grund* in the self-constitution of *Dasein* (authentic human existence) ap-peared one year later in 1929.[46] Heidegger, to be sure, is faithful to the text of the *Essay on Human Freedom* through most of the lectures; but his critical comments at the end make clear that, while he values Schelling's distinction between the dialectical principles of ground and existence, his own focus is exclusively on the operation of these principles within human conscious-ness. He is definitely not interested in Schelling's cosmological scheme whereby God achieves full self-awareness in and through creation, above all, in and through human beings.[47]

Part of this disdain for cosmology is due to Heidegger's conviction that the principle of sufficient reason (in German, *der Satz vom zureichenden Grund*) has been misused to turn ontology, the study of the nature of being, into onto-theology, the study of the relations between God as Creator and all God's creatures.[48] Hence, in *Vom Wesen des Grundes* he focuses on the notion of *Grund* as an internal principle of activity within an entity rather than an external cause for the existence of another entity. *Grund*, accord-ingly, represents a human being's principle of self-transcendence. That is, in virtue of his or her grounding in a primordial act of free self-constitution, the human being unconsciously projects a "world" or network of relation-ships in which it finds itself, together with other finite beings, from the first moment of self-awareness.[49] This is the human being's primordial exercise of freedom, within which context individual acts of conscious free choice subsequently take place.[50] Freedom is thus the *Abgrund des Daseins* or deeper ground of authentic human existence, but it is itself ungrounded or groundless, equivalently, its own act of causation or *causa sui*.[51]

Given this brief explanation of Heidegger's line of thought in *Vom Wesen des Grundes*, it is easy to see how he would find in Schelling's reflections on the human person as finite spirit, the dynamic union of the dialectical principles of ground and existence, confirmation of his own views on the self-constitution of *Dasein*. In both cases, the human being in the search for authentic personhood uncovers the basic structure of being and conforms himself or herself to it through a primordial free decision which Schelling describes as taking place at the beginning of creation or in any case in strict independence of historical circumstances here and now. Heidegger, too, wants this primordial exercise of human freedom, the grounding activity of self-constitution and world-constitution, to be independent of historical circumstances since history as the record of *Dasein's* dealings with other finite beings properly only takes place under the presupposition of this primordial act of grounding.

Yet questions can certainly be raised whether Heidegger's interpretation of Schelling's scheme in the *Essay on Human Freedom* is really accurate. Whereas Heidegger interprets Schelling to say that the human being continuously emerges out of the ground of his or her being to become an existent in virtue of a primordial free choice, Schelling, as I see it, rather proposes that the human being is a dynamic synthesis of the principles of ground and existence on the basis of a free choice which has to be somehow reaffirmed from moment to moment. There is, in other words, in Schelling's scheme as I understand it much more of a choice in the priority of the one principle over the other than Heidegger is willing to admit.[52] It is not simply that the human being recognizes the underlying structure of being and conforms himself or herself to it, as Heidegger suggests, but rather that the human being chooses which structure of being he or she wants and then has to abide by the historical consequences of that choice for herself or himself both as an individual and as a member of the human family.

Furthermore, one may well question whether Heidegger acted too quickly in simply dismissing the cosmological scheme of Schelling as a regression to earlier, now outdated, forms of metaphysical speculation. After all, in his subsequent philosophical development, Heidegger himself seems to have shifted from an anthropological focus on *Dasein* (authentic human being) to a new cosmological focus on *Sein* (being understood as the source of that grounding activity in human beings and indeed in all finite entities).[53] In his later work *Der Satz vom Grund* published in 1957, for example, he comments: "Nothing exists without a ground. Being and ground: the same. Being as that which grounds has itself no ground; it comes into play as the background of that game that as destiny (*Geschick*) tosses to us being and ground together."[54] Here it is *Sein* rather than *Dasein* that is primordially a grounding activity. But, as he comments in a letter to William Richardson, the reversal in his thought here "is in play with the matter itself."[55] That is, the being into which he inquired in *Being and Time* "cannot long remain something that the human subject posits."[56] As I interpret Heidegger here, this means that the grounding activity of *Dasein* sooner or later must itself be "grounded" in a still more comprehensive activity of grounding which, for example, makes roses to bloom (cf. below) as well as enables human beings mentally to project a world and uncover the ontological difference between being and beings.[57]

But this line of reflection implicitly restores the cosmological perspective of Schelling, albeit with an important qualification. Where Schelling and the German mystics, Boehme and Eckhart, clearly thought of the grounding activity or *Urgrund* in terms of the divine being in the first place and with reference to human beings and other finite beings only in the second place, Heidegger as a consciously secular thinker refused to connect being as a grounding activity with God as the Supreme Being in any way.[58] For him, this would be an unhappy regression into the thought patterns of classical metaphysics which distorted, as noted above, ontology as the study of being into onto-theology as the analysis of the relations between the Creator God and all God's creatures. But, admitting this key difference between Heidegger, on the one hand, and Schelling together with the German mystics, on the other hand, one should not overlook the remarkable similarity of their respective insights into the nature of Ultimate Reality. All of them in different ways are urging that Ultimate Reality is not a being, not even God as the Supreme Being; rather, it is an all-comprehensive activity which grounds the existence of entities, even the existence of God as the Supreme Entity.

Heidegger is perhaps the most insistent on this point. For, in his early period, he urged that *Dasein* not be understood as a substance in the classical sense but rather as an ongoing process of self-transcendence toward the world. Then, in his later reflections, he shifted his attention to being as that which universally grounds the existence and activity of finite entities while itself remaining groundless. Since it is not a being but by implication an activity which manifests itself or comes to self-expression in an event of some kind (*ein Ereignis*), e.g., the blooming of a rose, it has no need of any being to ground it or cause it to be. Being itself as a principle of existence and activity is thus the inner ground or intrinsic reason for the blooming of the rose.[59]

Schelling, on the other hand, operating out of a more classical perspective, used the notion of ground to reconceive the God-world relationship. For, God in Schelling's scheme is initially the *Urgrund* out of which the dialectical principles constitutive of the divine being and of creation as well eternally emerge. God's being, accordingly, is in process until the end-time of creation when the ultimate victory of the rational principle over the vital principle within the divine being and within creation will have been accomplished. But even then, in Schelling's mind, the divine life will continue, with Love as the underlying activity of the divine being still at work to support the existence of God as Spirit, the Absolute Identity of ground and existence within the divine being.[60] The human person, on the other hand, in Schelling's scheme, is the fragile, never permanently achieved, product of the activity of these dialectical principles within his or her consciousness. Even the decision to order the principles one way rather than another has to be confirmed over and over again within the individual's lifetime. For, the temptation to reverse the order of the principles is ever-present within human consciousness; hence, the decision to sustain the present order must be reaffirmed, at least subconsciously, all the time.[61]

I will end here with a final reference to Meister Eckhart. For, as we saw above, he too thinks of Ultimate Reality in terms of an underlying activity which binds God and creatures to one another in a mystical union. In the Sermon "See What Love," Eckhart repeats at intervals the daring claim that the believer and the divine "Son of God" share the same being, substance and nature. By that he means that the believer and the "Son of God" exist, to be sure, as separate entities, but in virtue of one and the same act of divine filiation. Likewise, the "Father" and the "Spirit" exist in the soul of the believer by reason of the same act of being by which they exist within the Godhead. Hence, one must conclude, the ground of the mind of the believer and the ground of the divine being or the Godhead must be one and the same. The ground itself, however, is not a substance since this would result in a pantheistic monism in which all differences between beings, even those between the divine persons, would disappear. Rather, the ground uniting the divine persons with all their creatures, but above all their rational creatures, is a common underlying activity. It is, moreover, infinite, not only because it originates within the Godhead, but also because it is omnipresent to all entities without exception, enabling them both to be themselves and to exist in relationship to one another.

Given this dynamic understanding of the notion of ground both in the German mystics, Eckhart and Boehme, and in the more modern thinkers, Schelling and Heidegger, we are now in a position to study the notion of creativity in the philosophy of Alfred North Whitehead. As will be evident in the next chapter, creativity in Whitehead's scheme is perhaps best understood as an underlying activity which is in itself infinite, that is, without any limitations in terms of space and time, but which grounds the existence of "actual entities," momentary subjects of experience which come into existence and are related to one another in virtue of that activity common to them all.

4

Creativity and the Extensive Continuum in the Philosophy of Alfred North Whitehead

The meaning of the term *Ultimate Reality* is not readily apparent within the philosophy of Alfred North Whitehead. For there are, so to speak, several candidates for that function within his overall conceptual scheme. In the chapter on "God" in *Science and the Modern World*, for example, Whitehead distinguishes between individual actual occasions (momentary subjects of experience which are the "building blocks" or fundamental units of reality within Whitehead's metaphysical scheme) and an underlying ontological activity of which the various "occasions" are instantiations or different forms of expression.[1] In one sense, this underlying activity is like the single infinite reality or "substance" in the philosophy of Spinoza in that it produces all the things of this world through the power of its own nature or essence.[2] But in another sense, it is not at all like substance for Spinoza since it is not itself that which exists, the one enduring reality in this world. Rather, it is a "general activity" which is individualized and thus comes into being in terms of the process of self-constitution for each actual occasion as noted above. This underlying activity, in other words, does not exist in itself as a substantial reality, but only in and through the more limited activities of self-realization characteristic of the various actual occasions or subjects of experience constitutive of reality here and now.

In the same chapter Whitehead also describes God as the principle of limitation for this underlying ontological activity.[3] For, in itself, the activity is capable of realization into innumerable actual occasions with no necessary order or connection between them. But, given the existence of God as "the ground of rationality" within the cosmic process, this underlying activity is necessarily restricted in its mode of operation. In a qualified sense, then, Whitehead is proposing here two metaphysical Absolutes. The one Absolute is an underlying activity which because of its impersonal and non-rational character is the vital source for literally everything that happens, both good and evil. The other Absolute is God who is, to be sure, not yet conceived by Whitehead as a transcendent entity but only as a principle of control or restraint within the cosmic process. Yet, even as a cosmic principle, God is needed to set limits to this spontaneous productivity and thus as far as possible "to divide the Good from the Evil, and to establish Reason 'within her dominions supreme.'"[4]

In *Religion in the Making*, published a year later, Whitehead repeats basically the same theme. He distinguishes three "formative elements" in the self-constitution of finite entities:

1. The creativity whereby the actual world has its character of temporal passage to novelty.
2. The realm of ideal entities, or forms, which are in themselves not actual, but are such that they are exemplified in everything that is actual, according to some proportion of relevance.
3. The actual but nontemporal entity whereby the indetermination of mere creativity is transmuted into a determinate freedom. This nontemporal entity is what men call God.[5]

Thus, in *Religion in the Making*, God (now conceived as a transcendent entity) still acts as a restraint or check on the spontaneity of the underlying ontological activity, here specifically named creativity. Furthermore, ideal forms or "eternal objects" also participate in the self-constitution of individual entities, but Whitehead makes clear that these ideal forms exist in the first place within God and only secondarily and derivatively in finite entities.[6]

In his magisterial work *Process and Reality*, however, Whitehead added further qualifications to this basic scheme. First of all, he names creativity (together with the notions of the One and the Many) the "Category of the Ultimate." In his own words, creativity is "that ultimate principle by which the many, which are the universe disjunctively, become the one actual occasion, which is the universe conjunctively."[7] He then adds by way of explanation: "The novel entity is at once the togetherness of the 'many' which it finds, and also it is one among the disjunctive 'many' which it synthesizes. . . The many become one and are increased by one." By that he means that each new actual occasion or momentary subject of experience constitutes itself out of a world of actual occasions which have already come into existence and then adds itself to that world of completed actual occasions. Finally, he notes: "This Category of the Ultimate replaces Aristotle's category of 'primary substance.'" Since primary substance for Aristotle represents that which in the first place exists, what Whitehead appears to be saying here is that creativity as an ongoing passage from the many to the one and back again to the many is Ultimate Reality, thus even more ultimate than the individual actual occasions which are constituted in virtue of that activity.

Many Whiteheadians, to be sure, would disagree with this interpretation of creativity and the Category of the Ultimate since in their minds Whitehead is offering here simply a descriptive generalization of the way the world process de facto works, not an ontological explanation of the way that it de jure must work. After all, "the final real things of which the world is made up" are actual occasions.[8] There is, therefore, no going behind actual occasions to locate something still more real or more ultimate. Yet, as I shall argue more in detail below, creativity for Whitehead is not a higher-level entity but a foundational activity which is operative in the more limited self-constituting activities of individual entities or actual occasions. Individual occasions come and go, but creativity as the underlying activity of the world process never ceases and in this sense is Ultimate Reality or the equivalent of primary substance for Aristotle.[9]

In the meantime, however, I call attention to the way Whitehead further specifies in *Process and Reality* his notion of God. Whereas in *Science and the Modern World* and in *Religion in the Making*, as noted above, he gives the impression that there may be two metaphysical Absolutes, namely, the underlying activity and God, here in *Process and Reality* he makes clear that there is strictly speaking only one Absolute, namely, creativity. In one place, for example, he notes that "every actual entity, including God, is a creature transcended by the creativity which it qualifies."[10] In another place, having noted that God supplies the initial motivation or "aim" for each newly developing actual occasion, he immediately adds that God is not for that reason to be considered the Creator of each finite occasion by willing it into being. Rather, creativity "creates" each actual occasion by being the underlying force in its individual process of self-realization, and God is influential in these acts of creation by being both "the aboriginal instance of this creativity" and therefore "the aboriginal condition which qualifies its action."[11] Finally, in discussing the relations between God and the world in the final section of the book, he says: "God and the World are the contrasted opposites in terms of which Creativity achieves its supreme task of transforming disjoined multiplicity, with its diversities in opposition, into concrescent unity, with its diversities in contrast."[12]

There is, then, no doubt that in *Process and Reality* Whitehead subordinated God to creativity within his overall scheme. God, to be sure, never began to exist at some point, like finite actual occasions. But God, too, exists only in virtue of creativity even as God radically conditions the way in which creativity operates in the world. Faced with this affront to traditional Christian belief in God as Creator of heaven and earth, theologically oriented Whiteheadians like John Cobb have tended to regard creativity as Whitehead's descriptive generalization of the way things are rather than his systematic or strictly ontological specification of the way that they have to be.[13]

My own approach in this chapter, on the contrary, will be to assume the opposite, namely, that creativity is indeed Whitehead's metaphysical Absolute, the specification of the way things have to be, but also to point out, as mentioned previously, that creativity is the metaphysical Absolute as an activity, not as an entity. Furthermore, precisely as an activity and not an entity, creativity could be the underlying nature of God, the dynamic principle or ground of the divine being, and as such likewise the ground of all finite beings. In this way, Whitehead's philosophy would seem to be a further development of themes already inchoatively present in Aristotle, Thomas Aquinas, and Meister Eckhart, as the preceding chapters of this book have tried to make clear.

Before setting forth my own understanding of creativity in detail, however, I should make clear why I believe that creativity is a genuine metaphysical Absolute, existing, to be sure, not in itself apart from actual entities, but in and through those same entities as their underlying metaphysical ground or vital source of existence. Here I will be greatly assisted by the antecedent work of John Wilcox, who carefully researched and critiqued many of the positions that have been taken on the ontological status of creativity in Whitehead's philosophy before advancing his own proposal, which is remarkably similar to mine.[14] That is, without elaborating on the relation between God and creativity, Wilcox argues that, for creativity to be genuinely ongoing, it must be numerically one rather than many, that is, that it must be a single foundational activity at work in all the self-constituting activities of individual actual occasions rather than simply a descriptive term for all those same particular activities of self-constitution taken individually. In effect, then, he is arguing as I am, too, that creativity is a metaphysical Absolute rather than simply an empirical generalization without further ontological grounding.

Out of the many Whiteheadians who clearly endorse the opposite idea, namely, that creativity for Whitehead is simply a descriptive principle, a statement of the way things are, rather than a metaphysical absolute, I will single out only one, namely, Donald Sherburne. Sherburne puts his analysis of the role of creativity in Whitehead's philosophy within the context of the problem of the One and the Many. "Creativity is simply the ultimate principle descriptive of the one-many relationship inhering in the coming-to-be of actual entities."[15] That is, out of the multiplicity of past actual occasions which are together the environment or context for each newly developing occasion there emerges a new ontological unity or novel entity. This new entity, however, inevitably adds itself to the overall environment for its successor occasion(s). Creativity is thus just the descriptive term for a self-perpetuating process with complementary functions: the first, that of bringing unity out of multiplicity; the second, that of immediately adding to the multiplicity so that the unity has to be created all over again.[16] Here I would agree with Wilcox that creativity, when thus presented simply as a descriptive principle rather than as a metaphysical Absolute, does not answer the question why such a self-perpetuating process should exist in the first place.[17] A deeper reason is required to explain why there is this drive for unity on a universal scale when every attempt to achieve this unity only results in still further diversity.

Robert Neville both agrees and disagrees. Even though he is not a Whiteheadian, he agrees with Sherburne and other students of Whitehead's thought that Whiteheadian creativity is nothing more than a descriptive principle of the way the world process works.[18] It does not, in other words, offer any deeper reason for the way things are. For, as Whitehead himself comments in *Process and Reality*, the ultimate reasons for things are grounded in actual entities and the decisions which they make both in terms of their own development and with respect to the self-constitution of future actual entities.[19] Yet, if creativity is already involved in each of these decisions, it cannot itself be explained in terms of such a decision.[20] Rather, says Neville, the deeper reason for the existence and operation of creativity is creation itself understood as the product of divine creative activity emanating from an otherwise totally unknown Source. Thus "God" for Neville is not a Supreme Being standing over against the world as its Creator, but rather an indeterminate reality which becomes the Creator God of Biblical revelation in and through the transcendent activity of creating.[21] Part of that transcendent divine activity is to set up the necessary conditions for the dynamic interrelation of God and the world of finite occasions, chief among them being creativity which continually recreates unity out of antecedent multiplicity and vice versa.

I certainly agree with Neville that creativity, when understood simply as a descriptive generalization of the way the world process operates, is no substitute for God and divine creative activity as the deeper ontological reason for the existence of this world. Yet I do not share his other conviction that creativity as a result is simply the contingent result of an activity emanating from "God" in a vague and indeterminate sense. Equally possible, it seems to me, is the hypothesis that creativity operates the way that it does in creation because it already operates that way within the divine life. Creativity, in other words, as an ongoing attempt to create new unity out of antecedent multiplicity or diversity, is the divine nature or principle of existence and activity for God as a (tri-)personal being; as such it underlies and sustains what Whitehead in *Process and Reality* calls the "primordial," the "consequent" and the "superjective" natures of God.[22] In the remainder of this chapter, accordingly, I will give my reasons for that proposal and also make clear how, in my judgment, creativity as the ground of the divine being is likewise the immanent ground of the universe as a whole and of every entity within it.

I will be working here at first with Whitehead's concept of God as presented in *Process and Reality*. Later in the chapter, I will sketch my own Trinitarian reinterpretation of Whitehead's concept of God and show how within a Trinitarian framework the claims for creativity as the underlying nature of God and the ground of the universe are even more readily apparent. I begin by calling attention to the fact that, even though Whitehead refers to God as an actual entity,[23] God within Whitehead's scheme, strictly speaking, is not a fixed entity in the classical sense but the subject of an ongoing activity or, as I suggested in Chapter 2, a subsistent activity. For that matter, every actual entity is a subsistent activity in that its being consists in its process of self-constitution. But, whereas finite actual entities eventually terminate their processes of self-constitution and become "superjects," objective data, for subsequent actual entities, God by definition is an actual entity whose process of self-development never ends. Hence, God never really becomes an entity in the classical sense, that is, a fixed objective reality, but always remains the living subject of an ongoing activity.

Keeping this in mind, we may now reflect more critically on what Whitehead could mean by calling God the "aboriginal instance" of creativity and the "aboriginal condition which qualifies its action."[24] God is, first of all, not simply identified with creativity, since creativity is also at work in the self-constitution of finite actual entities. But God, as I see it, likewise gives creativity a specific character or decisive pattern of operation simply because God is the entity in which it primarily operates and through which it becomes available to other entities. Its existence and operation in the self-constitution of finite entities, in other words, are an outgrowth of its antecedent existence and operation within the divine process of becoming, as I shall explain in detail later.

Beforehand, however, an objection should be answered. In *Process and Reality* Whitehead says: "God and the World are the contrasted opposites in terms of which Creativity achieves its supreme task of transforming disjoined multiplicity with its diversities in opposition, into concrescent unity, with its diversities in contrast."[25] Hence, creativity does not exist first in God and then in finite actual entities, but rather exists between God and the world of finite entities. Admittedly, Whitehead's language here is misleading; he seems to picture creativity as an actuality independent of God and the world. But, as Ivor Leclerc remarks in *Whitehead's Metaphysics*, such an understanding of the role of creativity in the world process would be an instance of the fallacy of misplaced concreteness; for creativity exists only in its instantiations or modes of being.[26] Thus, if God is its archetypal or primordial instantiation, creativity must exist first and foremost within God and be structured by its operation within God so as to affect its operation within finite actual entities. Creativity, accordingly, is in the first place the ground or vital source of the divine being and activity, and only in the second place the ground or vital source of the being and activity of all finite actual entities.

Yet, if creativity is thus the ground of both the divine being and the being of all creatures, what is the relationship between God and finite actual entities? Do they as a result constitute one unified reality? Whitehead's answer would seem to be no, since the net effect of the operation of creativity, as noted above, is to produce a new multiplicity: "The many become one, and are increased by one."[27] The unity achieved through the action of creativity is in each case the unity within a given actual entity, not between actual entities. God and the world of finite actual entities are thus at any given moment a simple multiplicity, not a unitary reality. But has Whitehead thought deeply enough on this question? If God and finite entities share a common ground or common principle of existence and activity, then creatures must somehow exist in God. They are grounded in the very same principle of existence and activity which makes God to be God. Finite actual entities, accordingly, exist in God if by "God" is meant the divine nature, that is, the principle of creativity as the ontological ground for the existence and activity of both God and themselves. At the same time, they exist apart from "God" as a personal being who is, after all, likewise a "creature" of creativity like themselves, grounded in that same underlying ontological activity.

Charles Hartshorne, Whitehead's most celebrated disciple, was likewise not content with Whitehead's understanding of the God-world relationship. Instead, Hartshorne conceived God and the world as a "Compound Individual" whereby the world is the "body" of God and God is the "soul" of the world.[28] As will be evident below, I myself prefer to think of God and the world of finite entities as constituting a cosmic community rather than a supraindividual entity as Hartshorne does. But I agree with him that the precise nature of the God-world relationship within Whitehead's metaphysical scheme needs to be clarified. For that purpose, I will make use of the work of another Whiteheadian, Jorge Luis Nobo. The focus of Nobo's research, to be sure, is not on the God-world relationship as such but rather on the role of the *extensive continuum* within Whitehead's metaphysics. But, as I shall indicate below, there is a natural bridge here likewise to reconceive the God-world relationship.

In his book, *Whitehead's Metaphysics of Extension and Solidarity*, Nobo claims that within Whitehead's system "creativity and extension [i.e., the extensive continuum] are indissoluble aspects of one ultimate reality—a reality underlying the becoming, the being and the solidarity of all actual entities," including God as the primordial actual entity.[29] Like Aristotelian prime matter, therefore, neither creativity nor the extensive continuum exist in themselves as individual entities. Rather, they are principles of being or essential conditions for the existence of individual entities. Thus they achieve actuality only in and through the actual entities in which they are instantiated or embodied. Yet both creativity and the extensive continuum are indispensable for the self-constitution of those same actual entities. That is, without the antecedent principle of creativity the actual entity would lack the power of internal self-constitution; without the extensive continuum, the actual entity would not exist in solidarity with other actual entities, past, present, and future, so as to constitute with them the broader reality of the world as an ongoing process. Hence, creativity and the extensive continuum are "two differentiable, but inseparable, aspects of the ultimate ground of the organic universe. This ultimate ground has no name of its own, other than the names used to designate its two indissoluble aspects. Accordingly, insofar as this ground is the whereby of all becoming, it is termed 'creativity'; and insofar as it is the wherein of all interconnected actual existence, it is termed 'extension.'"[30]

Nobo, to be sure, does not identify this "ultimate ground of the organic universe" with the divine nature or the ground of the divine being. But, as noted above, God, like finite actual entities, exists in virtue of the principle of creativity. Likewise, God, too, as the ever-expanding infinite actual entity, exists together with all finite actual entities within the extensive continuum.[31] Hence, creativity and the extensive continuum are the ontological ground of the divine being as well as the ontological ground of all finite beings. Yet, since creativity and the extensive continuum as principles or conditions of existence for entities do not exist by themselves but only in the actual entities in which they are instantiated or embodied, then, logically, they must primordially exist in their primordial instantiation, namely, God. They together constitute, accordingly, in the first place the ground of the divine being and then only in the second place the ground of finite actual entities.

This is not to say, of course, that first God alone exists and then afterwards finite entities come into existence. Since Whitehead insists in *Process and Reality* that God and the world reciprocally condition one another's existence and activity,[32] it is sufficient to think here in terms of a logical priority of creativity and the extensive continuum serving as the ground of the divine being before functioning as the ground of all finite beings. Even so, the question of the location of this double-faceted ground of the organic universe must also be answered. In my view, as noted above, it can only be answered by saying that creativity and the extensive continuum are located within God in the sense that they together constitute in the first place the divine nature or the ground of the divine being. Finite actual entities thus exist *in* God, understood as the ground of the divine being, even though they have their own entitative reality apart from God understood as the sole infinite actual entity.

Whitehead himself, to be sure, never made this distinction between the underlying nature of God and the personhood or entitative reality of God. This is perhaps to be explained by the fact that, as William Christian notes, the *concept* of God is a "derivative notion" within Whitehead's philosophy.[33] That is, Whitehead was primarily interested in working out a philosophy of becoming or process. Within that perspective, "God" was simply one of the instances, albeit the primordial instance, of the principles of becoming. Hence, if the existence of creativity and the extensive continuum are necessary presuppositions of the self-constitution of finite actual entities, they must somehow likewise be necessary for the ongoing self-constitution of God as the sole infinite or ever-developing actual entity.

Quite another perspective emerges if one consciously begins with the

Christian notion of God as triune, that is, as a community of divine persons, and then asks how in virtue of creativity and the extensive continuum they are nevertheless one God rather than three gods in close collaboration. For, then, one sees in a dramatic way how both creativity and the extensive continuum are conditioned by their primordial instantiation in God. That is, each of the three divine persons at every moment recreates itself out of the multiplicity of its past moments of experience. Likewise, together with the other two persons, each divine person recreates at every moment the unity of the divine community. Thus on both the individual and the communal levels of existence within God, creativity is operative: "[t]he many become one, and are increased by one."[34]

Similarly, in and through the dynamic interrelatedness of the three divine persons at every moment the extensive continuum comes into being as a "relational complex" linking past, present and future within the divine being.[35] Furthermore, if with Nobo we join the extensive continuum with the principle of creativity as "two differentiable, but inseparable, aspects of the ultimate ground of the organic universe," then the two together function as an underlying "force-field" for the ongoing interrelated activity of the three divine persons.[36] Finally, if, as noted above, creativity and the extensive continuum likewise condition the existence and operation of all finite actual entities, then this same "force-field" is also the ontological ground for the emergence and interrelated activity of successive generations of finite actual entities. In this way, as we shall see below, the three divine persons and all their creatures together make up an ever-growing cosmic society within the force-field constituted by creativity and the extensive continuum.

Once again, however, various objections to this hypothesis must first be met. For, if all three divine persons are needed to constitute the force-field for themselves and all their creatures, one seems to end up with an affirmation of tritheism, belief in three gods, not monotheism, belief in one God. Furthermore, if, as Whitehead proposes, "agency belongs exclusively to actual occasions,"[37] it is even more difficult to imagine how the three divine persons can exercise a unified agency, behave, in other words, as one God. For, if all three divine persons exercise agency, then they would seem to be three gods who have antecedently agreed to act in concert with one another when dealing with their creatures. But this, too, is tritheism, not monotheism: an alternative clearly unacceptable to orthodox Christian belief.

From a Whiteheadian perspective, what is finally at issue here is one's antecedent understanding of the category of *society* within Whitehead's metaphysical scheme. Societies, it will be remembered, are groupings of actual entities which make up all the objective "things" of common sense experience; but their precise nature and function within Whitehead's philosophy are somewhat ambiguous. Elsewhere I have presented a detailed analysis and critique of Whitehead's relatively sparse remarks on this subject in *Process and Reality*.[38] Here I present only a brief summary of my own position on this controversial issue. While complying with White-head's dictum that agency belongs exclusively to actual occasions (actual entities), I maintain that the net effect of all the interrelated individual agencies of actual occasions within a given society is a collective agency for the society as a whole which is sufficient to allow for its retention of a definite form or character over time. Stones, for example, retain a certain size and texture over time because their constituent actual occasions spontaneously co-produce the same common element of form or objective structure over successive generations. This common element of form for the society as a whole is then at every moment both the effect of the collective agency of the current set of actual occasions and the cause of its reproduction in the next set of occasions, in that the latter "prehend" or appropriate their predecessors not simply as an aggregate of individuals but as an objective totality with a common element of form (e.g., as together constituting a stone of a certain size and texture).

This is, to be sure, a minimal ontological agency, but only a minimal agency is required to keep the actual occasions constitutive of a stone functioning together as an organized whole. Where more complex forms of agency are required, above all, those which demand some form of corporate decision for the entire group of actual occasions, then the society in question does have need of a dominant subsociety or a "soul." But, even here, the dominant subsociety or soul exists for the sake of the totality just as the subordinate subsocieties exist for the sake of the organism as a whole. In my mind, for example, I constantly make decisions, not simply for me as a disembodied ego but for me as a body-soul unity. Thus even in those structured societies of actual occasions with a dominant subsociety, there is a collective agency at work. The agency of the dominant subsociety is fused with the interrelated agencies of all the subordinate subsocieties to produce the collective agency of the "compound individual" or physical organism as a whole.[39]

If, then, Whiteheadian societies can be said to possess an ontological unity over and above the unity of their constituent actual occasions, and if these societies likewise possess a collective agency derivative from the interrelated individual agencies of those same occasions, then there is no reason on systematic grounds to deny the possibility of a trinitarian understanding of God within Whitehead's categoreal scheme. Granted, he himself did not think along those lines, at least with any consistency. But there would seem to be nothing wrong with modifying his metaphysical scheme in this direction. In addition, as I hope to show below, there are distinct advantages to conceiving the God-world relationship in trinitarian terms once one has come to the realization that the world is an objective unity in its own right. For, if the world does not derive its unity from incorporation into the consequent nature of God (as Whitehead himself proposes in *Process and Reality*[40]), then it must possess its own intrinsic unity as a quasi-autonomous structured society of actual occasions. In that case, however, the world remains ontologically dependent upon God its Creator only if it is part of the even larger societal reality represented by the communitarian life of the three divine persons in their dynamic interrelation. The all-comprehensive society constituted by the three divine persons, in other words, must include within itself the enormous but still finite society of the world with all its myriad subsocieties and constituent actual occasions.

To explain further this new understanding of the God-world relationship, I will first sketch my own model for the divine communitarian life and then indicate how the world of creation fits easily and naturally into the exchange of life and love among the three divine persons. I use the word *model* advisedly, however, since we are dealing here with the mystery of Ultimate Reality which is only partly revealed in the pages of the Hebrew and Christian Bible. Moreover, the purpose of the model is not so much to explain the reality of God which will always be somewhat mysterious to human beings, but rather to give a new perspective on the God-world relationship which is of vital interest to human beings both in their dealings with one another and with respect to God as their common object of worship. Such a model, in other words, inevitably tells us far more about the ideal of human life in this world than about the divine life as such.

In general, I accept Hartshorne's notion of God as a sequential series of actual occasions (in technical language, a personally ordered series of living actual occasions). But, in line with my trinitarian hypothesis, I propose that each of the divine persons is such a personally ordered society of actual occasions and that their unity as one God is the unity of a more comprehensive or "structured" society. That is, all three of them exercise an individualized agency vis-à-vis one another and all their creatures, but the net effect of their interrelated individual agencies is to produce a common element of form or pattern of interaction which constitutes their unity as one God. They are, in other words, one God because they share without overlap one and the same intentional field of activity which in its basic structure never changes.

Whitehead in *Process and Reality* specified that a society is an environment for its constituent actual occasions.[41] The shape or structure of this environment is set up at any given moment by the interrelated agencies of those same actual occasions, but basically the same structure will be realized by the next set of occasions insofar as they "prehend" or appropriate the structure of the environment from their predecessors.[42] In this way, the society as an ordered environment or, as I would phrase it, a structured field of activity, endures with basically the same character over time even though its constituent actual occasions are constantly changing. The only difference that I am suggesting here in line with a trinitarian understanding of God is that the divine persons as three personally ordered societies of actual occasions constitute not three separate fields of activity but rather identically one and the same field of activity. None of them, in other words, has any reality apart from the other two persons. Whereas human persons living in community have a field of activity which is partly shared with others in the community and partly personal to themselves, the divine persons have nothing personal which is not at the same time communal, likewise proper to the other two persons. For, only in this way are they one God, one ontological reality, rather than three gods in close relationship with one another.[43]

But what is the subjective identity of each of the divine persons? How are the "Father," the "Son" and the "Holy Spirit" related to one another within the divine life?[44] Here I consciously choose roles for each of the divine persons which seem to be in accord with Whitehead's understanding of God and yet which are likewise grounded in the understanding of God presented by the Christian Bible. I argue, for example, that all three divine persons participate in what Whitehead calls the divine primordial nature, the divine consequent nature and the divine superjective nature, albeit in different ways. That is, while all three persons survey the vast realm of possibilities existent within their common field of activity at any given moment (the divine primordial nature), the "Father" alone "decides" which possibility is appropriate for that moment of their common history. Secondly, while all three share in the divine consequent nature, the "Son" alone "decides" to actualize the possibility chosen by the "Father" for their common life together. Finally, while all three share in the divine superjective nature, the "Spirit" alone "decides" to execute or implement this "decision" of the "Son" and thus to perpetuate their life together as a community of divine persons. Each divine person, accordingly, has an indispensable role in the maintenance of the divine life.[45]

Admittedly, this is only a speculative model for the inner-trinitarian life, not a privileged picture of the way things actually are. But, as I shall now explain, it does serve to make clear how this world of ours can be participant within the communitarian life of the three divine persons and yet retain its separate ontological identity as a very large but still finite "structured society" within the Whiteheadian scheme. For, as I see it, in virtue of the role which the "Father" plays within the divine life, the "Father" can be said to be Creator of heaven and earth (or in more philosophical language the subsistent principle of potentiality for the world of creation). That is, at every moment the "Father" offers not just to the divine "Son" but likewise to all newly developing finite actual occasions the equivalent of a corporate "initial aim," namely, a possibility of existence, to which the "Son" and all finite occasions must in some measure respond in order to exist. The "Son," on the other hand, in virtue of the "Son's" role within the divine life is the head of creation or the subsistent principle of provisional actuality here and now for the world of creation. That is, the "Son" together with all these finite occasions, in thus responding to the initial aim of the "Father" at every moment, actualizes what was merely potential in terms of the "Father's" offer. Finally, the "Spirit" in virtue of the role which the "Spirit" plays within the divine life is the sustaining power of the world process or the subsistent principle of ultimate actuality within creation. That is, the "Spirit," in executing and bringing to fruition the corporate decision of the "Son" and all finite actual occasions at every moment, guarantees that the joint process of the divine life and of all creation will perdure into the future.[46]

The net result of this scheme is, therefore, an understanding of the God-world relationship in which all finite actual occasions and the field constituted by their dynamic interrelation are included within the field of activity proper to the three divine persons. That is, by their self-constituting "decisions" at every moment, the divine persons have a direct influence on all finite occasions. As noted above, at every moment finite occasions respond to the initial aim of the "Father" in union with the "Son" and through the power of the "Spirit." A trinitarian structure, accordingly, pervades the field of activity proper to the created universe without being directly perceptible by finite actual occasions. All that most human beings, for example, consciously recognize is that by their decisions from moment to moment they are helping to give shape and pattern to their own human world and in a very modest way to the ongoing evolution of the entire universe. That their human world, and indeed all of creation, participates in the communitarian life of the three divine persons is a perspective available only to those who antecedently believe in the reality of a triune Creator God and reflect upon the workings of the divine persons in their lives.[47]

At the same time, finite occasions by their self-constituting decisions not only structure the world of creation but likewise add richness and diversity to the communitarian life of the three divine persons. Their collective response to the initial aim of the "Father," for example, adds nuance and subtlety to the response of the divine "Son" to the "Father" at that moment. Likewise, the "Spirit" at every moment empowers the response of a myriad number of finite actual occasions to the "Father" as well as the response of the divine "Son" to the "Father." Finally, the "Father" offers a more complex initial aim, given the fact of creation and the existence of so many finite actual occasions. Thus the world of finite occasions, as a subordinate field of activity contained within the all-comprehensive field of activity proper to the divine persons, both influences and is influenced by the communitarian life of the three divine persons. Together, the three divine persons and all their creatures constitute one world, one all-embracing cosmic society.

Elsewhere I have argued that finite actual occasions preserve subjective immediacy even after their brief moment of existence in the space-time continuum.[48] Through incorporation into the communitarian life of God, they too acquire subjective immortality like the three divine persons; they remain forever as the entities which they have de facto become through their self-constituting decision in the temporal order. Thus a human being (and indeed, with qualifications, every other created entity as well) is continually being "resurrected" as the successive moments of his or her life are progressively incorporated into the communitarian life of the three divine persons. Full "resurrection," of course, takes place only when one dies and thereby escapes the limitations of the space-time continuum so as to be reunited with all the past moments of one's life. Presumably at this critical moment one experiences simultaneously judgment and peace as one finally comes to terms with the full meaning of one's life on earth within the context of the cosmic society, the divine communitarian life. Details of this argument, however, which is partly based on the analysis of key texts in the final part of *Process and Reality* and partly grounded in an extension of Whitehead's thought originally proposed by Marjorie Suchocki, can be found in *Society and Spirit*.[49] My intention in these pages is simply to summarize this earlier research and put it in the context of the argument of the present book.

By way of conclusion, then, I will try to make clear how this trinitarian understanding of God within the context of Whitehead's categoreal scheme verifies what I have said earlier about the relation between the Infinite and the finite. The underlying nature of this triune God is explained in terms of categories derived from Whitehead's own scheme. That is, as I have indicated above, creativity and the extensive continuum together constitute the divine nature or principle of existence and activity. They are respectively the *whereby* and the *wherein* for the ongoing existence of the three divine persons and for the emergence of successive generations of finite actual occasions. As such, creativity and the extensive continuum are infinite. Creativity possesses the infinity of an ongoing activity which is continually instantiated in the occasions constitutive of the divine persons and of all their creatures. The extensive continuum likewise is infinite in that it extends beyond the finite limits of the present space-time continuum and includes all past worlds and all possible future worlds as well.[50]

The divine persons, on the other hand, are "finite," not in the negative sense that they are imperfect or lacking in what they should be, but rather in the positive sense that at any given moment each of them is a fully *determinate* actuality by reason of a self-constituting "decision." Admittedly, as noted above,[51] each occasion constitutive of a given moment in the life of one of the divine persons recapitulates its past history, namely, the feelings appropriate to all its predecessor moments, in and through its appropriation of the structural objectifications of all those subjective "decisions" in the divine field of activity. Thus, because the field itself remains basically the same from moment to moment, there is presumably little or no sense of a succession of separate moments or passage of time for any of the divine persons. Yet, even so, the "Father" at any given moment is not precisely the same as the "Father" of the preceding moment, and the same may be said of the "Son" and the "Spirit" in the successive moments of their existence. What does remain basically unchanged, of course, is the pattern of their interrelation as recorded in the structure of their common field of activity. In virtue of this enduring structured field of activity to which they all contribute, they are one God, one and the same ontological reality yesterday, today and forever.

Similarly, the world of creation is an immense but still finite reality. Being made up of finite actual occasions which are organized into a myriad number of subsocieties, the material universe is an incremental reality which continues to expand but which at any given moment is still a finite reality. Even with the supposition that no finite actual occasion ever perishes but that all occasions without exception somehow enjoy subjective immortality within the communitarian life of the three divine persons, one must still say that the world is finite. For, as Aristotle made clear in his discussion of the nature of the Infinite in the *Physics*, whatever exists as an actuality is by that very fact finite, a determinate reality.[52] Only processes are infinite in that they are ongoing or unfinished. Yet even here, at any given moment every process (including the process of the divine life within which the world process is contained) represents a finite achievement; its infinity lies in what is yet to come.

Is there then no actual infinite? The answer to this question depends upon whether one recognizes the difference between the indeterminate actuality of a universal "force-field" and the fully determinate actuality of an entity within that field. For, as noted above, creativity is infinite but only because it is an activity, not an entity. It is, to be sure, rendered finite or determinate through instantiation in specific entities at every moment. But in itself as an ongoing activity, that is, as a fluid or indeterminate ontological reality, it is infinite. Similarly, the extensive continuum is infinite because it too is not an entity but rather an all-inclusive context or field for the existence of entities. It exists, in other words, through the interrelated activity of entities but for that same reason cannot itself be an entity since it is the necessary context or environment for their dynamic interaction. One could also argue, as noted above, that the extensive continuum is infinite because it transcends what actually exists, namely, the space-time continuum of the present world, and includes worlds which only potentially exist here and now. But the deeper reason for the infinity of the extensive continuum is that like creativity it is not an entity, that is, a fully determinate actuality, but rather a principle or necessary condition for the existence of entities.[53] Together with creativity, it is the indeterminate ground of being for everything determinate that exists; in itself, therefore, it is infinite.

The notion of ground, accordingly, corresponds to what is real without being fully actual or determinate. As first Schelling and then Heidegger saw with transparent clarity, the ontological ground of a being cannot itself be a being without needing to be grounded in still another being.[54] Thus they both stipulated in different ways that the ontological ground of a being is not another being but rather a hidden dimension of the being in question. The ground is thus real without being fully actual. For, the determinate actuality of the being is its character as an existent, that which has emerged out of the ground. Without the underlying ground, however, the existent would never come to be. Hence, the ground is just as real as the existent. Yet it never achieves determinate actuality in itself but only in and through the existent.

Heidegger in his early works, to be sure, refused to think of the ground in broader terms as that which underlies the existence of all entities without exception. Rather, he focused exclusively on the ground simply as operative in *Dasein* (the human being in the act of self-transcendence) so as to project a "world" for itself at every moment. But in his later works, it will be remembered, he realized that this grounding activity of *Dasein* must itself be grounded in the primordial activity of being which grounds the activity of all beings but is itself ungrounded since it is not a being in need of being grounded. Schelling, on the other hand, in implicit fidelity with the German mystical tradition as represented by Jacob Boehme, recognized from the beginning that there must be an ontological ground for the existence of all finite entities which is located in God but not identified with God as an existent.

While Whitehead clearly did not think of creativity and the extensive continuum as together constituting "the ground of the organic universe," I agree with Jorge Nobo that that is in fact what they are. Furthermore, in further development of Nobo's thesis, I propose that this ground of the organic universe must be located somewhere and that, if it can only be located in existents, it must exist, first of all, in God as the primordial existent and then from that "location" likewise exist in all finite occasions as the ground of their existence and activity. Yet, as I made clear in the present chapter, the best way to imagine a common ground between God and creatures is to think of God as tripersonal rather than unipersonal. For, in that case, creativity and the extensive continuum can be seen to operate primarily within God and then secondarily between God and creatures. As noted above, each of the divine persons is an ever-new unity of all its previous moments of experience. Likewise, together with the other two persons, each divine person at every moment recreates the unity of the divine community. Thus, when creativity operates to bring unity out of an antecedent multiplicity of finite actual occasions in creation, it is operating in the same way in which it already functions within God. Similarly, the extensive continuum primarily exists in virtue of the dynamic interrelation of the three divine persons within the divine community. It serves as the "relational complex" for all actual occasions within creation only because it already is the "force-field" for the existence and interrelated activity of the three divine persons. In this way, through such a trinitarian reinterpretation of the God-world relationship within Whitehead's philosophy, I am consciously aligning the latter with the mystical tradition of the West as represented by Eckhart, Boehme, and eventually Schelling.

With this passing reference to the mystical tradition of the West, I can now bring the first part of the present book to a suitable conclusion. For, in the second part of the book, I will be equivalently investigating the mystical tradition of the East, that is, the notion of Ultimate Reality to be found in classical Hinduism, Buddhism, and Taoism. Specifically, in the notions of *Brahman*, Absolute Emptiness, and the Tao I will be looking for possible corollaries to the ideas developed in this part of the book. That is, I will likewise be asking whether the Infinite in these Asian religions is to be understood as a transcendent entity or whether it is rather an underlying ontological activity together with the field or ontological context in which that activity must inevitably be exercised.

Note

In contemporary Trinitarian theology, one of the key issues is the alleged sexist character of the traditional names for the divine persons, namely, "Father," "Son" and "Holy Spirit" (the latter referred to as He rather than She or It). Theologians like Elizabeth Johnson have urged that female names for the divine persons such as "Mother-Sophia," "Jesus-Sophia" and "Spirit-Sophia" should likewise be used as metaphors to designate the divine persons in their relations with their creatures.[55] Although in full agreement with Johnson on this point, I have resorted to another option, namely, that of using the traditional male names for the persons of the Trinity but enclosed in quotation marks to indicate their nonliteral or metaphorical status.

At the same time, I wish to call attention to the fact that the Whiteheadian understanding of a "personally ordered" society of actual occasions has no intrinsic reference to sex or gender. Not only animal organisms, but inanimate things like tables and chairs are likewise examples of personally ordered societies of actual occasions.[56] Human persons, to be sure, are sexually oriented but only because the personally ordered society of living actual occasions constituting the human soul is interactive with the various subsocieties of actual occasions making up a male or female human body. In the language of my own hypothesis in this chapter, the intentional field of activity constitutive of human consciousness inevitably reflects the experiences of life in a male or female body. Divine persons, on the other hand, in their dynamic relations with one another are sexless because their common intentional field of activity does not reflect the experiences of life in the body. Each of the divine persons is, in other words, an ongoing self-constituting center of activity in dynamic relation with two other such self-constituting centers of activity so as to constitute an all-comprehensive intentional field of activity which includes the whole of creation but is not itself a bodily reality. In this context, the terms "Father," "Son" and "Holy Spirit" are simply metaphors for the way in which these three self-constituting centers of activity interact with one another so as to share a common life.

The ultimate resolution for the issue of sexist language with reference to the persons of the Trinity, therefore, may well lie in the direction pointed out by Whitehead. The term *person* has to be purified of its imaginative link with life in a male or female body. As such, a person is simply an ongoing self-constituting center of activity within an intentional field structured by that individual's dynamic relations with other such self-constituting centers of activity. Admittedly, this does not correspond to the common sense understanding of personhood. But is not the common sense approach to personhood precisely the problem since it inevitably involves an imaginative link with life in the body? If the results of contemporary natural science have dramatically revealed to us that physical reality is not what it seems to be at first glance, perhaps it is time to develop appropriate conceptual tools for understanding more subtle spiritual realities like human and divine personhood.

PART II

Introductory Note

In this second part of the book, I will be exploring the notion of infinity within some of the major religious traditions of Asia, namely, classical Hinduism, Buddhism, and Taoism. Likewise, as in the first part of the book, I will be making that exploration with the aid of my own understanding of the categories of creativity and the extensive continuum from the philosophy of Alfred North Whitehead. Naturally, in this part of the book where I will be dealing with non-Christian and non-Western modes of thought, the danger of ideological imperialism referred to in the Introduction will be very great. As I have already experienced in submitting early drafts of these chapters to colleagues who are experts in the various Asian religions, the common complaint has been that my interpretation of the classic texts of each of these religions is interesting, but in many respects it clashes with the classic understanding of those same texts. I am reading the texts too much as a Christian trained in the thought patterns of the West and too little as a Hindu, Buddhist, or Taoist with the instinctive mind-set of an Asiatic.

Yet, as I indicated in the Introduction, this very difference of perspective may be valuable in promoting interreligious dialogue. Precisely because I am an "outsider" to the tradition in question and bring an unaccustomed set of philosophical categories to the analysis of the classic text, I am free to ask questions which in a sense are "off limits" to the Hindu, Buddhist, or Taoist. To the Advaita Vedanta Hindu, for example, who objects that activity in any form is totally absent from the notion of *Brahman*, I then ask: what then is *Brahman*, if it is neither an entity nor an activity? How can it be "the One without a second" if it is neither an all-encompassing entity nor an all-pervasive unifying activity? Likewise, to the practicing Buddhist, I pose the question in Chapter 6: what is the metaphysical ground or *raison d'être* for your belief in dependent co-arising as the universal condition of all experience and reality. What guarantee do you have that dependent co-arising will not cease in the next moment or sometime in the near future? Finally, to the Taoist, I am free to ask how being can indeed come from non-being, something from nothing. Granted that this is the clear meaning of the *Tao te Ching*, how can one justify its meaning apart from the authority of the text?

These questions, it seems to me, can be asked without danger of ideological imperialism, provided that one does not presume to have the correct answer on the basis of one's antecedent metaphysical scheme but instead is ready to learn and possibly to alter one's thinking on the basis of the other's response. In this way, both the questioner and the respondent are forced to deeper levels of reflection in the search for common under- standing. In virtue of my own study of the Asian religions, for example, I have been led to think more seriously about the notion of the Godhead within the Christian tradition and its place within a Christian under- standing of God as (tri-)personal. Likewise, reflection on Buddhist texts dealing with the non-self and dependent co-arising have led me to seek a correlation here with terms out of the philosophy of Alfred North White- head. In each case, the linkage is tentative and incomplete but the effort at further reflection is certainly rewarding.

In brief, then, for the expert in Advaita Vedanta Hinduism, classical Buddhism, Zen Buddhism and classical Taoism, the next few chapters may be less than satisfactory because various distinctions and qualifications in the interpretation of the classic texts have not been properly made. Yet my intention here is not to discredit the classic understanding of the text but only to raise the possibility of an alternate understanding based on a new set of questions out of another tradition and with a different mind-set. After all, as Paul Ricoeur noted some years ago, what is ultimately important in the history of interpretation is not the original intention of the author but the text itself as the source of ever new interpretations.[1] In that spirit of seeking an alternate rather than the definitive understanding of classic texts, I undertake now an analysis of the notion of infinity in classical Hinduism, Buddhism, and Taoism.

5

The Dynamic Identity-in-Difference of *Brahman* and *Atman*

Hinduism, as Frank Podgorski points out, is a generic term for many different spiritual paths to the Transcendent; it is a mosaic in which each piece of glass "attests clearly to a 'keen awareness of the transphenomenal dimension of reality.'"[1] In this chapter, accordingly, I will make no effort to survey all the various schools of Hindu philosophy; still less will I try to deal with the various rituals associated with the practice of Hinduism in India over the centuries. Instead I will focus on a few key texts out of classic Hindu religious literature (the Upanishads) which deal with the relation between *Brahman* and *Atman* and attempt to assess the meaning of these texts in terms of my own problematic in this book, namely, the notion of the Infinite as an underlying ontological activity which is actual only in its instantiations. In addition, I will offer some comments on the relationship between *Brahman* and *Atman* as set forth in the works of three great Hindu philosopher/theologians, namely, Shankara, Ramanuja, and Madhva. Once again, this is to focus only on a few representatives of a very rich philosophical and theological tradition. But, at the very least, I will be coming to terms with differing notions of the relationship between the Infinite and the finite, the One and the Many, within classical Hinduism.

Above all, in dealing with the philosophy of Shankara, I will be taking quite seriously the claim of the Advaita Vedantins, perhaps the best known school of Indian philosophy in the West, that Reality is ultimately one and that the apparent multiplicity of independent and self-sufficient beings is illusory. My own contention, on the contrary, will be that only in a qualified sense is this true. In my view, all beings are interrelated forms or manifestations of one and the same underlying activity; this activity then is what is ultimately real. Yet these beings are not for that reason illusory or unreal. For, the underlying activity does not exist by itself but only in and through these entities. Hence, there is real (and not just apparent) multiplicity along with a deeper ontological unity.[2]

75

As already indicated in the Introduction to this book, therefore, I will be working with a notion of non-duality in addressing the Infinite-finite problematic. Monism, as I see it, is not satisfactory because it absorbs the empirical Many into the all-encompassing unity of the One or the Infinite. Nor is dualism satisfactory since it implicitly renders the infinity of the One finite by juxtaposing the One to the finite Many. Hence, only non-duality with its affirmation of the mutual implication of the One in the Many and the Many in the One seems adequately to address the problem of the relationship of the Infinite and the finite. At the same time, the notion of non-duality which I will set forth in this chapter will be quite different from that endorsed by Shankara and other Advaita Vedantins. It will be certainly closer to the world view espoused by Ramanuja and Madhva, as I shall indicate below. But, even here, certain differences in perspective will inevitably remain.

The Upanishadic texts which I plan to analyze are the *mahavakyas*, the "great sayings" of the Brahmanical tradition. Traditionally, they are four in number, one for each of the four *Vedas*. But I will follow Raimundo Panikkar on this point and expand their number to six.[3] Likewise, I will often use Panikkar's commentary on these *mahavakyas* as a starting-point for my own reflections. The first Great Saying, taken from the *Chandogya* Upanishad, is *ekam evadvitiyam,* one only without a second.[4] As Panikkar comments, the other *mahavakyas* make sense only in terms of this initial statement, which affirms the uncompromising primacy of the One. "Nothing short of the One can be ultimate truth."[5] The context of this saying is the conversation between a young man named Svetaketu and his father, Uddalaka, after the young man has returned from twelve years of study in the Brahmanical tradition. The young man soon learns that he has not penetrated to the heart of this tradition in the manner already known to his father. He has not learned, in other words, the deeper meaning of being. For, just as things made from copper, clay, or iron are in the end only different modifications of one and the same material substance, so, says the father, in the beginning "this world was just Being (*sat*), one only, without a second." Some, to be sure, argue that all things came from non-being. But, says Uddalaka, this is patently false: "How from Non-Being could Being be produced?"[6]

We will return to this conversation between Svetaketu and his father for still another of the Great Sayings of the Upanishads in due course. For the moment I wish to reflect upon the significance of this first Great Saying. The first and most obvious question is what is meant by being in this context. In terms of the problematic of this book, is it an entity or an activity? Or is it both simultaneously? Or is it neither an entity nor an activity since it is absolutely transcendent to all conceptual categories? As we will see in the latter half of this chapter, philosophers of the Advaita Vedanta school such as Shankara affirm the last of these three alternatives. I myself will argue in this chapter that it is an activity, indeed, the most fundamental activity of all, the activity of be-ing or existing. As such, it is foundational to all other more particular activities and has no distinguishing characteristics of its own. But it is the reason why reality is ultimately one rather than multiple. For, as the pure act of being, it is in a sense the sole reality. All entities are real only to the extent that they participate in its reality.

Eliot Deutsch comments: "*Reality* is that which cannot be subrated [called into question] by any other experience." But he then adds: "The only experience, or state of being, whose content cannot be subrated in fact and in principle by any other experience—which no other experience can conceivably contradict —is the experience of pure spiritual identity; the experience wherein the separation of self and non-self, of ego and world, is transcended, and pure oneness alone remains."[7] As I see it, the only reality which is simply identical with itself and yet which serves as the ground for the existence of self and non-self, the ego and the world, is the pure act of being, the activity of existing.

To illustrate this point, I now make reference to two of the celebrated "creation hymns" within the *Rig Veda*, one of the four canonical sets of sacred texts within Hinduism. We read, for example, in the "Nasadiya Sukta": "At first was neither Being nor Nonbeing. . . . The One breathed without breath, by its own impulse. Other than that was nothing else at all. Darkness was there, all wrapped around by darkness, and all was Water indiscriminate. Then that which was hidden by the Void, that One, emerging, stirring, through power of Ardor, came to be."[8] Thus, prior to the emergence of the One (understood as the primal entity), there was only a Void or nameless ground of being, the ontological source for the existence, first, of the One and then of the Many which proceed from the One. The author pictures it as *temporally* prior to the emergence of being and non-being; as I shall indicate below, it may be just *logically* prior to entities of various kinds (e.g., gods and mortals) since as the pure act of being it is their common principle of existence and activity.

Similarly, in the "Hiranyagarbha," another creation hymn out of the *Rig Veda*, reference is made to the Golden Germ or, as it is also translated, the Golden Egg out of which Prajapati, the Lord of all creatures, is born.[9] As Panikkar comments, "Vedic thought here struggles with the primordial problem of the piercing into the very nature of the Godhead and the luminous discovery of its dynamism and life."[10] God, after all, is a relative term. God, in other words, is "God" only to creatures, not to God's own self or being. Hence, God becomes "God" only with the dawn of creation. And yet, previous to creation there seems to be an internal divine life, "a birth inside the ultimate mystery itself,"[11] and it is this logically prior moment to which the "Hiranyagarbha" points with its reference to the Golden Germ. This, too, is being in the sense of the first Great Saying, that singular reality which precedes the birth of the gods and mortals and thus precedes the conventional distinction between being and non-being. Yet is being in this context an entity or an activity? With his reference to the Godhead and the internal divine life, Panikkar seems to be asserting that being is an activity. But, faithful to the sacred text, he also refers to it in more entitative terms as the "enclosure" where God is not yet God or as the "womb" of the Ultimate.[12]

At this point I will set forth in more detail my own hypothesis, namely, that being understood as a non-dual reality is not a being but rather an underlying ontological activity which exists only in its instantiations. Admittedly, as noted above, this is not the understanding of non-duality espoused by Advaita Vedantins. But, in line with all the possible meanings for the notion of non-dualism,[13] it would seem to be a legitimate interpretation of the term. For, an activity, after all, is non-dual in that it is both itself and something else at the same time. That is, it never exists in itself as an entity separate from other entities; it exists only in and through the entities which it empowers to exist. It is thus involved with all of them as the principle of their self-constitution and yet at the same time identical with none of them since it is an activity and not an entity. Similarly, it transcends the conventional distinction between being and non-being since it can equally well be said both to be and not to be at the same time. It *is not* in that it is not an entity, and it *is* in that it is the internal principle of existence and activity for everything that is. Finally, as a never-ending activity, it is a timeless or eternal reality, unchanging in itself even as it is the principle of movement or change within the entities which it thereby empowers to exist.[14]

Keeping this hypothesis in mind, we turn now to a consideration of another Great Saying, *prajnanam brahma*, consciousness is *Brahman*.[15] To the question "Who is this one?" the answer is given in the *Aitareya* Upanishad: "We worship him as the Self (*Atman*)." Then, to the second question "Which one is the Self?" the further answer is given: "He whereby one sees, or whereby one hears, or whereby one smells odors, or whereby one articulates speech, or whereby one discriminates the sweet and the unsweet."[16] The author apparently has in mind to identify the universal Self and the individual self, that is, to claim that the self of the individual is only a transient manifestation of a cosmic reality, the universal Self. Furthermore, the author continues, the universal Self is also Brahma, Indra, Prajapati and the other gods. The universal Self is likewise the five gross elements (namely, earth, wind, space, water, and light) and all the material combinations thereof, both living and non-living. He concludes: "All this is guided by intelligence, is based on intelligence. The world is guided by intelligence. The basis is intelligence. Brahma is intelligence [consciousness]."[17]

As R. C. Zaehner points out, "the basic doctrine of the Upanishads is the identification of *Brahman* with *Atman*, that is to say, of the changeless essence that upholds the universe . . . with the same changeless essence that indwells the human spirit."[18] But what is this essence? Is it an activity or is it an entity? Is it both an activity and an entity or is it neither of the two? On the basis of the text alone, this is difficult to answer. For the *Aitareya*

Upanishad begins with the creation of the universe by the Self (*Atman*) and ends, as noted above, with the identification of the Self with everything in the world. If the Self be regarded as an entity, then logically pantheism or monism seems to result. All other entities are only phenomenal manifestations or forms of the one transcendent entity. On the other hand, if the Self be regarded as an activity, namely, the activity of consciousness or intelligence, then the distinction between entities can be maintained. As the text itself maintains, everything is guided by intelligence and based on intelligence. But intelligence itself is not an entity but an activity; hence, it can be possessed by many entities simultaneously.

There are problems, to be sure, with this interpretation since not all entities are capable of exercising intelligence. Thus, for an inanimate entity to be guided by intelligence, one must assume the existence of a transcendent entity or Creator God who employs intelligence first to bring the world into existence and then to conserve it. This question of a difference between a divine Self and human selves will be dealt with in a later *mahavakya*. But for now, I wish to reflect more deeply on the notion of consciousness or intelligence as an activity. Panikkar's comments are helpful here. "Consciousness is not a substance, but an action, an act. Brahman *has* no consciousness, and thus no self-consciousness. Brahman is consciousness."[19] How are we to make sense of this statement? One possible explanation might be the following. When individuals through various forms of yogic meditation abstract from all objects of consciousness and even from themselves as individual subjects of consciousness in order to focus simply on the activity of being conscious, taken by itself, then conceivably at that moment they are experiencing *Brahman*. Furthermore, since it is thus experienced in abstraction from any individual subject of consciousness, human or divine, it is concomitantly experienced as in itself an eternal and unchanging reality, namely, as "one only, without a second."[20]

Elsewhere in his commentary, Panikkar likewise notes: "A multiplicity of thoughts as well as the many objects and contents of consciousness do not disrupt but rather reinforce the unity of consciousness. Consciousness is both one and a unifying force."[21] Here I call attention to what seems to be implied in Panikkar's thought. Consciousness is uniquely one *because* it is a unifying force or activity. If it were one of the objects of consciousness needing to be unified within the act of consciousness, or if it were simply an individual subject of consciousness, it would not be "one without a second." Only because it is the unifying activity at work in all individual subjects of consciousness so as to gather into unity the objects of consciousness for each of these subjects, is it simultaneously both the one and the many, transcendent unity and empirical multiplicity.

Here one might object with Advaita Vedantins that *Brahman* is devoid of activity because it is a symbol for "the experience of the timeless plenitude of being."[22] Reference to activity within this context is meaningless because there is nothing to be gained or lost in virtue of such activity. Yet, as already noted in the Introduction, the logically opposed concepts of timeless being and of ceaseless becoming are experientially indistinguishable; in neither case is there for the individual a sense of before and after. Furthermore, as Michael von Brück points out, *Brahman* "is derived from the root *brh* and means 'growth,' 'expansion.' In Vedic times it meant the holy word of the ritual sacrifice or prayer. Thus it is also used to present or invoke numinous power. The root meaning points to a force which unfolds."[23] Hence, even etymologically, *Brahman* could symbolize unceasing activity as well as timeless being, provided that that same activity was not need driven or goal oriented as is most often the case among humans and other finite beings.[24]

On the other hand, one cannot ignore the fact that an activity never seems to exist by itself but always within some entity who is the subject of that activity; consciousness or intelligence as an activity implies a subject of consciousness or intelligence. Keeping this in mind, I turn to a third *mahavakya*, namely, *atman brahman*, this self (*atman*) is *brahman*.[25] The context of this utterance is a discussion of the symbolism of the letters of the word *Aum*, each of which stands for a different level of consciousness. "A" is the normal waking state; "u" is the dreaming state; "m" is the deep-sleep state; and the silence after the pronunciation of all three letters as one word is the ultimate state of the Self (*Atman*) which is identical with *Brahman*. The individual self who achieves this fourth level of consciousness "with his self enters the Self" or *Brahman*.[26]

As Panikkar points out, there is a long prehistory to the identification of *Atman* and *Brahman* here in the *Mandukya* Upanishad. The term *Atman* initially meant the immediate subject or self in a concrete empirical way but eventually it came to mean "the ultimate subject or self of the whole of reality."[27] *Brahman*, on the other hand, first connoted prayer and/or ritual in the *Vedas* and then later in the Upanishads came to stand for the cosmic force or ultimate ground of the universe. Here they are taken together as one reality. And yet, as Panikkar points out, they are not completely identical. In terms of the problematic of this book, I offer the following further interpretation. If *Brahman* be understood as an activity rather than as an entity, then *Atman* can be considered the subject of that activity. That is, *Brahman* is the unifying activity of consciousness and *Atman* is the primordial subject of consciousness. Thus, without being totally identified, the two are always linked. For, as I have stated repeatedly in preceding chapters of this book, the underlying ontological activity is actual only in its instantiations. It is not an entity existing in itself, but rather the principle of existence and activity for entities, in this case, the primordial Self (*Atman*).

Given this interpretation of *Brahman* and *Atman*, what the third *mahavakya* may be said to affirm is that *Atman*, the cosmic or divine Self, is co-terminous with *Brahman*, the cosmic force at work everywhere in the universe. Hence, wherever *Brahman* is operative in the self-constitution of finite entities, above all, in the self-constitution of human consciousness, there the cosmic Self is also present. The self within the individual (*atman*) is then, in terms of this theory, one with the cosmic Self (*Atman*) since both are grounded in *Brahman* as the source of their mutual existence and activity.

It should be carefully noted, however, that in terms of this hypothesis the union of the individual self with the cosmic Self is the union of two entities which are ontologically independent of one another. The individual self is not simply the appearance or phenomenal reality of the cosmic Self. It enjoys its own independent existence and activity even though it stands in the closest possible union with the cosmic Self in virtue of their common ground in *Brahman* as the underlying ontological activity. On the other hand, the individual self is one ontological reality with *Brahman* since *Brahman* is its internal principle of existence and activity. Accordingly, as we shall see below in a subsequent *mahavakya*, the individual self rightly says to itself: "I am *Brahman*." *Brahman* exists in and through me as an individual self.

As we shall see below, this interpretation of *Brahman* and *Atman* runs directly counter to that posed by Shankara and other Advaita Vedantins who affirm that there is only one reality, namely, *Brahman-Atman* and that all sense of individual selfhood is a result of illusion (*maya*). Yet even for Vedantins the term *Brahman-Atman* is not a pure tautology. If, as noted above, *Brahman* is pure consciousness, then *Atman* is the subject of that consciousness. Ultimate Reality is then not only objective, something to be somehow known, but also subjective, someone who knows; in fact, it is primarily the knower rather than the thing known.[28] Furthermore, if the fundamental Upanishadic quest is to know the knower rather than some transcendent object of knowledge, then the only available avenue to knowledge of Ultimate Reality lies in heightened self-awareness, penetration into the depths of the individual self. Thus, even if with the Vedantins one affirms that in the end there is only one cosmic Self, that is true only because one simultaneously realizes that one's own deeper self is the cosmic Self.

What is at stake here then is not a formal or purely logical identity but a dynamic identity between *Brahman* and *Atman* (understood as primarily the cosmic Self but likewise the individual self). Panikkar explains this complex interrelationship in terms of individual drops of water and the ocean. "All things, including human beings in a specialized manner, can be said to be drops of water, participants in or reflections of the single One, beings of the Being."[29] As Panikkar correctly points out, the drops of water are primarily water and only secondarily individual drops. But the problem with this example is that the ocean is still an entity, albeit a much larger entity than individual drops of water. What my own hypothesis suggests, however, is that *Brahman* is not an entity but an underlying ontological activity resident in each of the "drops of water," first, to make them the individual entities that they truly are and then to bring them together to make up the ocean. Thus *Brahman* is not their aggregate or sum total as the ocean is the sum total of its innumerable drops of water. Where Panikkar's example seems to lead to monism, the assimilation of all particular entities into one all-comprehensive entity, my distinction between *Brahman* as an underlying activity and *Atman* as the subject of that activity preserves the non-dual character of *Brahman* and *Atman*. That is, *Brahman* both is and is not identical with *Atman* as the entity in which it is instantiated, and *Atman* both is and is not identical with *Brahman* as its principle of existence and activity.

The next *mahavakya* to be considered is *aham brahmasmi*, I am Brahman.[30] As Panikkar comments, the difference between this Great Saying and *Atman-Brahman* is that here one moves from third-person language to first-person language.[31] In the other *mahavakya*, one is still thinking objectively in terms of the relationship between *Brahman* and *Atman* in general. But in this Great Saying the writer recognizes that, in virtue of being an individual self (*atman*), he is identified with *Brahman*, the cosmic force at work in the entire universe. As he comments, "in the beginning this world was *Brahma*. It knew only itself (*atmanam*): 'I am Brahma.'" Likewise, the gods and seers came to realize that they, too, are *Brahma*. He then concludes: "Whoever thus knows 'I am Brahma!' becomes this All; even the gods have not power to prevent his becoming thus, for he becomes their self (*atman*)."[32] Is this "self" or soul of the world and of all the entities within it, however, itself an entity or an underlying activity? As Robert Hume points out, in the mind of the author it quite probably was both.[33] My argument, however, is that, if it is taken to be an entity, then monism logically results. On the other hand, if it is taken to be an underlying activity (like the soul in the body), then non-dualism is possible. For, in that case, while *Brahman* exists in me and indeed in everyone and everything else as well, it exists in me in a unique way so that my personal identity is to be this particular manifestation of *Brahman*, the principle of movement and activity everywhere in the world. I am, therefore, *Brahman*.

Once again, in offering this interpretation of the text, I am consciously taking issue with the standard position of Advaita Vedantins who argue that in the end there is no individual self but only the cosmic Self (*Brahman-Atman*). Panikkar, moreover, seems to side with the Vedantins on this point. For he first urges that *aham brahmasmi* effectively means, not "I am He," but rather "I am you."[34] But he then adds: "The *you* cannot be my projection, my creation, my creature. That would be idolatry. The relation must be reversed. The *you* begins to dawn as the authentic I."[35] Thus the deeper identity of the individual self is to be the cosmic Self. I myself, however, would say that the individual self is a particular manifestation of *Brahman* and as such one with the cosmic Self but not identical with it. For, both the individual self and the cosmic Self are manifestations of *Brahman* as the underlying ontological activity or energy principle at work everywhere in the world.

In effect, then, as I see it, both the cosmic Self and the individual self can say in truth: *aham brahmasmi*, I am *Brahman*. But, even though they both are manifestations of *Brahman*, they are not equal manifestations, much less the same manifestation of *Brahman*. For, they are separate selves, the one finite and the other infinite. *Brahman* is their common ground which allows them to stand, as noted above, in the closest possible relationship. That is, in discovering its own deeper self (*atman*), the individual human being likewise encounters God or the cosmic Self. But he or she encounters God as the Other, even the totally Other (given the fact that God is transcendent), but not as herself or himself. For this reason, I cannot accept Panikkar's statement: "God in this sense is not the Other but the I, the absolute I, the ultimate I of every act."[36]

This is, of course, not simply Pannikar's own judgment but likewise the conclusion of Shankara and other Advaita Vedantins. Yet, in my judgment, this assertion seems to endorse monism rather than non-dualism since in the end there exists only the reality of *Brahman-Atman*. According to my understanding of the *Brahman-Atman(atman)* relationship, on the other hand, non-dualism is retained. For, besides the reality of *Brahman* as the transcendent One, there exists the Many in terms of the entities empowered to exist in terms of the activity of *Brahman*. Yet the Many are not thereby simply other than *Brahman* since *Brahman* is the immanent principle of their interrelated existence and activity. Accordingly, non-dualism is achieved in that *Brahman* both is and is not the entities in which it is instantiated, and at the same time those entities both are and are not *Brahman*.

For basically the same reasons, I find myself likewise resisting Panikkar's interpretation of a fifth Great Saying, *Tat tvam asi*, That art thou. In this perhaps most celebrated of the Great Sayings in the Upanishads, Uddalaka gives his son Svetaketu a series of instructions on the true nature of *Brahman*, all of which end with the same refrain: "That which is the finest essence—this whole world has that as its soul. That is Reality (*satya*). That is *Atman* (Soul). That art thou, Svetaketu."[37] In his commentary, Panikkar addresses Svetaketu in imagination:

> You are not the I, Svetaketu, there is only one I, only one I capable of saying in truth I am, *aham-asmi*, I am Brahman, *aham-brahman*. This is the *paramatman*, the ultimate *atman*. It resides in you, is you, and is you in such a way that only by realizing it can you become and are you, your-self.[38]

Panikkar is using the language of I-Thou relationships here. But, as far as I can judge, within his interpretation of the text there is no I-Thou relationship, since the reality of the human Thou as the counterpart to the cosmic I does not ultimately exist. My own position, on the contrary, would not only allow but demand an I-Thou relationship between God as the cosmic Self who addresses all finite selves as Thou even as they achieve their own individual identity in addressing God as Thou. Thus my own interpretation of the Fifth Great Saying would run as follows. *Brahman* is the ontological ground or principle of existence and activity for both Svetaketu and God in their mutual I-Thou relationships. In virtue of *Brahman*, God as the cosmic Self (*Atman*) becomes an I in saying Thou to Svetaketu; but, likewise in virtue of *Brahman*, Svetaketu becomes an I in saying Thou to God as the cosmic Self (*Atman*). *Brahman* in itself, however, is neither an I nor a Thou but an It, their common ground or principle of unity.

Perhaps this last statement may be clarified by analyzing the oft-repeated refrain in Uddalaka's discourse to his son Svetaketu: "That which is the finest essence—this whole world has that as its soul. That is Reality. That is *Atman*. That art thou, Svetaketu." "That" in each case refers to *Brahman* which the poet describes as "the finest essence." It is the finest essence presumably because it is imperceptible, invisible to the senses. Uddalaka illustrates this point by asking his son to split the seeds within a fig only to find nothing inside. Either the finest essence is something microscopic beyond the power of human sight or it is not any *thing* at all but rather an activity which is only perceived when it is instantiated in something which is active or someone who is active. Activity as such escapes the power of perception because our human senses grasp only things or material bodies in motion, never their ontological source or principle of activity as such.

Yet *Brahman* understood as pure activity is everything in this entire world. The whole world has *Brahman* as its Soul or immanent principle of activity. Hence, *Brahman* is Reality, not in the sense of the sum-total or aggregate of all the things in this world, but rather in the sense of that invisible power or activity which makes them to be a world or ontological totality. It is pure consciousness, provided that one understands by that term not a cosmic mind as such, but rather the unifying activity of consciousness which is present in God as the cosmic Self but also present in Svetaketu and other finite selves as likewise their principle of consciousness. For this reason, that (*Brahman*) is *Atman*, the cosmic Self. But for the same reason, that art thou, Svetaketu, a finite self.

Naturally, one can find innumerable texts in the Upanishads which resist my interpretation here. In the celebrated "honey wisdom" of the *Brhadaranyaka* Upanishad, the writer repeats over and over again the same refrain: "This shining, immortal Person who is in this earth, and, with reference to oneself, this shining, immortal Person who is in the body—he, indeed, is just this Soul (*Atman*), this Immortal, this Brahma, this All."[39] *Purusha*, the cosmic Person, is thus equated with the soul of the individual human person, with *Brahman* and with the All. As noted above, the author in all likelihood did not distinguish here between an impersonal and personal ground of being but instead thought of Ultimate Reality as simultaneously personal and impersonal. But, from the perspective of my own hypothesis in this book, I would argue that the statement requires further qualification. Strictly speaking, *Purusha* is not *Brahman* since *Purusha* is an entity within the universe, not the cosmic power which sustains all the entities in the universe, including *Purusha*. But, on the other hand, *Brahman* is *Purusha*; it becomes actual in the cosmic Person. Yet *Brahman* is everything else as well since *Brahman* is likewise their underlying principle of existence and activity. Hence, not *Purusha*, but *Brahman* is strictly speaking the All, the transcendent One.

One could counterargue, of course, that as the cosmic Person or the cosmic Self, *Purusha* must be co-terminous with the All and everything in it. But to be co-terminous with the All is not to be the All. If *Purusha* be seen literally as the All, then monism results. For, then, there is only one entity, the cosmic Person, and everything else is merely a phenomenal appearance of that one supernal reality. On the other hand, if *Purusha* is simply co-terminous with the All, then other selves can co-exist with *Purusha* within the All. *Purusha* as the cosmic self is then united with all finite selves within the universe in an ongoing I-Thou relationship. *Purusha* is the cosmic I to whom all finite selves, both individually and collectively, are Thou. For each of the finite selves, on the contrary, *Purusha* is the cosmic Thou. But, seen from either perspective, the ontological duality of the I-Thou relationship remains. *Purusha* never becomes one self with any of the finite selves to which it is united in the way that *Brahman* is one self with the finite selves of which it is the intrinsic principle of existence and activity. The principle of unity for the universe, in other words, is not an entity but an underlying activity, not *Purusha* but *Brahman*.[40]

The last Great Saying out of the Upanishads cited by Panikkar is the word *Om (Aum)*. In many ways equivalent to the Hebrew word *Amen* or the English phrase "So be it," it indicates agreement with or personal acquiescence in the prayer just recited or in the ritual just performed. But in some Upanishads it evidently symbolizes the reality of *Brahman*, as in the expression "*Om* is brahma; *Om* is the whole world."[41] Panikkar comments that the sound *Om* is truly imperishable. "But *om* is not only the sound. It is also the silence following the utterance of *om* . . . And yet this ontic silence is still connected with the word, for this is that empty, soundless *om* which is the highest Brahman, the ultimate wisdom, the groundless ground, the absolute Mystery."[42] As I see it, what Panikkar is implying here is that *Om* is primarily not a written but a spoken word. Furthermore, even as a spoken word, it is less the word itself than the activity of uttering the word, an activity which presumably has no beginning or end. But, thus understood as an activity rather than a verbal entity, that is, as an uttering rather than an utterance, *Om* quite properly symbolizes the reality of *Brahman* as I have presented it in these pages. It is in itself soundless because any sound is already the product, the entitative result, of the underlying activity of uttering the word. Thus, like *Brahman*, *Om* as an activity exists only in its instantiations, the word *Om* as spoken by human beings at different times and places.

In the few remaining pages of this chapter, I will compare and contrast the understanding of the *Brahman-Atman (atman)* relationship presented here with the much more celebrated interpretation of that same relationship offered by Shankara and two other philosophers out of the so-called medieval period of Indian philosophy: namely, Ramanuja and Madhva. These three are chosen, not only because they are three of the best known Indian philosophers of all time, but also because they each represent a different solution to the problem of the relationship between the Infinite and the finite. At the same time, no effort will be made to analyze and critique the philosophical system of each of these thinkers in full detail. Nor will I attempt to evaluate the extensive secondary literature on these authors. For my purposes, it will be enough to compare and contrast my own understanding of the *Brahman-Atman* relationship with that of three famous Hindu philosopher/theologians.

"Vedanta philosophy," comments Surendranath Dasgupta, "is the philosophy which claims to be the exposition of the philosophy taught in the Upanishads and summarized in the *Brahma-sutras* of Badarayana."[43] The earliest commentary on the *Brahma-sutras* that is still available was written by the celebrated Indian philosopher, Shankara (c. 788-820 C.E.). Though Shankara also wrote commentaries on a number of Upanishads, I will limit myself to what he says about the *Brahman-Atman* relationship in the *Brahma-sutras*. Beforehand, however, it might be advisable to note some of the cosmological theories that he rejects. The *Samkhya* school of metaphysics, for example, argued that unconscious primal matter as composed of three attributes or *gunas* (goodness [*sattva*], passion [*rajas*] and darkness [*tamas*]) in various combinations produces all the persons and things of this world without any conscious guidance from a god or spiritual principle. Against this theory, Shankara contends that the teleological development of nature from an unconscious source is unintelligible.[44] The *Vaisesika* school argued that the present world is caused by the combination of indestructible atoms in virtue of an unconscious karmic principle (*adrsta*) derived from a previous cosmic epoch, against which Shankara once again claims that this is insufficient to explain the evident order and purposefulness of nature.[45]

Against Buddhist thinkers of a realist persuasion who say that the world is composed of aggregates of entities which exist momentarily, Shankara argues that there is no reason given for these momentary entities to come together as aggregates.[46] Likewise, against Buddhist thinkers of an idealist persuasion who contend that the world is, like a dream, an illusory product of the human imagination, Shankara argues that this is clearly contrary to common-sense experience in which ideas of things are clearly distinguished from the things themselves and in which dream states are clearly distinguished from waking states.[47] Finally, against those who would argue that God is simply the operative or efficient cause and that matter is the material cause of the world, Shankara argues that this position inevitably reduces the transcendence of *Brahman* as the Lord. For the Lord is thus either acting on the world out of internal need or in any case affected by what happens in the world.[48]

In conscious opposition to all these rival cosmological theories, Shankara sets forth his own quite radical proposal, namely, that to the enlightened individual there exists only the reality of *Brahman*, hence, that the independent existence of the world and all finite selves within it is ultimately illusory. At the beginning of his commentary on the *Brahma-sutras*, for example, Shankara defines *Brahman* as "[t]hat omniscient omnipotent cause from which proceed the origin, subsistence and dissolution of this world."[49] But this is only a provisional or "accidental" definition of *Brahman* until one realizes that the world as such does not really exist, that only *Brahman* exists. As Shankara comments, "for him who sees that everything has its Self in Brahman the whole phenomenal world with its actions, agents, and results of actions is non-existent."[50]

As already noted, Shankara likewise affirms that things external to the human mind really exist: "In every act of perception we are conscious of some external thing corresponding to the idea, whether it be a post or a wall or a piece of cloth or a jar, and that of which we are conscious cannot but exist."[51] Hence, Shankara is not a subjective idealist for whom only mind exists. But, in his view, what is empirically real is unreal from the perspective of *Brahman*, namely, that which is permanent, eternal and infinite. "The world that is distinguished from true reality (*sat*) and from complete non-reality (*asat*) has then an apparent or practical reality, which is called *vyavaharika*. *Vyavaharika* is the level of *maya* [illusion] that denotes the totality of errors caused by *avidya* [ignorance]."[52] Without trying to explain the causes of *maya* and *avidya* within human life, we may say that for Shankara the one in search of enlightenment must first recognize that the effect is non-different from its cause, hence, that *Brahman* is both the material and the efficient cause of the world.[53] But full enlightenment comes only when one realizes that there really is no cause-effect relationship, that *Brahman* alone exists.[54]

Similarly, before achieving enlightenment, the individual sees himself or herself as separate from other individuals and subject to mortality. After enlightenment, the individual recognizes that he or she is *Brahman* and therefore one with all of reality and immortal. Shankara comments: "As therefore the individual soul and the highest Self differ in name only, it being a settled matter that perfect knowledge has for its object the absolute oneness of the two; it is senseless to insist (as some do) on a plurality of Selfs, and to maintain that the individual soul is different from the highest Self, and the highest Self from the individual soul. For the Self is indeed called by many different names, but it is one only."[55]

Furthermore, being thus enlightened, the self has an experience of *Brahman* as *saccidananda*: that is, as being (*sat*), consciousness (*cit*), and bliss (*ananda*). "These are not so much qualifying attributes of Brahman as they are the terms that express the apprehension of Brahman by man. *Sacci-*

dananda is a symbol of Brahman as formulated by the mind interpreting its Brahman-experience."[56] The world, in other words, is only an extrinsic symbol of *Brahman*; only in a qualifed sense is *Brahman* known through the world because, as noted above, the cause-effect relationship between *Brahman* and the world is ultimately non-existent. But the individual self who has reached the state of enlightenment, on the other hand, is an intrinsic symbol of *Brahman*. For, in a state of enlightenment, the individual self is simultaneously experiencing itself and *Brahman* as one, albeit in a human way. This is why *saccidananda* is considered the "essential definition" (*Svarupa-laksana*) of *Brahman*; it gives a true insight into the all-encompassing reality of *Brahman*.[57]

Here it should be remembered, of course, that when the enlightened self experiences being, consciousness, and bliss, it is not experiencing its own being, consciousness, and bliss, but rather being, consciousness, and bliss independently of any reference to itself or to anyone or to anything else. To quote Eliot Deutsch, "Brahman is that state which *is* when all subject-object distinctions are obliterated. Brahman is ultimately a name for the experience of the timeless plenitude of being."[58] Where the experience of the world in an unenlightened state is always pluriform and therefore illusory, the experience of *Brahman* or the Self is always unitary and therefore true. Reality is ultimately One.

By way of commentary and critique, I would argue that the term *Self* in Shankara's philosophy requires further scrutiny. As noted above, the Self for Shankara is the underlying reality of the world and all the things in it; likewise, the Self is the reality of the individual self. But is the Self as thus understood an entity or an activity? The term *Self* is a noun and therefore would seem to imply that the Self is an entity. But this leads logically to monism; in the end, there exists only one thing. If the term *Self*, however, actually has reference to a foundational activity which is the principle of existence and movement for all entities, then non-dualism would seem to be vindicated. For, the underlying activity both is and is not the entities in which it is instantiated, and the entities both are and are not identical with the underlying activity which is their common ground or source of existence and movement. Reality is One, not because it is grounded in a transcendent entity, but because it is grounded in a transcendent unifying activity.

Yet, one may object, if *Brahman* is an underlying activity rather than an entity, why does Shankara refer to it as the Self? My answer would be that this foundational activity never exists in itself but is always instantiated in entities, notably, in individual selves. Hence, it would be normal in thinking of a foundational activity to imagine it as the activity of a supreme entity, namely, the Lord (*Ishvara*). Consistent with his whole philosophy, however, Shankara is quick to point out that this superimposition (*adhyasa*) of the image of a Creator God on *Brahman* is the effect of Nescience (*avidya*).[59] *Brahman* in its true nature is not an entity in relation to other entities but that which transcends all entities so as to be their common ground. Yet if one probes what is meant by the term *common ground*, then only a transcendent activity seems to be suitable. For, a common ground is created by entities in dynamic interrelation. But only a principle of existence and movement common to all the entities can bring about their dynamic interrelation and thus create the common ground. Hence, the underlying principle for the unity of reality is not an entity, not even an absolutely transcendent divine being, but a foundational activity common to all the entities, finite and infinite alike, making up the world.

One final objection to this admittedly somewhat unconventional interpretation of *Brahman* in the philosophy of Shankara and other Advaita Vedantins is that as a totally transcendent reality *Brahman* "has no genus (*jati*), no quality (*guna*), no relation (*sambandha*), no activity (*kriya*)."[60] Only on the empirical or phenomenal level is *Brahman* active with respect to the world, and even here its activity is not governed by desire or need but only by playfulness or sport (*lila*).[61] On the absolute level, however, where the world no longer exists, there is no need for activity on the part of *Brahman*. My response would be that even on the absolute level *Brahman* still *is*, that it is, in fact, pure "is-ness," that Reality whose essence or being is existence itself.[62] Thus, while it is not an entity with a specific form of activity such as a Creator God active in the world, as the pure act of existence it is (ontologically speaking) an activity and as such the unchanging ground or ultimate source of all the multiple activities of entities in the world.[63] Furthermore, as noted earlier in this chapter, while unchanging being and unceasing becoming are conceptually opposed to one another, experientially they are indistinguishable since in both cases one experiences no sense of before and after. Thus, to the enlightened individual, "Brahman is a state of silent being; it is also a dynamic becoming."[64]

I turn now to a consideration of the philosophy of two other celebrated Indian philosopher/theologians who offer a different understanding of the *Brahman-Atman* relationship on the basis of their own reading of the pertinent texts: namely, Ramanuja (1017-1137 C.E.) and Madhva (1197-1276 C.E.). They both reject Shankara's position that *Brahman* is the sole reality or the Absolute Self. But they differ from one another in that, while both say that unconscious matter (the *prakrti* of the Samkhya school) and finite selves (*jivas*) really exist, Ramanuja claims that they exist as the "body" of God and Madhva asserts that they exist as separate from God but under divine control. Thus Ramanuja is regarded as a qualified non-dualist (*Vishishtadvaita* Vedantin); for, in the end, there exists only the reality of God with matter and finite selves as part of the divine being.[65] Madhva, on the other hand, is a *Dvaitin* or dualist. For, even though he asserts that God is the Regulator or Controller of creation, he nevertheless maintains the separate identity of matter and finite selves from God's own being.[66]

Both men likewise wrote commentaries on the *Brahma-sutras* of Badarayana in which the above-mentioned views on the *Brahman-Atman* relationship come sharply to the fore. With respect to *Brahma-sutra* I, l, 2, for example, in which *Brahman* is defined as that from which the origin, subsistence and dissolution of this world proceed, Ramanuja comments: "'That from which,' i.e. that highest Person who is the ruler of all; . . . who is omniscient, omnipotent, supremely merciful; from whom the creation, subsistence, and reabsorption of this world proceed—he is Brahman: such is the meaning of the Sutra."[67] Similarly, Madhva in his commentary on the same passage notes that he of whom the sacred text here speaks is unquestionably *Vishnu* since all the names of God in Scripture ultimately refer to *Vishnu*.[68] Thus both authors implicitly affirm that *Brahman* (or *Vishnu*) in this passage is the Highest Self, but not the sole or Absolute Self. As noted above, of course, Ramanuja and Madhva would disagree between themselves with respect to the way in which the world thus originates from *Brahman* (*Vishnu*). For Ramanuja, *Vishnu* is both the material and the efficient cause of the world; for Madhva, *Vishnu* is simply the efficient cause of the world. Both, however, would agree that *Vishnu* exercises perfect control over all finite entities.

Thus, in *Brahma-sutra* II, l, 14-20, where Shankara argues for the non-difference of cause and effect and therefore for the ultimate identity of *Brahman* and the world, Ramanuja claims that *Brahman* sometimes exists in an unmanifest "causal" state in which sentient and nonsentient beings are indistinguishable from himself and at other times exists in a manifest or "effected state" in which these same finite beings have distinct names and forms.[69] Even in the "effected state," however, finite entities are under *Brahman's* pervasive control.[70] Yet *Brahman* is not thereby affected by what happens in the world as his "body" any more than the soul is directly affected by bodily changes and imperfections. For, the pleasures and pains experienced by the soul are the effect of *karma*, not the result of life in the body. Hence, since *Brahman* is in no way connected with *karma*, "it is all the less connected with evil of any kind."[71] Thus *Brahman's* only motive for producing the world is divine sport or play (*lila*).[72] Even more so does Madhva assert that *Vishnu* as the transcendent efficient cause of the world is supremely unaffected by what happens in the world since *Vishnu* controls and orders the world out of the abundance of his bliss which is the unmistakeable sign of his power and infinity.[73]

To sum up, therefore, Shankara, Ramanuja and Madhva each struggled to make sense out of the *Brahma-sutras* and the various Upanishadic texts which describe the *Brahman-Atman* relationship. Each was able to cite certain texts in support of his own interpretation of that relationship, but each likewise had to deal somehow with texts that stood in apparent contradiction to his theory. Of the three authors, Madhva has possibly the closest affinity to classical Western Christian theology in which the ontological independence of the created universe and the finite self from God is likewise strongly affirmed. Shankara, on the other hand, as George Thibaut points out, is possibly closest in spirit to the Upanishadic texts themselves in their emphasis on the mystical reality of *Brahman* as the All.[74] Ramanuja, finally, is probably closest in spirit to the thinking of Badarayana himself in the composition of the *Brahma-sutras* since the latter, as Thibaut notes, was presumably quite influenced by the belief in a personal God implicit in the *Bhagavadgita* and other "theistic" works of that period.[75]

In terms of the problematic of this book, the work of Shankara is perhaps the most important since he espoused the most radical solution to the problem of the Infinite and its relation to finite reality. Admittedly, to defend this position, he had to argue that there is a higher knowledge of *Brahman* to which only the enlightened have access. Hence, all those texts which speak of *Brahman* as simply the transcendent cause of the universe reflect in his mind the lower, provisional knowledge of *Brahman* which is destined to be superseded. But at least he recognized that the Infinite cannot simply be the Highest Self presiding over a world of finite selves. For, as genuinely other than the Highest Self, the finite selves effectively render the Highest Self finite, that is, less than everything, as required by the Upanishadic definition of the Infinite as One without a second.[76]

Ramanuja, to be sure, likewise wrestled with the issue of the nature of the Infinite. Furthermore, unlike Shankara he did not distinguish between higher and lower forms of knowledge of *Brahman*. Hence, he was obliged to reconcile with one another all the conflicting statements in the Upanishads about *Brahman* and *Atman*. Yet his solution leaves several philosophical questions unanswered. If the created universe and all finite selves are the "body" of *Brahman*, for example, then *Brahman* as the *antaryami*[77] or "soul" would seem to be still only part, albeit the governing part, of the composite reality. On the other hand, if one insists with Ramanuja that *Brahman* is not just a part of the cosmic totality but the whole of that totality, then its "parts," namely, unconscious matter and finite spirits, logically are reduced to "modes" or accidental modifications of its own substantial reality.[78] It alone really exists as a self-sufficient reality, and the alleged reality of unconscious matter and finite spirits is ultimately illusory.

As I see it, only if *Brahman* is regarded as an underlying activity constitutive of the existence and interrelated activity of the various kinds of entities in the world can it be identified with the whole, the All, without danger of ontological monism. For the universe or the All is the totality of entities in existence. But what makes them to be an organized totality rather than a random aggregate of individual entities is *Brahman* as an underlying unifying activity. Furthermore, since each of the entities exists through participation in *Brahman*, *Brahman* is logically more ultimate than any of the entities in which it is instantiated. At the same time, *Brahman* does not exist by itself, since it is not an entity but a principle of existence and activity for entities. They, in turn, cannot exist either as individuals or as members of the totality, the All, without *Brahman* as their ultimate cause or *raison d'être*.

Madhva, finally, avoided in large measure the problem of the Infinite by stipulating that *Vishnu* as the Highest Self is simply the efficient cause of the material world and all finite selves which exist as ontological realities in their own right. Yet he too insisted that *Vishnu* is present in the world and present to the finite self through his creative power. "'He is present in all, awakening in each its *shakti.*' Yet the Supreme Being remains independent. He alone possesses the unthinkable supreme power. The *shaktis* he grants to others is his."[79] If Madhva had reflected that this creative power of *Vishnu* is thus in altered form likewise the creative power of all the persons and things of this world, then he might possibly have come to the conclusion that it is the *shakti* of *Vishnu* rather than *Vishnu* himself which is truly infinite or unlimited in scope. *Vishnu*, in other words, is present to his creation only in virtue of a power or activity which is not limited to its operation in *Vishnu*. Hence, the *shakti* mediates between *Vishnu* and the world of creation as their common ground or ontological source of existence and activity. It exists, to be sure, primarily in *Vishnu* as its primordial instantiation; but it likewise genuinely exists in finite entities as their *shakti* or source of energy. Hence, it is the sole infinite reality in a world of entities which are inevitably limited by one another's existence and activity.

Armed with these insights into the nature of the *Brahman-Atman (atman)* relationship, we may bring this chapter on classical Hinduism to a close. It is now time to reflect on the life and teachings of another great Indian philosopher and ascetic, Siddhartha Gautama, who as the Buddha or the Enlightened One paradoxically both challenged and confirmed the Upanishadic tradition in which he was trained before his illumination under the Bodhi tree.

6

The Buddhist Doctrine of Dependent Co-Arising

While there is general agreement among scholars about the main lines of the Buddha's family background, his life and eventual death, there is much less agreement about his philosophy or world view. As Huston Smith comments, this situation can be traced to a number of factors. First of all, he himself wrote nothing and discouraged his disciples from writing down his oral discourses. As a result, there is a gap of 150 years between his own spoken words and the first written records. Secondly, there arose afterwards a great profusion of texts attributed to the Buddha but actually composed by members of various schools of Buddhist thought which had arisen in the intervening years. Thirdly, partisan interpretations of the master's thought were thus inevitably intermixed with faithful transmission of his actual words. But fourthly and most importantly, the Buddha himself showed little interest in metaphysical questions even though the Four Noble Truths, the Eightfold Path and other principles of Buddhist doctrine all presuppose an understanding of reality quite different from the conventional Hinduism of his day.[1]

Yet scholars likewise seem to agree that for the Buddha reality was characterized by three "marks" or "signs": suffering (*dukkha*); impermanence (*anicca*); and no-self (*anatta*), that is, the absence of a permanent form or soul in humans (and indeed in all living beings).[2] The first mark reflects the first Noble Truth, namely, that life is usually painful and in the end disappointing. The second mark suggests that nothing in the external world remains the same for long; reality is an ongoing process rather than a fixed state of being. Finally, the third mark takes note of the fact that process or becoming is likewise characteristic of the human psyche. Contrary to standard Hindu belief, there is no self (*atman*) which underlies the various states of consciousness and thus represents a principle of continuity or enduring self-identity for the human being.

Underlying these three marks or signs of the human condition, however, is a still more fundamental reality, namely, "dependent co-arising," since it is in virtue of dependent co-arising that life is considered to be painful, transient, and insubstantial or formless. This insight into the true nature of things the Buddha formulated as follows:

> When this is present, that comes to be;
> from the arising of this, that arises.
> When this is absent, that does not come to be;
> on the cessation of this, that ceases.[3]

As David Kalupahana comments, this understanding of universal causality as objective, necessary, invariable, and inherently conditioned "was the Buddha's answer to both the eternalist theory of the Substantialists, who posited an unchanging immutable 'self' (*atman*), and the annihilationist theory of the non-Substantialists, who denied continuity altogether."[4] Furthermore, in a remarkable way, it skirted further metaphysical issues such as the nature of causality, the identity or non-identity of the cause and the effect in each instance of causality, etc., and simply clung to the empirically verifiable fact that nothing arises or ceases to be in total isolation from other beings.

At the same time, implicit in the formula for dependent co-arising, as I see it, is the notion of unceasing activity as the experiential ground or objective reason why individual beings continue to arise and cease to be in dependence on one another. This underlying activity, to be sure, does not exist in itself apart from the entities in which it is embodied or instantiated. But it de facto serves as the ongoing principle of continuity when one pair of entities comes into being and another pair ceases to be. Otherwise, there is no reason why new entities should come into existence or already existing entities should cease to exist.[5] Still less is there reason why they should come into existence and cease to be in radical dependence on one another. The term "dependent co-arising," therefore, while it does not refer to a transcendent entity, does refer to a transcendent activity which, as already noted, is actual only in its instantiations. While not itself an entity, it is the deeper reason why there are entities in the first place.[6]

Furthermore, one might well argue that the three universal marks or signs of reality are likewise fully comprehensible only in terms of such an unceasing underlying activity. That is, life both in the world of nature and in the world of the psyche is in continuous flux. But the deeper reason for the continuous flux is that reality is an ongoing process of becoming which is verified both in the continuous changes taking place in the world of nature and in the successive moments of consciousness. Finally, life is painful until one learns to "let go" and peacefully merge with this never-ending stream of activity both within and around oneself.

In the first part of this chapter, accordingly, I will consciously make use of this insight as a hermeneutical tool for analyzing a number of key texts out of the Indian Buddhist tradition. Afterwards, I will examine the writings of Kitaro Nishida, the founder of the Kyoto School of Buddhist philosophy in Japan, and once again raise the issue whether an underlying ontological activity lies at the base of Nishida's speculations about "pure experience" and "the logic of the place of nothingness." In this way, I hope to give further confirmation to the basic hypothesis of this book, namely, that the Infinite is an activity rather than an entity, here within the context of Indian and Japanese Buddhism.

The first classical text from the Indian Buddhist tradition is the Buddha's discourse to Kaccayana out of the *Samyutta Nikaya*.[7] Gautama is asked by Kaccayana to explain what is meant by a "right view." Gautama replies to the effect that a right view is the middle way between those who hold that there is no becoming but only unchanging being and those who believe that there is no being but simply discontinuous becoming. Anyone, says Gautama, who has observed the coming-to-be of things cannot believe that reality is totally discontinuous; whereas anyone who has witnessed the passing-away of an entity realizes that reality is not absolutely permanent and unchanging. Hence, the right view is the middle way which recognizes that reality is a continuous passage from potentiality to actuality with entities arising and ceasing-to-be in strict dependence on one another.

David Loy's comments on the experience of non-duality are helpful to understand the point of the Buddha's remarks here. As Loy notes, the terms *being* and *becoming, permanence* and *impermanence*, do not exclude but rather imply each other since they both refer to basically the same experience interpreted from different perspectives:

> Consider a solitary rock out of an ocean current, protruding above the surface. Whether one is on the rock or floating past it, it is the relation between the two that makes both movement and rest possible. Obviously, the current will be measured by the rate of movement past the rock, but the rock can be said to be at rest only if there is something else defined as moving in relation to it.[8]

Only conceptually, therefore, are being and becoming opposed to one another, and even here one cannot understand being without reference to becoming and vice versa. For each is defined as the absence of the other: being is the absence of change or becoming, and becoming is the absence of permanence or being. Thus in a curious way each requires the indirect presence of the other to be fully intelligible.

Furthermore, the attempt to explain movement or causality in terms of initially separate entities which are then linked with one another by causal interaction always ends in failure. For, upon closer inspection, the entities in question turn out to be already in movement, and the sharp distinction between cause and effect disappears as one comes to recognize the co-dependence of everything upon everything else. Furthermore, this all-encompassing web of causal conditions is paradoxically experienced by the individual entity as absolute freedom to be itself within the larger cosmic reality. As Loy remarks, "each nondual event—every leaf-flutter, wandering thought, and piece of litter—is whole and complete in itself, because although conditioned by everything else in the universe and thus a manifestation of it, for precisely that reason it is not subordinated to anything else but becomes an unconditioned end-in-itself."[9]

In the second half of his discourse to Kaccayana, Gautama illustrates this paradoxical condition of dependent co-arising in explaining how human suffering arises and how it can be eliminated. For, out of initial ignorance of the inner workings of the law of dependent co-arising, human beings find themselves burdened by various karmic dispositions and disordered behaviors. The latter, in turn, give rise to various states of unhappiness and suffering for individuals with the result that they end up bound to *samsara*, the cycle of deaths and rebirths. Suffering is eliminated and a new sense of freedom is experienced, on the other hand, when one recognizes the workings of the law of dependent co-arising in one's life and peacefully accepts one's "place" in the network of causally conditioned events. For, then karmic dispositions are healed, the sense of oneself as separate from the world in which one lives disappears along with self-centered feelings and desires, and samsara is transfigured through the experience of *nirvana*.[10] That is, the cycle of deaths and rebirths is no longer repellent, and one experiences true freedom and inner peace.

From the perspective of the hypothesis of this book, one could further interpret this discourse of Gautama to Kaccayana as follows. The right view for the understanding of reality is indeed the middle way which recognizes that reality is neither unchanging being nor chaotic becoming but mutually conditioned becoming or dependent co-arising. That is, from the observation of innumerable instances of change, one comes to see that nothing ever comes into existence or ceases to be on its own; it is always a link in a chain of mutually conditioned events that stretch out to infinity. All that stands out from this analysis is the fact of dependent co-arising within the experience of continuous activity. One should therefore give up any attempt to explain the deeper reality of things and simply rest in the experience of continuous activity in which everything is conditioned by everything else.

To such an understanding of the nature of reality, I myself would add that the experience of continuous activity is, as a matter of fact, an experience of the Infinite. The very fact that it is continuous means that it has no beginning or end and thus is, at least in principle, boundless or infinite. But I would also claim that one does not have to recognize it precisely as an experience of the Infinite in order for it to be in fact an experience of the Infinite. Presumably the Buddha himself and certainly most contemporary scholars of Buddhist philosophy would not want to call it an experience of the Infinite, because this would be considered an implicit return to metaphysical speculation, from which the Buddha obviously tried to extricate himself and from which the mainstream of Buddhist philosophy has generally sought to remain free. But, as I see it, this is because notions of the

Infinite are usually reified in terms of a transcendent entity or some other reality which exists in itself. My own proposal, however, is that the Infinite is properly understood only as an activity which never exists in itself but only exists as a principle for entities in dynamic interrelation. It is infinite because it transcends them all even as it is immanent within each of them.

Furthermore, as one rests within this experience of continuous activity, whether it be formally recognized as an experience of the Infinite or not, a new sense of freedom and a feeling of inner peace is experienced, as the Buddha himself made clear.[11] Self-awareness is not thereby lost; only the feeling of being a separate self is abandoned. One gives up, in other words, the sense of being an objective observer of the stream of activity going on around and within oneself and becomes instead a willing participant in that same underlying movement or activity. One thus shares in the reality of the Infinite even as one paradoxically realizes more deeply than ever the "emptiness" of all things, oneself included.

With this reference to emptiness as the appropriate description of the Buddha's experience of enlightenment, I pass now to consideration of the thought of Nagarjuna, perhaps the most celebrated of all Indian Buddhist philosophers. Living and writing in the latter half of the second century of the Common Era, Nagarjuna, as Kalupahana comments, tried to recover the true teaching of the Buddha after intervening centuries of metaphysical speculation on the master's teaching by various schools of Buddhist philosophy had somewhat obscured the master's basic message.[12] As a result, his *Mulamadhyamakakarika* treatise to which we now turn is effectively a commentary on Gautama's discourse to Kaccayana, analyzed above.

It would be fruitless to try to comment upon the entire treatise, since many of its chapters deal with fine points of Buddhist doctrine in dispute among the various schools of thought at the time but not pertinent to the question of this chapter, namely, whether the notion of ceaseless activity underlies Nagarjuna's discussion of dependent co-arising. I will limit myself, therefore, to an analysis of a few selected topics which bear upon that theme. In the first two chapters of the treatise, for example, Nagarjuna deals with the conventional notions of causality and movement and shows that they are logically inconsistent. This then allows him to appeal to a new empirically grounded understanding of both causality and movement which transcends the rival explanations of the various schools.

To be specific, in the first chapter Nagarjuna initially notes that there are no existents that have arisen "from themselves, from another, from both, or from a non-cause."[13] This is not to say that there are no empirically observable existents, but only that their existence cannot be explained in terms of self-causation, external causation, a combination of the two, or some unknown non-cause. As he indicates in the following verse, there are indeed conditions for the existence of whatever is perceived to exist; but these conditions do not function as ontological causes of the entity in question since they too exist only in conjunction with the effect being produced. Both cause and effect, in other words, arise and cease to be together; thus neither enjoys ontological priority over the other. As Nagarjuna comments, "these are conditions, because depending upon them these [others] arise. So long as these [others] do not arise, why are they not non-conditions?"[14] No entity is in itself either a cause or an effect; it is labeled such only because of a tendency in human beings to analyze fluid existential situations in terms of fixed causes and effects.[15]

Similarly, in Chapter 2, Nagarjuna uses dialectical reasoning to prove (a) that there are in the end no subsistent movers or things moved apart from actual movement, and (b) that movement itself is inconceivable apart from things that here and now are in motion. Thus he categorically denies that there is any permanent or unchanging substantial reality underlying the experience of movement. All that is given to experience is the fact of movement in terms of movers and things moved. As he says, for example, in the first verse, "separated from what has been moved and has not been moved, present moving is not known."[16] Movement apart from things that are being moved or are currently at rest is unimaginable. And yet, "movement is in the present moving, and not either in the moved or in the not moved."[17] Movement is not in the mover, but rather the mover is in movement or "the present moving."

The reality here is the reality of movement although concretized in terms of a given entity in motion here and now. Otherwise, one ends up in logical contradictions, speaking of a two-fold movement in the present moving ("that by which there comes to be present moving and, again, the movement itself"[18]) or of two movers to account for these two movements, or of a mover apart from any movement at all. In the end, there is only movement which has no beginning and no end since movement is implied in both beginning to move and ceasing to move.[19] Yet movement does not exist by itself but only in an entity that here and now is in motion. Hence, movement is neither identical with nor simply different from entities in motion. By implication, then, movement is both the same as and different from entities in motion. It is the primordial example of what Loy and others call the non-dual character of reality.

I turn now to the twenty-second chapter of the treatise in which Nagarjuna asks whether the Buddha as *Tathagata* (the one "thus gone") is immortal like the *atman* of Hindu metaphysics. His answer is neither yes nor no. For to claim that the Buddha is immortal is implicitly to assert that the Buddha has a transcendent "self-nature" which is distinct from the "aggregates" of which he was composed during his earthly life. Yet "the *tathagata* is neither the aggregates nor different from them. The aggregates are not in him; nor is he in the aggregates."[20] On the other hand, it is equally false to claim that the Buddha was annihilated when the aggregates dissolved at the moment of death, because this, too, goes beyond the empirical evidence into the realm of metaphysical theory. Nagarjuna continues: "'Empty,' 'non-empty,' 'both' or 'neither'—these should not be declared. It is expressed only for the purpose of communication."[21] As Kalupahana comments, Nagarjuna is rejecting any theorizing about the "empty" or the "non-empty": "Neither the empty nor the non-empty should be reified. These terms are used only for communicating or expressing an experience which, being dependent (*pratityasamutpanna*), has not static self-nature (*svabhava*), and as such cannot be demarcated and reified."[22]

Nagarjuna concludes Chapter 22 with the following provocative statement: "Whatever is the self-nature of the *tathagata*, that is also the self-nature of the universe. The *tathagata* is devoid of self-nature. This universe is also devoid of self-nature."[23] In line with my own hypothesis, I would urge that what Nagarjuna is implicitly proposing here is that the *tathagata* like all human selves is an instance of ceaseless activity, what Nagarjuna calls "dependent co-arising." Furthermore, the universe as a whole is nothing more than various forms of dependent co-arising. Dependent co-arising, however, does not exist in itself as a metaphysical entity apart from the concrete entities that "dependently co-arise." Strictly speaking, it exists only in these empirical entities that arise and cease to be with such rapidity. Yet it is not for that reason created anew at every moment. For, as noted earlier, dependent co-arising has no beginning or end; it simply exists as pure movement or activity in the present. Hence, it logically must endure from one moment to the next as the implicit ground or *raison d'être* for all the specific forms of dependent co-arising in the world.

This last statement is undoubtedly the most controversial feature of my hypothesis since it seems to reintroduce metaphysical speculation into the carefully contrived non-metaphysical statements of both the Buddha and his faithful disciple Nagarjuna. Yet, if it is a metaphysical statement, it is one which is empirically verifiable. For all that it proposes is that there is one constant in human experience both of the self and of the world. That one constant is activity or dependent co-arising. It is, to be sure, constantly assuming new forms both within the self and within the world. Hence, it is empty of any "self-nature" or entitative reality which would allow one to think of it apart from its various manifestations. But sustained attention to the data of consciousness allows one to realize that, simply as an activity, it is indeed constantly, if indirectly, present to all experience. As we shall see later, it is in fact the purest form of experience in which the distinction between the experiencing subject and the object experienced is not yet felt or, still less, reflected upon.

I turn now to Chapter 24 in which Nagarjuna discusses the ontological status of the Four Noble Truths and other stable features of institutional Buddhism, given the experience of all-pervasive emptiness. If these, too, are "empty," do they have any enduring value or significance for the followers of the Buddha? In answer to this question, Nagarjuna first notes the distinction between two truths: "truth relating to worldly convention and truth in terms of ultimate fruit."[24] He then adds: "Without relying upon convention, the ultimate fruit is not taught. Without understanding the ultimate truth, freedom is not attained."[25] The Four Noble Truths and the other features of institutional Buddhism, therefore, belong to the realm of worldly convention; they are only provisionally true. Yet without them one does not normally learn the ultimate truth (or acquire the ultimate fruit) which is the experience of emptiness. Finally, without understanding the ultimate truth or having the experience of emptiness, one does not attain freedom, that is, *nirvana*.

The Four Noble Truths, accordingly, do not possess of themselves "self-nature" (*svabhava*) or self-sufficient reality. They are merely instrumental to the attainment of an experience which is self-authenticating. That is, once one has the experience, one realizes intuitively that the genuine experience of emptiness (or *nirvana*) is inseparable from the experience of dependent co-arising and vice versa. For, the experience of emptiness is grounded in the experience of things that continually arise and cease-to-be and thus are seen to be "empty" of enduring value and significance. Only then, when one has concretely experienced the emptiness of things that continually arise and cease-to-be, can one truly experience freedom (or *nirvana*).[26]

In this same context, Kalupahana suggests that the notions of dependent co-arising and emptiness are "abstract concepts derived from concrete empirical events, 'the dependently arisen' (*pratityasamutpanna*) and 'the empty' (*sunya*) respectively."[27] In line with Gadjin Nagao's interpretation of Nagarjuna and the Madhyamika tradition,[28] I would prefer to say that dependent co-arising and emptiness are not abstract concepts or logical universals but rather names for one and the same foundational experience, albeit seen from two different perspectives. Admittedly, the experience of dependent co-arising and/or emptiness is given in and through the more concrete experience of something which is dependently co-arisen and thus empty. But, as I commented above, the experience of dependent co-arising would seem to be the experience of pure activity which accompanies, even in some sense precedes, the experience of the subjective self or the object of consciousness. It is, accordingly, not an abstraction from the concreteness of experience but rather its most concrete moment prior to the movement of reflection or the felt distinction between oneself and the object experienced. One never departs, therefore, from the Four Noble Truths and the specific experiences on which they are based, namely, the experience of "suffering, its arising, its ceasing and the path [leading to its ceasing]."[29] For, only in and through these more specific experiences can one attain enlightenment, that is, the experience of pure activity or dependent co-arising which, as noted above, is simultaneously an experience of emptiness or freedom (*nirvana*).[30]

This leads naturally to an analysis of Chapter 25 of the *Mulamadhyamakakarika* in which Nagarjuna sets forth his understanding of freedom (or *nirvana*). He begins by noting that freedom normally connotes relinquishing something or ceasing from some activity in order to be genuinely free. Yet what does one relinquish or give up if everything is "empty" (or, on the contrary, if everything is "non-empty," that is, a manifestation of an all-pervasive substantial reality)?[31] Freedom, accordingly, is "unrelinquished, not reached, unannihilated, non-eternal, non-ceased and non-arisen."[32] It simply *is* as the sole constant in human experience even though it is seldom recognized as such by human beings in their preoccupation with the persons and things of ordinary experience. For, in itself, it is neither existent nor non-existent.[33] That is, as the experience of unlimited activity or movement, it is never experienced in itself but always in conjunction with persons that move or with things that are moved. Hence, concludes Nagarjuna, "the life-process [*samsara*] has no thing that distinguishes it from freedom [*nirvana*]. Freedom has no thing that distinguishes it from the life-process."[34] The key phrase here is "no thing." The life-process and freedom are not separate "things" with their own characteristics and/or attributes. Rather, they are mutually self-implicating dimensions of one and the same foundational experience. Genuinely to experience the one is invariably to experience the other.

As Kalupahana comments, however, Nagarjuna should not be cited in support of the view that the life-process and freedom (*samsara* and *nirvana*) are identical unless one reflects carefully on what type of identity one is implicitly proposing.[35] For, it is in any case not a straightforward logical identity, but rather a dynamic, non-dual identity in which *samsara* and *nirvana* are experienced as both the same as and different from one another. For, depending upon one's subjective response to the unending cycle of births and deaths as represented by *samsara*, one will experience either *nirvana*, a new sense of freedom, or on the contrary a sense of bondage. Similarly, Nagarjuna cannot be cited in support of the theory that *samsara* and *nirvana* are opposite states of being, so that liberation consists in passing from one state to the other. For freedom (*nirvana*) is never experienced except in conjunction with the life-process (*samsara*). *Nirvana*, in other words, is a this-worldly, not an other-worldly, experience.

For this same reason, Nagarjuna emphatically denies that he or anyone else knows that the Buddha exists after death.[36] To assert that the Buddha exists after death or that the Buddha does not exist after death are metaphysical statements which cannot be verified in view of the strictly this-worldly experience of *nirvana*. Likewise, in the final chapter of the *Mulamadhyamakakarika*, Nagarjuna refuses to speculate on the existence or non-existence of the individual human being after death, or on the infinity or non-infinity of the world. All these are metaphysical claims which cannot be either verified or disproved on the basis of the experience of the life-process (*samsara*) and/or freedom (*nirvana*). He concludes: "Thus, because of the emptiness of all existents, where, to whom, which and for what reason views such as the eternal could ever occur?"[37] As Kalupahana remarks, these metaphysical views arise because of an urge on the part of human beings to know where they came from and where they are going after this life is ended.[38] Natural as these questions may be for human beings, they cannot be immediately answered on the basis of the experience of *samsara* and/or *nirvana*. All that is directly experienced is the unending cycle of births and deaths (*samsara*) with emptiness or freedom (*nirvana*) as its natural concomitant once one accepts that fact with true equanimity.

To sum up, then, Nagarjuna was not in the first place a metaphysician, trying to explain the experience either of dependent co-arising or of emptiness. Rather, as both Kalupahana and Nagao insist in different ways, he used various forms of dialectical reasoning only to expose the inconsistencies implicit in antecedent schools of Buddhist philosophy. In his own positive statements, he preferred to point his readers toward certain key experiences, e.g., the experience of movement and/or causality, and to allow them to conclude for themselves what they were really experiencing. At the same time, his very appeal to experience does not preclude the possibility that this same experience is multi-dimensional, specifically, that in and through the experience of particular entities that constantly arise and cease to be one likewise experiences an underlying activity that implicitly serves as their ontological ground or dynamic source of existence. One has, in other words, an implicit experience of something unlimited and unconditioned in and through the explicit experience of what is finite and conditioned. Furthermore, it is this "feel" or "taste" for the Infinite which allows one to conclude that it is an experience of *nirvana* as well as an experience of *samsara*, that is, an experience of freedom or the "emptiness" of all empirical reality even as one still feels deeply the unending cycle of births and deaths within this world.[39]

Before turning to a consideration of Japanese Buddhism, I wish to reflect upon the significance of a few verses out of the Heart Sutra which are treasured by Mahayana Buddhists everywhere:

> [F]orm is emptiness, and the very emptiness is form; emptiness does not differ from form, form does not differ from emptiness; whatever is form, that is emptiness, whatever is emptiness, that is form.[40]

Reality, in other words, is both emptiness and form in equal measure and at the same time. Even though emptiness as indeterminate reality is the logical contradiction of form as determinate reality, they are one and the same "self-contradictory" existential reality. But what precisely is a "self-contradictory" existential reality? As I see it, every entity is both subject and object at the same time. As subject, it has the capacity to represent itself under different forms; but, for that same reason, in itself it is formless or empty. As object, it possesses a definite form here and now. Its full reality, therefore, is to be paradoxically both form and emptiness at once; otherwise, it would not be a dynamic *subject of experience* but simply an inert *object of thought*.

Perhaps the easiest way to understand and appreciate this paradoxical approach to reality is to realize what is happening as one reflects, first, upon the notion of emptiness and then upon that of form, and then once again upon emptiness and one more time upon form. The mind, in passing back and forth between these two logically opposed concepts, experiences itself as in continuous movement or activity. It both is and is not a determinate reality at any given moment. For it is the dynamic synthesis of these two concepts, though not in the Hegelian sense of being a third entity, which somehow "sublates" the antecedent thesis and antithesis into its own more comprehensive reality. Rather, it is their synthesis in that it is the existential subject which links the objective notions of form and emptiness together, synthesizes them into its own dynamic self-contradictory identity as something both determinate and indeterminate at the same time.[41]

Finally, the mind as the "place" where this synthesizing activity occurs is not thereby co-terminous with reality as a whole. Rather, this synthesizing activity presumably occurs in many other "places" at the same time, that is, in other minds and indeed in any other entity where form and formlessness are paradoxically joined together in a self-contradictory existential identity. The mind, in other words, is a "window" on reality as a whole: not, however, in the sense that it reflects internally what exists as an independent reality outside the mind,[42] but in the sense that it is itself an instance of an activity which is going on everywhere in the universe at the same time. Hence, to reflect upon the mind as an instance of pure activity is to gain an insight into the nature or deeper reality of the universe as a whole.[43]

Armed with this interpretation of the above-cited lines out of the Heart Sutra, we may now come to grips with the thought of Kitaro Nishida (1870-1945), the founder of the Kyoto School of Buddhist philosophy. I will first analyze certain passages out of Nishida's classic work *An Inquiry into the Good*, above all, out of Part One of that book, entitled "Pure Experience." I will then indicate how Nishida's concept of pure experience developed into a logic of place (*basho*), as evidenced in the essay written shortly before his death, "The Logic of the Place of Nothingness and the Religious World View." My intention here, of course, will not be to set forth Nishida's philosophy in its entirety, but rather to see whether Nishida's basic line of thought verifies the hypothesis of this chapter and indeed of the entire book: namely, that the Infinite is an underlying ontological activity which becomes finite in its various manifestations, above all for our purposes, in the dualism of subject and object within the human mind.

Nishida begins Part One of *An Inquiry into the Good* by giving an informal definition of pure experience: "the state of experience just as it is without the least addition of deliberative discrimination." He then adds immediately:

> The moment of seeing a color or hearing a sound, for example, is prior not only to the thought that the color or sound is the activity of an external object or that one is sensing it, but also to the judgment

of what the color or sound might be. In this regard, pure experience is identical with direct experience.44

In virtue of this example, one might readily conclude that pure experience is limited to momentary perceptions. Nishida, however, quickly notes that "all mental phenomena appear in the form of pure experience."45 Thus thinking, willing and feeling as well as perceiving count as pure experience if one is fully identified with whatever it is that one is perceiving, thinking, willing or feeling. Key to pure experience, therefore, is the "strict unity of concrete consciousness" in which the distinction between subject and object is not yet (or no longer) present.46 What one is experiencing, accordingly, is activity which is not yet or no longer the activity of the subject vis-à-vis the object or vice versa, but simply an activity which is unfolding according to its own dynamic in one's consciousness.

As Nishida comments, "[w]hen a consciousness starts to emerge, a unifying activity—in the form of a feeling of inclination—accompanies it. This activity directs our attention, and it is unconscious when the unity is strict or undisturbed from without; otherwise it appears in consciousness as representations and diverges immediately from the state of pure experience."47 We are, in other words, not aware of ourselves as perceiving, thinking, willing or feeling until we experience an interruption in the flow of that activity. At that moment, the concrete unity of consciousness is broken and we begin self-consciously to assign meanings to and/or make judgments about the contents of consciousness. But the concrete unity of consciousness is restored as we once again become absorbed in the object of consciousness, lose ourselves in its concrete actuality.

The full details of Nishida's analysis of pure experience are not important for our purposes. What is important for that end is his conclusion that "immediate reality" at the time of pure experience is invariably "an independent, self-sufficient, pure activity."48 Activity, in other words, is common to both the subject and the object of consciousness; it is their underlying ontological substrate. Generalizing upon this conclusion, Nishida then argues that "the unifying power at the base of our thinking and willing and the unifying power at the base of the phenomena of the universe are one and the same."49 This leads him to conclude a few pages later that "reality is the activity of consciousness."50 In my judgment, Nishida erred here in thus "idealizing" the data of experience; it is sufficient to say that the same ontological activity which is at work in the self-constitution of human consciousness is likewise at work in the self-constitution of the objects of human consciousness. There are, moreover, things that exist in their own right quite apart from human consciousness, even apart from collective human consciousness. What is solely important is that human consciousness and the objects of human consciousness are emergent out of a common ontological ground which is pure activity.

Nishida, to be sure, argues that Nature as a truly concrete reality does not come into being without having a unifying activity. "Nature therefore possesses a kind of self, too."[51] But, as noted above, when he inquires into the reality of this selfhood within Nature, he concludes that "the unifying self behind nature is not some unknowable entity totally unrelated to our consciousness but actually none other than the unifying activity of consciousness."[52] Then, to avoid the charge of solipsism, he postulates that the consciousness of the individual human being is only part of a universal consciousness whose spirit or unifying activity is God.[53] Thus human beings and all other things in this world are "manifestations" of God and "only God is true reality."[54] Our individuality, however, is not a "mere phantasm; rather, it is part of God's development, one of God's activities of differentiation."[55]

As already noted in preceding chapters of this book, it is very important to distinguish between the personhood of God and the underlying nature of God when trying to set forth the proper relation between God and the world. Everything that Nishida proposes about God as the unifying activity of the world can properly be predicated of the divine nature which is the ontological ground for the existence of God as well as for human beings and all other finite beings. At the same time, in virtue of that same divine ground of being, God possesses a consciousness numerically different from the myriad individual consciousnesses of human beings and other living organisms. The unlimited consciousness of God, accordingly, incorporates the *objective* contents of the consciousnesses of all finite living beings without *subjectively* identifying with these more limited forms of consciousness and thus reducing them simply to "manifestations" of itself; in this way, one avoids all the theoretical problems associated with pantheism and the ontological independence of finite entities vis-à-vis an all-encompassing God.

Keeping in mind Nishida's key insight, however, namely, that pure experience and/or immediate reality is "self-sufficient, pure activity," we may now take up his logic of place (*basho*) which is most clearly set forth in the essay "The Logic of the Place of Nothingness and the Religious World View." Nishida begins by noting that "religion is an event of the soul."[56] Yet it is not thereby a purely subjective experience for the individual human being. Rather, it has to do with the consciously active self in a manner which, as he sees it, transcends the empirical logic set forth by Aristotle and the transcendental logic proposed by Immanuel Kant. For, it is a question of *interactivity* whereby the self and the other, the subject and the object of human consciousness, are simultaneously constituted in a dialectic of mutual negation and affirmation of one another.[57] That is, each individual act of human consciousness is a contradictory self-identity in that it simultaneously both affirms and denies its own existence. Likewise, the world as the "other" of human consciousness is a transformational process exhibiting the contradictory self-identity of space and time, that is, of simultaneity and succession.[58] Thus the individual act of human consciousness is in the end nothing more than the self-expression of the world, and the world exists only in terms of the self-expression of the individual act of consciousness.[59]

To explain these paradoxical statements, I will now briefly set forth Nishida's critique of empirical and transcendental logic. Within the framework of Aristotle's empirical logic, "the world is predicated as an attribute of a self-identical unity, or grammatical subject; that is why the predicates become the activities of objectively real units, or substances."[60] The really real for Aristotle, in other words, is the concrete individual thing which is the ultimate referent of the grammatical subject and its array of predicate-attributes. Yet, thus understood as the grammatical subject of various predicates, the concrete individual thing is still only an inert object of thought, not the dynamic subject of its own self-affirmation. Aristotle, in other words, is implicitly dealing with a logical abstraction rather than with a living reality. Within Kant's transcendental logic, on the other hand, the categories or transcendental predicates are conceived as really real in that they structure and order the empirical data provided by the senses. Furthermore, in combination, they make up the "noetic field" within which the ego or human self-consciousness is dynamically reconstituted at every moment.[61] But, says Nishida, the self that Kant has in mind here is the theoretical universal self, not the empirical individual self. Like Aristotle with his empirical logic, therefore, Kant in his transcendental logic never attains to the empirical individual except as an abstract object of thought.

Within Nishida's own concrete or "existential" logic, on the other hand, the world is to be understood as a "transformational matrix" in which the empirical individual here and now negates itself and yet thereby expresses itself.[62] The individual self negates itself in that it recognizes that it is merely a single self-determination of the world understood as a noetic field or transformational matrix; yet its own individual identity or existential reality consists in being precisely just that dynamic self-expression of the world. Furthermore, in conjunction with other selves or "monads," the self effects a gradual transformation of the world. That is, the selves together form the world "interexpressively" through their mutual negation and affirmation. The world then "transforms itself by having the monads [selves] as its centers."[63] In contrast to Aristotle, therefore, the self for Nishida is active rather than passive; in contrast to Kant, the self is existential and historical rather than theoretical and universal.

Furthermore, it is only this existential-historical self which can have a religious consciousness, can experience God as an event in the soul. For, as Nishida comments in Chapter 2 of his essay, "it is only when a person becomes conscious of a profound existential contradiction in the depth of his own soul—when he becomes aware of the bottomless self-contradiction of his own self—that his own existence becomes religiously problematic."[64] To be specific, the moral self implicitly presupposes its own immortality, as Kant suggests in the *Critique of Practical Reason*. That is, the self evaluates its actions in terms of the "categorical imperative" which as a dictate of reason transcends space and time. The religious self, on the other hand, is keenly aware of its own mortality, not simply at some future date, but even now insofar as it is no more than a momentary self-determination of the world as a transformational matrix. As Nishida comments, "[a] deathless being is not temporally unique, and that which is not temporally unique is not individual. The self truly realizes its own temporal uniqueness as it faces its own eternal negation."[65] Yet, as it faces its own eternal nothingness, the religious self becomes self-aware in a new way; in judging itself to be nothing, it attains "a deeper subjectivity behind judgment that in some sense transcends death and participates in eternal life."[66]

It is in this context, moreover, that the empirical individual has genuine contact with God. God, too, of course, exists in virtue of an absolutely contradictory self-identity. For, if God is to be truly absolute, then God cannot share existence with the individual self or anything else. To be truly absolute, God must either exist alone or in some sense cease to exist as God in order to exist as this or that empirical individual. For only thus can God remain the Absolute, that which has no other entity opposed to itself. Yet this means that God is not only absolute being but likewise absolute nothingness. As Nishida notes, "in respect of the absolute, if there were something outside it, negating and opposing it, it would not be the absolute. The absolute must rather possess absolute self-negation within itself. In this respect, the absolute must be absolutely nothing."[67]

The paradox of the relationship between God and the religious self, then, is that each must negate itself by identifying with the other in order to attain its own unique self-identity or self-affirmation. Nishida quickly adds that this is not a form of pantheism. Rather, it is an instance of what commentators on the *Prajnaparamita Sutra* term the dialectic of "is" and "is not."[68] Everything, God included, exists in virtue of an absolute contradiction; it must be both itself and its opposite at the same time. Nishida makes this point even clearer by claiming that God, to be truly God, must likewise be Satan. Satan represents the ultimate limit of the self-negation of God. God becomes Satan insofar as God identifies with the individual self in its refusal to admit its dependence on God for its creaturely act of self-affirmation. God, in other words, allows the individual self to affirm its independence of God even though it can make that act of self-affirmation only through God's own act of self-negation in allowing it to be in the first place.[69] Thus, for different reasons, both God and the religious self are an absolutely contradictory self-identity of good and evil. God is such through identification with rebellious creatures; the creatures, through non-identification with God.

As noted above, Nishida explains this paradoxical relationship of God and the religious self in terms of the dialectic of "is" and "is not" in the *Prajnaparamita Sutra*. Still another option was open to him, however, which I wish to explore at this point. That option would have been to distinguish more carefully between the personhood of God and the underlying divine nature. For, there is an obvious contradiction in saying that God truly becomes the existential self and yet remains God at the same time; God is then equivalently both terms of the I-Thou relationship at once. On the other hand, there is no apparent contradiction in saying that the divine nature or the ground of the divine being is at the same time the ground of the existence and activity of the existential self. It is immanent within the existential self as its underlying principle of activity; yet it is transcendent to the existential self in that it is likewise the divine nature or principle of activity for the divine being.

In this second case, then, God and the existential self stand as separate entities in an I-Thou relation with the divine nature serving as their common ground or principle of existence, linking them together in an ongoing dialectic of mutual affirmation and negation. Each, in other words, employs the divine nature to achieve its own unique identity through an act of self-negation, that is, through definition in terms of the other. God becomes God, that is, creative and expressive being, only in virtue of the existential self as created and responsive being. The existential self, in turn, achieves its true identity only in terms of its renunciation of the claim to self-sufficiency or full independence of God. Each therefore conditions the existence and activity of the other, but both act only in virtue of their common ground in the divine nature as a principle of existence and activity.

For basically the same reasons, God as a transcendent personal being does not have to become Satan in order to preserve the divine omnipotence and omniscience, as in Nishida's scheme.[70] Rather, it is the existential self which becomes Satan in that it chooses the stance of independence from God rather than that of interdependence with God. It can make this choice, to be sure, only because of its grounding in the divine nature as the principle of activity common to both God and itself. In this qualified sense, God may be said to become Satan in that the divine nature empowers the creature to choose independence of God rather than interdependence with God. But, as Nishida himself concedes, God as a personal being never behaves like Satan in dealing with creatures. That is, God does not respond vindictively to this rebellion on the part of the existential self; instead God always acts out of compassion and love for the creature still in need of enlightenment with respect to its true self-identity.[71]

This same distinction between the divine nature and the personhood of God, as I see it, likewise makes clear the relationship between God and the world in Nishida's thinking. As noted above, Nishida refers to the world as a "transformational matrix" in which the existential self paradoxically affirms itself in an act of self-negation and, together with other existential selves, thus reshapes the "world" understood as the concrete field or context for their mutual interaction. What is this transformational matrix, however, if not the divine nature, that is, the underlying principle of activity for the interaction of God with the existential selves and for the existential selves in their ongoing relations with one another? Since it is operative within all of them and between all of them as their common ground, it equivalently sets up a field for their dynamic interrelation. It itself, however, as simply a principle of activity and in no sense of the word an entity, is Absolute Nothingness. Only its effects, in other words, are entitative; in its own nature as a principle of activity or "transformational matrix," it is strictly non-entitative. For the same reason, of course, it never exists in itself but always in conjunction with the entities which it thus empowers to exist and to relate to one another within a given context or "world."

Nishida himself seems to support this understanding of the God-world relationship in his admittedly somewhat ambiguous reference to the "trinitarian" structure of the existential self:

> As an individual center of the world of the absolute present, each self is a unique monad that mirrors the Father, the absolute One. Conversely, each self is the *Verbum* of the Father, as the self-expression of the absolute One; and each self forms the creative world as a spirit vector of the world. In this way the personal self is grounded in the world's own trinitarian structure.[72]

Nishida focuses here on the way in which the individual self reflects in its activity each of the persons of the Trinity. But implicit in his thinking is the notion of Absolute Nothingness as the transformational matrix out of which all individual selves emerge and become related to one another.

As Donald Mitchell comments, "Nishida could see this trinitarian structure in the world where all selves and other forms of existence are expressions or self-determinations of one matrix. . . . Each self is unified in Absolute Nothingness in a relation of trinitarian-like interrelatedness with all other selves and forms of the world."[73] Yet Mitchell insists, quite rightly in my judgment from a Christian perspective, that Absolute Nothingness or the Void is not beyond God. It does not antedate, in other words, the existence of the three divine persons in the way that it antedates the existence of individual entities in this world. Rather, "the Void is the kenotic dynamic of the Trinity, the kenosis of the Trinity, experienced from the near side [of the God-world relationship] as the ground of our existence and indeed of the fullness of all creation. In other words, the Trinity is *not* derivative from the kenosis of the Godhead. Rather, the Godhead *is* the kenosis of the Trinity."[74]

Mitchell might have been helped here if he had employed the distinction between the divine persons and the divine nature as I have done throughout this book. The divine nature, in other words, does not antedate the existence of the divine persons any more than the persons antedate the existence of the nature. Rather, the divine persons relate to one another as one God in virtue of the divine nature, and the divine nature exists or is actualized in terms of the interrelated activity of the persons. Furthermore, as Mitchell points out, the divine nature likewise serves as the ground of being or vital source for the existence and interrelated activity of all finite entities so that they, too, in their own way reflect the trinitarian structure of the world.

To sum up, then, I would argue that Nishida's underlying premise in both *An Inquiry into the Good* and many years later in the essay "The Logic of the Place of Nothingness and the Religious Worldview" is the same, namely, that Ultimate Reality is not an entity, not even God as the Supreme Being, but an underlying activity which makes all entities, God included, to be themselves and to relate to one another according to the aforementioned dialectic of affirmation and negation. In *An Inquiry into the Good*, to be sure, Nishida focuses more on the issue of "pure experience" in which "immediate reality" can be reflexively grasped. Yet, as indicated above, when he seeks to set forth the ontological foundations for this affirmation of "pure experience" and "immediate reality," he ends up with the assumption of a universal consciousness which is somehow identified with God as its unifying Spirit. This is tantamount to pantheism unless one implicitly assumes that by "God" here is meant a divine activity rather than a divine being. It is the divine activity or the underlying nature of God that unifies and coordinates all particular consciousnesses (including the consciousness of God understood as a personal being) into a single all-embracing "universal consciousness" or shared consciousness.[75]

Similarly, in "The Logic of the Place of Nothingness and the Religious Worldview," Nishida is always implicitly working with the notion of an underlying ontological activity which sets God and the existential self in dialectical relation to one another through mutual self-affirmation and self-negation. Nishida's "existential" logic, for example, is superior to the empirical logic of Aristotle and the transcendental logic of Kant only because it accurately reflects the workings of that underlying ontological activity in the paradoxical relations between God and the existential self. That is, in virtue of this genuinely "existential" logic, one is finally coming to terms with God and existential selves as *interactive subjects of existence and activity* rather than as simply *interrelated objects of thought* within one's world view or metaphysical scheme. But God and existential selves are thus truly interactive only because they are empowered to interact with one another in virtue of an underlying activity common to them both. Since this principle of activity is primordially located in God as Creative Being and only secondarily operative in creatures as created beings, it is properly described as the divine nature which is then shared with all creatures. But, insofar as it transcends the entitative reality of God so as to be likewise the underlying nature or principle of activity for all creatures, it can in a qualified sense be regarded as Ultimate Reality even beyond God as a personal (or tripersonal) being. Yet, even then, it is still Ultimate Reality not as an entity but as a transcendent activity which allows God and creatures to co-exist and relate to one another within a common world.[76]

Within the Kyoto School of Buddhist philosophy can be counted many other distinguished philosophers besides Kitaro Nishida: Keiji Nishitani, Shin'ichi Hisamatsu, Hajime Tanabe, Shizuteru Ueda and Masao Abe, to name only the most prominent. I have limited myself in this chapter, however, to the preceding analysis of Nishida's thought since my intention has been not to provide an overview of the philosophical orientation of the entire school but only to note in the writings of its most prominent member regular (even if most often implicit) reference to an underlying ontological activity which underlies the relation between subject and object in human consciousness and the relation between God and the existential self in the context of the world or "universal consciousness." In brief, then, my argument is that even more strongly than the Buddha himself, as far as we are able to judge from the discourse to Kaccayana out of the *Samyutta Nikaya*, and more strongly than Nagarjuna in his celebrated *Mulamad-hyamakakarika*, Nishida seems to confirm the basic hypothesis of this chapter and this entire book, namely, that the Infinite, that which in the end must be counted as Ultimate Reality, is an activity, not an entity (not even God as the Supreme Being). In the next chapter, I will pursue this same theme within the context of one more Asian religion, namely, Taoism, with its understanding of Ultimate Reality as the Tao, both named and un-named.

7

The Secret of the Tao

Of all the classics of Chinese literature available in English translation, certainly the *Tao Te Ching (Classic of the Way and Its Power)* holds a position of pre-eminence. Wing-tsit Chan, author of the widely used *Source Book in Chinese Philosophy*, notes that there are more than forty different English translations of the book.[1] One reason for its popularity, as Holmes Welch comments, is quite possibly its brevity; not only the translator but likewise the reader is powerfully attracted by a well-known work of such modest proportions.[2] But still another reason is its obscurity. Because it is written in Archaic Chinese, no one can be really certain what it says; still less can one be certain what it means. As a result, new translations and commentaries abound.[3]

These prefatory remarks appear necessary as I undertake in this chapter an examination of Ultimate Reality in Chinese Philosophy, specifically, in the *Tao Te Ching* and in another great classic of early Taoism, the *Chuang Tzu*. My point in the analysis of key passages out of these two works will not be finally to set forth the definitive meaning of the Tao, but simply to extend the basic hypothesis of this book into the area of Chinese philosophy. That hypothesis, it will be remembered, is that the Infinite as such is not an entity but an activity, an activity which serves as the ontological ground for all entities, both created and uncreated. In previous chapters, I outlined how this notion of the Infinite as an activity underlying the existence and operation of entities is implicit in the thought of major Western thinkers such as Aristotle, Thomas Aquinas and Alfred North Whitehead; likewise, I made clear how this same notion of the Infinite could be seen as clarifying the notion of *Brahman* in classical Hinduism and the notion of *Sunyata* (Emptiness) in classical Buddhism. The present discussion of Chinese philosophy is thus intended only to fill out this picture of various systems of metaphysics sketched in the preceding chapters so as eventually to make some observations about the usefulness of this notion of the Infinite as unending activity for contemporary interreligious dialogue.

In the first part of the present chapter, accordingly, I will cite and offer an interpretation of various passages out of the *Tao Te Ching*, using the translation provided by Wing-tsit Chan in his *Source Book*. The much-quoted first chapter runs as follows:

> The Tao (Way) that can be told of is not the eternal Tao;
> The name that can be named is not the eternal name.
> The Nameless is the origin of Heaven and Earth;
> The Named is the mother of all things.
> Therefore let there always be non-being so we may see their subtlety,
> And let there always be being so we may see their outcome.
> The two are the same,
> But after they are produced, they have different names.
> They both may be called deep and profound (*hsuan*).
> Deeper and more profound,
> The door of all subtleties![4]

My basic interpretation of this passage is that the Tao itself is pure movement or activity, and that *non-being* (or potentiality) and *being* (or actuality) are its two essential dimensions. For all movement or activity inevitably involves both non-being and being in that it is a continuous transit from potentiality to actuality.[5]

Thus, as Lao Tzu (or in any case the author of the text[6]) comments, non-being and being are the same; that is, they are complementary dimensions of one and the same underlying reality. But, once an entity is produced in virtue of this activity, non-being and being (or potentiality and actuality) can be logically distinguished. The entity in question is, after all, an actuality; but the underlying activity out of which it emerged and upon which it depends for the exercise of its existence remains a potentiality. That is, the underlying ontological activity never becomes an actuality in its own right but instead serves as the dynamic principle for the existence of things that do exist in their own right. Hence, the underlying ontological activity, as Lao Tzu comments, is "the door of all subtleties," the universal principle of potentiality for all the actualities of this world with their more specific potentialities.[7]

Being, therefore, corresponds to the Tao that can be named in that being is manifest in various entities or actualities. Non-being, on the other hand, corresponds to the Tao that cannot be named since it is only indirectly manifest in those same beings as their principle of potentiality. Hence, while "being and non-being produce each other," as noted in Chapter 2 of the *Tao Te Ching*,[8] non-being enjoys an ontological priority over being because it is more closely associated with the Tao that cannot be named, that is, the indeterminate "origin of Heaven and Earth."[9] The Tao that can be named, on the other hand, is "the mother of all things" because it acquires a type of actuality or specification as a maternal principle in and through the entities to which it gives birth.[10] In this way, as noted above, the Tao that can be named corresponds to being rather than non-being in that it can be grasped by the mind as something actual rather than as simply nothing, that is, as pure potentiality.

Still other metaphors are used by Lao Tzu to describe the relationship of being to non-being. After having categorically stated in Chapter 40, for example, that "All things in the world come from being. And being comes from non-being,"[11] he then complicates the issue with the following passage out of Chapter 42:

Tao produced the One.
The One produced the two.
The two produced the three.
And the three produced the ten thousand things.
The ten thousand things carry the yin and embrace the yang,
    and through the blending of the material force (*ch'i*)
    they achieve harmony.[12]

Ellen Marie Chen claims that the One (*Yu*) is being in opposition to the Tao itself understood as non-being or pure potentiality (*Wu*).[13] The two, she adds, are most likely *yin* (the "female" cosmic principle at work in the world) and *yang* (the "male" cosmic principle); the three is their harmonious interaction in any given entity. She then concludes: "What is clear from chapter 42 is that the world of ten thousand things, as the world of many, issues forth from the 'one,' which itself comes from the nothingness of Tao. Thus Tao as zero begets being as the 'one,' and being as the 'one' through 'two' and 'three' gives rise to all things in the world."[14]

What is important for our purposes in this chapter, however, is to recognize that neither the Tao itself, nor the One, nor the two and the three, are entities. All of them are principles of existence and activity for "the ten thousand things," the material entities of this world. The Tao, for example, is here identified with *Wu*, the principle of potentiality for all movement and activity. The One is identified with *Yu*, the corresponding principle of actuality within movement and activity. The One, in turn, begets still another pair of principles, *yin* and *yang*, which are related to one another respectively as receptivity and activity. Finally, their harmonious combination in terms of the three as *ch'i*, material force or energy, results in the creation of an entity, one of "the ten thousand things."

Why such an elaborate hierarchy of principles is needed to explain the origin of "the ten thousand things," that is, the material entities of ordinary experience, is difficult to say. But, undoubtedly, it is rooted in the difficulty of imagining how something comes into existence out of nothing. In Greek and Western medieval philosophy, a transcendent entity or actuality always precedes and accounts for the existence of contingent beings. But in Chinese thought, as Chen points out,[15] non-being or pure potentiality precedes and logically accounts for actuality or determinate existence. I myself would argue that this is because the primordial Chinese insight is into the reality of becoming rather than into the reality of being. Unlike being, becoming understood as movement or activity necessarily gives priority to potentiality over actuality. For whatever actuality movement or activity possesses is always provisional. By definition it is always enroute to further stages of actualization; otherwise, it would cease to be movement or activity.

As we have already noted above in Chapter 1, Aristotle evidently grasped this insight into the nature of motion in Book III of the *Physics*. But it is likewise clear that he did not grasp all its logical implications. For, if he had done so, he would have been logically compelled to revise his cosmology, grounded as it is in a philosophy of being(s) rather than a philosophy of becoming. That is, for Aristotle, actuality precedes and logically accounts for potentiality. Whatever is "moved" from potentiality to actuality is moved by another entity already in act. Hence, to account for movement or activity among entities in need of actualization, he had recourse to a causal scheme whereby things that are "moved" are related to their respective external "movers," until one arrives in thought at an Unmoved Mover, a being which is pure actuality and thus logically requires no Mover beyond itself to account for its continued existence and activity.

He did not, in other words, make use of his own insight into the necessarily unending character of motion to stipulate that reality is primarily becoming, not being. Thus he failed to see that self-contained activities or entelechies (*entelecheiai*) do not have to be "moved" from potency to act in virtue of an external agent. Rather, as ongoing subjects of their own processes of self-realization, they continually move themselves from potency to act. By their immanent processes of self-actualization, in other words, they exemplify the ontological priority of potentiality over actuality. What they will become is more important than what they are here and now.[16]

There are several other attempts to describe or name the Tao in the *Tao Te Ching*. All of them, of course, are simply analogies intended to grasp somehow the reality of that which has no fixed actuality in and of itself because it is pure activity. In Chapter 4, for example, the author says:

> Tao is empty (like a bowl),
> It may be used, but its capacity is never exhausted.
> It is bottomless, perhaps the ancestor of all things.
> . . . .
> Deep and still, it appears to exist forever.
> I do not know whose son it is.
> It seems to have existed before the Lord.[17]

The first line reminds one of the Buddhist notion of emptiness (*sunyata*), discussed in Chapter 6. Like Buddhist emptiness, the emptiness of the Tao is simultaneously a fullness. As Lao Tzu comments in the second line, "it may be used, but its capacity is never exhausted." A normal container or bowl is either empty or full but cannot be both at the same time. Unlike an entity, however, an activity as a combination of non-being and being is paradoxically both empty and full at the same time. For, on the one hand, it exists only in its instantiations; hence, it is empty of actuality or "self-nature" (*svabhava*), as Nagarjuna pointed out in the *Mulamadhyamakakarika*.[18] On the other hand, it transcends each of those entities in which it is instantiated since it is their common principle of existence and activity. Hence, it possesses a fullness or lack of limits to which no entity as a (presumably) fixed reality can lay claim.

A few lines later, we read: "Deep and still, it appears to exist forever. I do not know whose son it is. It seems to have existed before the Lord." Likewise, Chapter 25 begins: "There was something undifferentiated and yet complete, Which existed before heaven and earth. Soundless and formless, it depends on nothing and does not change. . . . I do not know its name. I call it Tao."[19] Do these texts imply that the Tao is an Absolute, a reality existing in itself apart from the world?[20] Throughout this book, I have consistently argued that the Infinite as an underlying ontological activity does not exist in itself apart from the entities in which it is instantiated. Here, too, therefore, I would argue that the Tao as the Infinite of Taoist metaphysics may indeed be conceived as an Absolute independent of all finite entities, but that in fact it never actually exists except as a principle of existence and activity for some entity (e.g., God or "the Lord") or set of entities (e.g., the world).

For only as an underlying activity can the Tao be truly infinite, that is, both totally immanent within and yet completely transcendent of the entities in which it is instantiated. As we have seen above in dealing with Advaita Vedanta Hinduism and Zen Buddhism, entities inevitably limit one another; what is one entity is not another entity. But an activity can be totally immanent within entities as their principle of existence and activity; yet, at the same time, it is transcendent of all of them since it exists within each in a different way. Hence, I would argue that the Tao as the generalized principle of potentiality for the things of this world is only in thought, and not in reality, separable from the things of this world.

Indirect confirmation for this proposal seems to be given in the following lines out of Chapter 11:

> Thirty spokes are united around the hub to make a wheel,
> But it is on its non-being that the utility of the carriage depends.
> Clay is molded to form a utensil.
> But it is on its non-being that the utility of the utensil depends.
> Doors and windows are cut out to make a room,
> But it is on its non-being that the utility of the room depends.
> Therefore turn being into advantage, and turn non-being into
>   utility.[21]

In each of these examples, it is clear that non-being cannot exist in itself apart from being, some form of actuality. Yet that same being or entitative reality has no utility or advantage without the potentiality implicit in non-being, what it is not.

The bowl, for example, is a vessel of a certain size and shape. Yet its "advantage" lies in its capacity or potentiality to hold what it is not, namely, liquids or foodstuffs. A wheel is useful for transportation only because it is round; yet its roundness is paradoxically made possible by straight spokes radiating out from a hollow round center, an emptiness at the core of its being. Finally, a room is functional for human habitation only because it has doors and windows which, strictly speaking, are not part of the room but openings into the room to allow for light and the passage of human beings into and out of the room. Everything that exists, therefore, is a combination of being and non-being, actuality and potentiality. For only thus does it have any utility or function in the world of "ten thousand things." Even more importantly for our purposes, however, only thus does the entity in question reflect its grounding or source in the Tao which in itself is a combination of being and non-being, actuality and potentiality.

Still another metaphor often employed to describe the reality of the Tao is water. "Water is good; it benefits all things and does not compete with them. It dwells in (lowly) places that all disdain. That is why it is so near to Tao."[22] Elsewhere Lao Tzu comments: "There is nothing softer and weaker than water, And yet there is nothing better for attacking hard and strong things. For this reason there is no substitute for it."[23] As Wing-Tsit Chan comments, the implicit emphasis here is on ethics rather than on metaphysics.[24] That is, the human being who acts in accord with the Tao is compared to the quiet but irresistible force of running water. But a clue to the deeper reality of the Tao as an activity rather than an entity seems to be given in the image of running water rather than stagnant water. It is running water, for example, that, in following the law of gravity, seeks "lowly" places. Furthermore, in thus gaining momentum, running water is able to dislodge and wear down what is initially hard and strong, resistant to the flow of water around it. Hence, even though it appears to be soft and weak in flowing around obstacles in its path, running water proves to be over the passage of time the most powerful of natural forces (or activities) over which nothing else in this world prevails.

Pursuing the same basic metaphor Lao Tzu comments: the Tao "may be compared to rivers and streams running into the sea."[25] Nothing escapes its all-pervasive influence and activity. But, if this is so, then not only running water but also the countryside or terrain through which the water flows is a temporary instantiation or momentary form assumed by the Tao as an underlying activity. Thus, just as ice is water whose natural movement has been temporarily suspended, so all the different entities of this world are, so to speak, crystallized forms of one and the same underlying activity. Our attention, accordingly, is drawn to running water as a metaphor for this underlying activity because of its obvious fluidity by comparison with other entities. But, in point of fact, not just the water but also the countryside through which it is flowing is pulsating with activity. Everything is in constant movement. Flowing water merely illustrates what is happening everywhere without our adverting to it.

Knowing how to work with the Tao rather than to assert oneself against it is the key to understanding the Taoist ideal of *wu-wei*. Literally translated as "non-action," it does not mean inactivity or idleness but rather "'taking no action that is contrary to Nature'—in other words, letting Nature take its own course."[26] Just as running water seems to follow the path of least resistance in its downward path to a still larger body of water, so human beings who are in tune with the natural rhythms of Nature as operative in the people and things around them will lead more tranquil lives and in the end will succeed better at what they do than those who deliberately try to impose their will on others around them. As Lao Tzu comments, "[t]he use of force usually brings requital."[27] Or, as Holmes Welch rephrases the insight, "when anyone, ruler or subject, tries to *act* upon humans individually or collectively, the ultimate result is the opposite of what he is aiming at. He has invoked what we might call the Law of Aggression" whereby an equal or greater force is used to resist the violent measures of the other.[28]

This does not mean, of course, that the use of force is never justified. There are times when force must be employed to prevent injustice. But it must be used with restraint and a sense of regret. I quote Chapter 30 of the *Tao Te Ching*:

A good (general) always achieves his purpose and stops,
But dares not seek to dominate the world.
He achieves his purpose but does not brag about it.[29]

Likewise, in the following chapter, Lao Tzu notes that when the good ruler is victorious in battle, "he does not regard it as praiseworthy, For to praise victory is to delight in the slaughter of men. . . . For the slaughter of the multitude, let us weep with sorrow and grief, For a victory, let us observe the occasion with funeral ceremonies."[30]

What is ultimately important, then, is not the bare use of force but one's attitude toward it. If our attitude in the use of force is bloodthirsty and aggressive, then the conflict between ourselves and our opponent(s) will end in mutual destruction. If, on the other hand, our use of force is restrained and compassionate, then the hostility of our opponent(s) may shortly abate and the conflict will be brought to an end. The vicious circle of mutual aggression will have been broken by growth in mutual sympathy and forebearance.[31] In any event, "[w]hatever is contrary to Tao will soon perish."[32] The prolonged use of force will inevitably have disastrous consequences for both sides.

In matters of state, therefore, rulers and other policy-makers should imitate the "female" principle both in Nature and in human sexual relations:

The female always overcomes the male by tranquillity
And by tranquillity she is underneath.
A big state can take over a small state if it places itself below the
    small state;
And the small state can take over a big state if it places itself below
    the big state.
Thus some, by placing themselves below, take over (others),
And some, by being (naturally) low, take over (other states).[33]

In both cases, the key point is to remain tranquil and responsive to the subtle workings of the female principle in the situation at hand. One would expect women to be more naturally responsive to the activity of this principle in their lives. But, as Lao Tzu suggests here, men too can be alert to what the Tao under the dimensionality of non-being or the female principle is gently urging for the conduct of their lives. "To act, but not to rely on one's own ability, To lead [others], but not to master them—This is called profound and secret virtue (*hsuan-te*)."[34]

Lao Tzu frequently refers to the Tao in feminine terms. In many cases, the Tao is called Mother.[35] In other places, the vagina is called the "gate" or "root" of Heaven and Earth.[36] Ellen Marie Chen suggests that the *Tao Te Ching* "as a thought form traces its original inspiration to the existence of a matriarchal society" which antedates the rise of Confucianism and a male-dominated society with its emphasis on reason and order.[37] Whether or not one agrees with Chen on this point depends, to some extent at least, on when one dates the composition of the *Tao Te Ching* and whether one regards Confucianism as a reaction to Taoism or vice versa.[38] What seems incontestible, however, is that in the *Tao Te Ching* the Tao is linked with mothering and/or the feminine principle of generativity.

Hence, even in its relatively passive or receptive dimension as non-being (*Wu*), the Tao should be understood in terms of activity rather than as static nothingness.[39] As noted above in the discussion of the ethical ideal of *wu-wei*, those who are instinctively in tune with the Tao are not inactive but highly productive. Like women in the act of sexual intercourse, those in harmony with the Tao are only apparently passive and inert. In the end, their quiet productivity results in the "birth" of something new and worthwhile. Thus I concur with Chen in her conclusion: "*Tao* as the ground of the changing world is not itself immutable or unchanging. Rather, all things change because *Tao* is itself change."[40] But I would add that, paradoxically because it is *ceaseless* activity, the Tao appears to be immutable. That is, because it has no beginning or end, the movement of the Tao is an unchanging reality responsible for all the manifest changes taking place in this world.[41]

One last metaphor for the reality of the Tao remains to be discussed. That is the image of the infant or the uncarved block of wood (*p'u*),[42] both of which symbolize one's "original nature" to which one must continually return in order to maintain peace of mind and the proper balance in the practical decisions of life. As Kenneth Kramer comments:

> For Lao Tzu there are three stages in human growth—the infant, the adult and the sage. We could refer to these as *original nature* (the natural pre-self-reflective innocence of infancy), *human nature* (the conditioned self-reflective experience of mature consciousness), and *Tao-nature* (the un-self-reflective emptiness of spontaneous aware-ness). The True Sage actualizes a process of mystical reversal, and returns to the original nature or *p'u* (the uncarved block). This reversal is characterized by "reversion" in which the action of the Tao comes through weakness, through appearing to fall backward.[43]

From a metaphysical perspective, one may say that this reversion to one's original nature as symbolized by the infant or the uncarved block of wood is a matter of getting in touch with the non-being which is the wellspring or source for one's being or overt activity. For if, as noted earlier, "all things in the world come from being, and being comes from non-be-ing,"[44] it is apparent that new being or fresh activity can only occur after the movement from an already fixed state of being to non-being has taken place, if only for a moment.[45]

Thus the movement of the Tao is in terms of pulsations or vibrations. That is, there is first a movement from non-being to being and then a reverse movement from being to non-being so as to initiate the cycle all over again.[46] The Sage who understands well the natural rhythm of the Tao schools himself or herself to rest in the tranquility of non-being momentar-ily before asserting himself or herself again in terms of being or overt activity. In this way, one allows the natural creativity of the Tao to influence one's decisions and/or behavior-patterns. The being or pattern of the next moment does not have to duplicate the pattern of the preceding moment because in the interval one has momentarily reverted to the repose of non-being from which all new being or a new pattern of existence and activity must inevitably arise. Lao Tzu expresses the matter thus:

> All things flourish,
> But each one returns to its root.
> This return to its root means tranquillity.
> It is called returning to its destiny.
> To return to destiny is called the eternal (Tao).
> To know the eternal is called enlightenment.
> Not to know the eternal is to act blindly to result in disaster.[47]

Yet, from a purely logical perspective, there is a basic ambiguity here in this understanding of the activity of the Tao. For on what rational grounds can one trust one's "original nature" or the spontaneous activity of the Tao as non-being to make the right decisions in life? Why should submitting to an impersonal principle of creativity be more helpful in making important decisions than a fully deliberate weighing of the reasons for and against a given option? The movement from non-being to being, after all, is in principle equally fulfilled when one performs an objectively evil action, harmful to oneself and others, as well as one that is evidently good, that is, beneficial to oneself and others.[48]

According to Holmes Welch, Lao Tzu simply presupposed that life in society tends to corrupt human beings who in terms of their "original nature" are free from hostility and aggressiveness.[49] But can this presupposition be justified empirically? That is, are human beings naturally peace loving and friendly? Furthermore, if in remaining quiet the Sage refrains from passing judgment on the propriety and impropriety of the actions of others,[50] does he or she not run the risk of being considered insensitive or inhumane? Lao Tzu himself seems to concede the point:

> Heaven and Earth are not humane (*jen*).
> They regard all things as straw dogs.
> The sage is not humane.
> He regards all people as straw dogs.[51]

As Chan notes, this may simply be Lao Tzu's emphatic way of opposing the rival Confucian doctrine of humanity and righteousness.[52] In addition, the clear innuendo is that Lao Tzu regards himself as likewise a "straw dog," that is, an image used in religious rituals which is afterwards thrown away or burnt up. But it still illustrates how, in allowing Nature to take its course, one must steel oneself against its apparent aberrations as well as enjoy its blessings. "Gentle rains or spring floods, the havoc of a landslide or the beauty of mountain mist—all are parts of the whole to which the Sage himself belongs."[53] Even more so in human affairs, one must be extraordinarily patient with oneself and others in waiting for excesses of various kinds to be naturally adjusted, for all wrongs to be righted.

It is always dangerous to make comparisons between thinkers in different cultures. But it is interesting to note that Alfred North Whitehead in his philosophy distinguished carefully between creativity and God as the principle of limitation for the exercise of that same creativity. According to Whitehead, creativity as the underlying metaphysical activity is responsible for everything that exists, both good and evil. God, however, as the source of order or rationality within the world process is silently at work "to divide the Good from the Evil, and to establish Reason 'within her dominions supreme.'"[54] Lao Tzu and his contemporaries, to be sure, presumably did not believe in a Creator God with a providential care for all creatures. As Chan points out, the notion of a Supreme Being within the Shang dynasty (1751-1112 B.C.E.) was gradually replaced by the concept of the Mandate of Heaven or cosmic order within the Chou dynasty (1111-249 B.C.E.).[55] But the philosophical issue at stake here is not thereby resolved: namely, whether one should trust the direction of one's life to an impersonal principle of process or creativity unless it is somehow linked with the providential activity of an all-wise and all-loving God in this world. For only in this way do human beings not have to wait for the inevitable workings of the Tao painfully to adjust excesses of various kinds in human affairs. Instead, with divine guidance and assistance, they can work with the Tao in its gentler manifestations and thus conceivably prevent many excesses in human behavior from taking place at all.

In the remaining pages of this chapter, I will investigate the understanding of the Tao to be found in another celebrated classic of early Taoism, namely, the *Chuang Tzu*, written in whole or in part by the Chinese philosopher of the same name.[56] In the celebrated second chapter of this book, Chuang Tzu makes reference to the coinherence and interaction of entities with one another in a manner quite similar to the Indian philosopher Nagarjuna:

> There is nothing that is not the "that" and there is nothing that is not the "this." Things do not know that they are the "that" of other things; they only know what they themselves know. Therefore, I say that the "that" is produced by the "this" and the "this" is also caused by the "that." This is the theory of mutual production.[57]

Herbert Giles translates the first sentence of this passage somewhat differently: "There is nothing which is not objective; there is nothing which is not subjective."[58] According to either translation, however, there is a mutual bonding of two distinct realities with one another in and through the invisible activity of the Tao. They produce one another because they are both manifestations of the Tao. Much like the notion of "dependent co-arising" in the *Mulamadhyamakakarika* of Nagarjuna, therefore, the concept of "mutual production" for Chuang Tzu undercuts all conventional understandings of cause and effect. There are no independent causes and effects. Everything is both cause and effect of everything else.[59]

A dramatic illustration of this notion of mutual production through the action of the Tao is provided by Chuang Tzu at the end of Chapter 2:

> Once I, Chuang Chou, dreamed that I was a butterfly and was happy as a butterfly. I was conscious that I was quite pleased with myself. But I did not know that I was Chou. Suddenly, I awoke, and there I was, visibly Chou. I do not know whether it was Chou dreaming that he was a butterfly or the butterfly dreaming that it was Chou. Between Chou and the butterfly there must be some distinction. [But one may be the other.] This is called the transformation of things.[60]

Constituting both subject and object within the dream and linking them together in dynamic interaction is the underlying activity of the Tao. Hence, from the perspective of the Tao, the philosopher is unable definitively to decide whether he is a man who dreamt that he was a butterfly or a butterfly who even now is dreaming that it is a man. There is clearly an entitative distinction between a butterfly and a man. But both entities are necessarily involved in the activity of dreaming. Thus both are manifestations of one and the same underlying activity, that is, the Tao as the principle of the transformation of things.

Chang Chung-yuan comments: "The awareness of the identification and interpenetration of self and nonself is the key that unlocks the mystery of *Tao*."[61] He then distinguishes between the Confucian ideal of *jen* or fellow-feeling based on rational discrimination of one's responsibilities to others, beginning with one's own relatives but eventually including all other beings in this world, and the Taoist ideal of *Tz'u* or great sympathy in which "subject and object are totally and immediately interfused and the self is transformed into selflessness."[62] Whereas the Confucian ideal of *jen* evidently presupposes a high degree of self-awareness, the Taoist experience of *Tz'u* implies a radical loss of self-awareness. This is the realm of non-being, says Chung-yuan, which a human being attains either by sudden enlightenment or gradual illumination as a result of prolonged meditation.[63] In either case, however, it is primarily an "ontological experience, nondifferentiated and nondiscriminated,"[64] rather than the result of discursive reasoning.

I would only add that the experience is "nondifferentiated and nondiscriminated" because it is presumably the experience of an activity rather than the experience of an entity. That is, entities are always at least somewhat discriminated and differentiated from one another in experience. Hence, if, as Chung-yuan claims, one truly experiences a reality which is nondifferentiated and nondiscriminated, one must be experiencing an activity prior to the distinction into the subject and object of the activity. Like Chuang Tzu in his celebrated dream, one is both subject and object at the same time because one is directly and immediately identified with the activity of dreaming. Self-awareness returns only after the activity of dreaming is finished. As Chuang Tzu says elsewhere in Chapter 2, "when we dream, we do not know that we are dreaming. . . . Only after we are awake do we know that we have dreamed."[65]

Self-awareness, to be sure, is likewise an activity of which one is the subject. But the focus of mental attention is on the division between oneself and the object; Chuang Tzu, for example, awakening from his dream asks himself whether he is a man who dreamt that he was a butterfly or a butterfly who currently is dreaming that it is a man. He raises, in other words, the question of self-awareness: who or what am I? In the "pure experience" of dreaming,[66] however, one is simply the activity of dreaming without discrimination or differentiation into subject and object of a dream. In Taoist terms, one is in the realm of non-being where the Tao is experienced as "transformation" or pure activity. Furthermore, when through sudden enlightenment or gradual illumination one fully awakens to the underlying reality of non-being, then one knows that life as a whole "is a great dream."[67]

Likewise, in Chapter 6 Chuang Tzu seems to think of the Tao as an underlying activity or process of transformation immanent in all the things of this world: "Tao has reality and evidence but no action or physical form. It may be transmitted but cannot be received. It may be obtained but cannot be seen."[68] It has reality and evidence in and through the things of this world which are continually active, in process of transformation. Yet, for that same reason, it cannot be singled out as one activity among the many which are constitutive of this world. Likewise, it has in itself no physical form since it is the underlying dynamism by which all the entities of this world take on a definite form. In being thus omnipresent and supremely active in a world of things, it remains itself unnoticed and invisible, the (back-)ground or ontological source for all the changes that catch the eye.

Yet Chuang Tzu immediately adds: "It is based in itself, rooted in itself. Before heaven and earth came into being, Tao existed by itself from all time."[69] Here one may well question whether Chuang Tzu (like Lao Tzu in the passages from the *Tao Te Ching* quoted above) has not confused logical and temporal priority in thinking about the relation of the Tao to the things of this world. Certainly as their ontological ground or source of existence and activity, the Tao is logically prior to any of the things of this world. But it does not follow that it is likewise temporally prior to these same entities. In fact, if one claims that the Tao is temporally prior to the things of this world, then one seems to have reified the Tao, mentally converted it into a transcendent reality (e.g. the Void) which originally existed in independence of the things of this world. For an activity never exists in itself; it is always instantiated in some entity which thus acts or is acted upon. Hence, if the Tao is thus imagined to exist by itself, it has indeed been reified, mentally converted into an entity in opposition to other entities.

Yet, strictly speaking, in that case one can no longer say that the Tao is the Tao, that is, that which is immanent in all things and yet completely identified with none of them. For, while this is proper to an understanding of the Tao as pure activity, it is not appropriate to an understanding of the Tao as an entity. Entities by definition stand in opposition to one another as separate centers of activity. They may participate in the same activity, but each participates in that activity in a different way. If then the Tao is conceived as a transcendent entity existing prior to the creation of heaven and earth, then not the Tao itself, but the activity which makes the Tao to be the Tao is immanent within all the things of this world. For only an activity can mediate between entities, that is, serve as their common ontological ground or source of existence and activity, and yet be itself at the same time. Hence, the Tao is no longer the Tao if it is conceived as a transcendent entity.

If my hypothesis here is correct, then Chuang Tzu's apparent confusion of the distinction between the logical and temporal priority of the Tao to the things of this world may also account for a rather difficult passage in the *Chuang Tzu* on the "great beginning" or origination of all things:

There was a beginning. There was a time before that beginning. And there was a time before the time which was before that beginning. There was being. There was non-being. There was a time before that non-being. And there was a time before the time that was before that non-being. Suddenly there is being and there is non-being, but I don't know which of being and non-being is really being or really non-being. I have just said something, but I don't know if what I have said really says something or says nothing.[70]

Admittedly, what Chuang Tzu is dramatically illustrating here is the difficulty in thinking about the relationship between being and non-being. Logic seems to fail as one tries to grasp what is inherently mysterious. Yet some light could have been thrown on this relationship if he had consciously distinguished between a logical and a temporal priority of non-being over being. For then he would not have had to ask himself about a "time" before the origination of all things, even before non-being as the first stage in the actualization of being.

If Chuang Tzu, for example, had probed more deeply into his own insight that the Tao is the principle of transformation for all the things in this world, he would have realized that the Tao is indeed logically but not temporally prior to the things that exist. As the ontological source of their being and activity, it co-exists with the things that it empowers to exist. But it does not exist in itself since it is only a principle of transformation for the things of this world; it is not itself a thing, not even a transcendent "thing" or Creator-God. But was there then an absolute beginning, a sudden emergence first of non-being and then of being from pure nothingness, as Chuang Tzu seems to imagine? This would appear to be impossible for the following reasons. First of all, as non-being, that is, as a principle of transformation or continuous activity, the Tao must be eternal, without beginning or end. For, as Aristotle argued in the *Physics*,[71] motion can have no beginning or end since motion is already presupposed in the transition from a state of rest to a state of movement and vice versa. Yet, if non-being is eternal, then being in some form or other (either God or the world or God and the world in dynamic interaction) must likewise eternally exist. As already noted, non-being or potentiality never exists in itself but only in conjunction with being or actuality in some form or other.

Thus Chuang Tzu found it so difficult to imagine a "time" before anything existed because such a "time" is metaphysically impossible. There never was a "time" when absolutely nothing existed, because otherwise to this day nothing would exist. From strict nothingness, nothing proceeds. Only from non-being in the sense of potentiality does being or actuality proceed, and even here the priority of non-being or potentiality to being or actuality is logical rather than temporal. In point of fact, non-being always co-exists with being as its immanent ground or ontological source of existence and activity. Both being and non-being, therefore, are manifest in everything that exists. Being is manifest in the entity's actuality, that which it already is. Non-being is indirectly manifest in its potentiality to become something else. Of the two, non-being is the more mysterious since the potentiality of an entity to become something else becomes apparent only as it is beginning to pass from one state of actuality to another. In "the rustlings of leaves and the twilight of the evening," says Kuang-Ming Wu, one feels the presence of non-being in Nature.[72]

In this sense, as already noted above in analyzing the first chapter of the *Tao Te Ching*, the Tao that cannot be named is properly identified with non-being; whereas the Tao that can be named is linked with being or the One as "the mother of all things." On this most fundamental point, Lao Tzu and Chuang Tzu are clearly in accord, as the following passage from the *Chuang Tzu* makes clear:

> In the great beginning, there was non-being. It had neither being nor name. The One originates from it; it has oneness but not yet physical form. When things obtain it and come into existence, that is called virtue (which gives them their individual character). That which is formless is divided [into yin and yang], and from the very beginning going on without interruption is called destiny (*ming*, fate). Through movement and rest it produces all things.[73]

Virtue or power (*te* in Chinese) is the result of the Tao becoming particularized or individuated in a given entity.[74] Hence, from non-being comes being or the One. But the One itself must become the Many, the "ten thousand things," each of which exists in virtue of its inherent power of *te*. Among human beings, of course, the Sage is the one who through habitual non-action (*wu-wei*) paradoxically possesses the virtue or power of *te* most fully.

Chan adds that the formless One is divided into *yin* and *yang*, the characteristically "female" and "male" forces within Nature. Here it would be tempting to extend our analysis of Ultimate Reality within Chinese philosophy to such Neo-Confucian philosophers as Chou Tun-I who in his *Explanation of the Diagram of the Great Ultimate* sets forth a cosmological scheme remarkably similar to that employed by Lao Tzu and Chuang Tzu. That is, he first postulates the existence of the Non-ultimate (*Wu-chi*) and the Great Ultimate (*T'ai chi*). He then continues: "The Great Ultimate through movement generates yang. When its activity reaches its limit, it becomes tranquil. Through tranquillity the Great Ultimate generates yin. When tranquillity reaches its limits, activity begins again."[75] Finally, through the interplay of *yin* and *yang* the "Five Agents" (Water, Fire, Wood, Metal and Earth) arise which in combination produce all the material things of this world. But, as Chan comments, Chou Tun-I in his cosmology probably followed the *Book of Changes (I Ching)* more than the *Tao Te Ching* or the *Chuang Tzu*. He was then clearly influenced by classical Taoism but in the end remained faithful to the broad lines of Confucian thought.[76]

Hence, it seems best to restrict the present analysis of Ultimate Reality within Chinese philosophy to these two classics of early Taoism in which the primitive notion of the Tao as pure activity comes so clearly to the fore. For, in this way, classical Taoism can likewise be cited in support of the basic hypothesis of this book: namely, that the Infinite or Ultimate Reality is best described in terms of an unending activity rather than as a Supreme Being. Within a theistic perspective, of course, the Supreme Being or God is the primordial subject of that unending activity. But, insofar as this activity is likewise the ground or source of existence and activity for still other finite beings, then the activity enjoys an ontological priority over all the entities in which it is instantiated, including God. The activity, to be sure, never exists in itself. Hence, its distinction from God as the primordial subject of that activity is purely logical, not in any sense temporal. But it does in any case represent for Jews, Christians, and Muslims a new and different dimension to the full reality of God which, as I shall argue in the next and concluding chapter of this book, needs to be brought forward and examined more carefully in contemporary interreligious dialogue.

Conclusion

The Divine Matrix

In trying to describe the interpenetration of reality and appearance in *Creativity and Taoism*, Chang Chung-yuan recalls a celebrated parable which Fa-tsang, the founder of the Hua-yen School of Chinese Buddhism, delivered to the Emperor and the royal court on one occasion. Pointing to the statue of a golden lion in the vicinity, Fa-tsang commented:

> Gold symbolizes reality, and the lion . . . symbolizes appearance. Reality is formless by itself but assumes any form that circumstances give it. Similarly, gold has no "nature of its own" but is shaped into the form of a lion as its appearance. On the other hand, the lion is merely a form or an appearance, which has no reality of its own—it is entirely gold.[1]

When one is impressed by the quantity of gold thus represented, the figure of the lion fades into insignificance. On the other hand, when one's eye is drawn to the artistry of the sculpture, the fact that it is made of pure gold is for the moment forgotten. Ideally, one should advert to both the form and the precious metal at the same time and appreciate the harmony between appearance and reality. At that moment, says Chung-yuan, one will experience inner peace in sensing the interpenetration of reality and appearance.

In similar fashion, the intent of this book has been to bring into focus the dialectical relationship between the Infinite and the finite within various metaphysical schemes and/or religious worldviews, both East and West. The Infinite certainly corresponds to reality in the parable of Fa-tsang since by definition the Infinite encompasses all that is real, both past, present, and future. Likewise, in itself the Infinite (like reality in the parable) is formless; for by assuming a form the Infinite paradoxically becomes finite or determinate. On the other hand, the finite certainly corresponds to what Fa-tsang meant by appearance. For, like the figure of the lion, the finite really exists. Yet its deeper reality is to be the temporary manifestation of something else which never exists by itself but always comes to expression in and through a quasi-infinite number of forms or appearances.

Like seeing the gold and the figure of the lion at the same time, therefore, the deeper perception of reality is to recognize the presence of the Infinite in the finite and thus to acknowledge the provisional or in any case limited character of the finite. One cannot, to be sure, see the Infinite in the finite entity in the same way that one actually sees the gold in the statue of the lion. Hence, it is much more difficult to remain sensitive to the presence of the Infinite in the finite. But, once one has truly felt that presence on one occasion, the experience tends to repeat itself. One has become enlightened with respect to the true nature of reality, and the world is never quite the same again.

Even more importantly, however, the purpose of this book has been to determine the nature of the Infinite that is thus revealed in all the finite persons and things of this world. My argument has been that the Infinite as such cannot be an entity but must be an activity. For, if the Infinite is an entity, then logically nothing else exists except as an accidental modification of the one, all-comprehensive, substantial reality. As Aristotle notes in *On Generation and Corruption*, the component parts of a compound substance are governed by the substantial form proper to the totality; hence, they are separate substances only potentially, not actually.[2] Thus, if finite entities exist within God or some other transcendent entity, then those same finite entities do not really exist in themselves with their own substantial form but exist instead only as parts of the all-comprehensive divine being with its substantial form.

One might counterargue here that this line of thought represents a purely quantitative or spatial understanding of the Infinite. The Infinite, however, is to be understood in qualitative rather than merely quantitative terms. An infinite being is that which both contains and transcends all the perfections to be found in finite beings. As already noted in Chapter 2, Christian thinkers like Augustine and Aquinas did indeed revise the classical Greek understanding of the Infinite as the Void or the totally indeterminate in favor of a new notion of the Infinite as that which is fully determinate in itself but incomprehensible to the human mind because qualitatively superior to anything finite. Thus God as Infinite Being is fully actual with no potentiality or indeterminacy and yet absolutely transcendent of anything finite.

Yet, as I also noted in Chapter 2, while the divine being as the pure act of existence may *objectively* encompass the perfections of all finite entities, God as the subject of the divine act of existence cannot *subjectively* exercise creaturely perfections in the same way that the creatures themselves do. God, in other words, cannot be both the subject of the divine act of existence and the subject of the act of existence proper to a creature at the same time without contradiction. God cannot, for example, be simultaneously both the I and the Thou of the divine-human relationship without destroying the ontological reality of the human Thou.

The human being, then, in his or her subjectivity stands outside of God as the divine subjectivity and thereby limits God, equivalently renders God "finite," even though the divine subjectivity is infinitely superior to the creaturely subjectivity. Put in other terms, God may objectively understand what it means to be human better than any human being that ever lived. But God cannot in virtue of one and the same subjectivity be both a divine and human subject of existence at the same time. Two subjectivities are needed, the one divine and the other human, for a genuine I-Thou relation between the divine and the human to take place.[3] But the net effect of this exchange is to render the divine "finite" in the face of the finite Other, the human being in his or her subjectivity. The subjectivity of God is limited by the subjectivity of the human being and vice versa.

As noted above in Chapter 6, Kitaro Nishida analyzed this self-contradictory relationship between God and the human being in his essay "The Logic of the Place of Nothingness and the Religious World View." That is, God must cease to be the Absolute (in this context, the Infinite) in order to allow the creature to be itself as an ontologically independent reality. Yet God is at the same time truly God, the Lord of creation, only when creatures exist in ontological dependence on the divine being. Thus God both is and is not the Absolute, in relation to creatures. Similarly, the creature first achieves true self-identity when it acknowledges the ontological ground of its being in God. It receives, in other words, from God the power to exist in independence of God as well as in interdependence with God. But, even when it chooses to exist in independence of God, it can make that choice only because of God's antecedent self-negation as the Absolute or the Infinite in allowing it to exist in the first place.

The truly Infinite within this dialogical situation, then, is neither God nor the human being as separate entities but the world as a "transformational matrix" in which God and human beings encounter one another and by their exchange give new shape and order to the world itself. Yet, as I also argued in Chapter 6, what is this transformational matrix if not the divine nature which is the ontological source or common ground both for the existence of God as a personal being and for all creatures? Out of the "absolute nothingness" of the divine nature, therefore, both God as a personal being and all finite beings emerge and are dialectically related to one another. As a *transformational* matrix, however, absolute nothingness is not simply a field or spatial context for the interaction of God and creatures. Rather, it is in the first place an underlying activity which empowers God to be God, creatures to be themselves, and God and creatures to be dynamically interrelated within the "world." Thus the Infinite, once again, turns out on closer examination to be not an entity, not even God as the divine entity, but an activity in which the existence both of God and all creatures is grounded.

The temptation to think of the Infinite in entitative terms, however, is very strong as the chapter on Hinduism earlier in this book made abundantly clear. The Upanishads, after all, only set the parameters of the problem; they do not indicate precisely how the Infinite is related to the finite and vice versa. That is, as my analysis of the first *mahavakya* made clear, they affirm unequivocally the primacy of *Brahman*, the One without a second. Yet they also insist, as in the second and third *mahavakyas*, that consciousness is *Brahman* and that *Atman* as the subject of consciousness or the Self is likewise *Brahman*. Here the ambiguity of the relationship between the Infinite and the finite is quite evident. Is *Brahman* primarily an activity, that is, the activity of being conscious, or is it primarily an entity, that is, the *Atman* or Self who is conscious? If *Brahman* is understood to be the activity of consciousness, then *Brahman* and *Atman* are distinct yet dynamically one since *Brahman* is that principle whereby *Atman* is a conscious self. On the other hand, if *Brahman* is itself an entity, then *Atman* is just another name for the all-encompassing entitative reality of *Brahman*.

Furthermore, as the fourth and fifth *mahavakyas* indicate, there is the further ambiguity whether *Atman* means the divine or cosmic Self, the self within the individual human being, or both in a manner still to be determined. If *Brahman* is understood to be an entity and thus in the end identical with *Atman* as the cosmic Self, then the ontological independence of the human being as an individual *atman* is severely compromised. For, in saying "I am *Brahman*," the individual human being implicitly renounces his or her reality as an independent subject of existence and professes to be nothing more than a transient manifestation or accidental modification of *Brahman* as the Supreme Being. On the other hand, if *Brahman* is understood to be the underlying activity of consciousness whereby the cosmic Self is an unlimited subject of existence and the human self is a limited subject of existence, then by saying "I am *Brahman*" the individual human being only claims to be in dynamic union with the cosmic Self in virtue of their mutual groundedness in the reality of *Brahman* as a principle of existence and activity.

According to this second interpretation, *Brahman* is a non-dual reality in that it both is and is not the cosmic Self and the individual self at the same time. It is both of them together and each of them separately in that it is their common nature or underlying principle of activity. It is neither of them in that it is an activity, not an entity as they are entities. The cosmic Self and the individual self, on the other hand, are likewise non-dual realities in that they both are and are not what they seem to be. They are distinct entities. The one is strictly limited in its exercise of consciousness; the other as a divine being possesses unlimited consciousness. Yet from another perspective they are not distinct in that they both are *Brahman*, that is, manifestations or instantiations of one and the same underlying activity. Yet, precisely as an activity rather than an entity, *Brahman* never exists in itself and by itself. It is simply the principle of consciousness for both the cosmic Self and the human self and as such the bond of unity between them.

As likewise indicated in Chapter 5, however, the great philosophers of the Vedanta philosophical tradition did not come to these same conclusions. Rather, in different ways they all tended to think of *Brahman* in quasi-entitative terms and thus to subordinate the reality of the visible universe to the all-comprehensive entitative reality of *Brahman*. Shankara, to be sure, carefully distinguished between higher and lower forms of knowledge with respect to *Brahman*. In the lower or provisional form of knowledge, *Brahman* is the transcendent cause of the universe and of all the entities within it, including all human beings. In the higher form of knowledge based on the experience of *saccidananda*, the empirical self and indeed the entire material world are recognized for what they truly are: namely, illusion (*maya*), the result of "superimposition" (*adhyasa*) of the non-self on the self which thus conceals the true reality of the self as *Brahman*. Hence, *Brahman* as the true Self of all things alone exists and Reality is ultimately One.

In all these remarks, to be sure, Shankara does not give any theoretical definitions of *Brahman* but simply points to an experience of total Oneness (namely, *saccidananda*) in which all distinctions between subject and object of consciousness have disappeared. My own argument would be that this is an experience of an activity which lies at the base of human consciousness and indeed of reality as such. Out of this "transformational matrix," to use the language of Nishida, comes everything that exists, hence, both subjects and objects of consciousness. Humans become aware of it as a "pure experience," logically prior to the division into subject and object of normal consciousness. Shankara does not make these claims but, as noted above, simply says that *Brahman* is the true Self of everything that exists. Yet, in not making clear what he means by *Brahman* as the true Self of all finite entities, he lays himself open to the charge of monism. *Brahman* is then readily conceived as the only *entity* that exists. As I see it, only if one thinks of *Brahman* or the true Self as a principle of activity resident within entities rather than itself an entity can one logically affirm non-dualism rather than monism.

Ramanuja and Madhva, on the other hand, did not employ this distinction between lower and higher forms of knowledge and/or experience of *Brahman*. Hence, in line with those passages from the Upanishads which seem to describe *Brahman* in entitative terms, they consistently thought of *Brahman* (or *Vishnu*, since they both were devotees of *Vishnu*) as the Highest Self rather than the sole or Absolute Self. Hence, for both of them the world of finite entities is real, not illusory as with Sankara. Ramanuja claimed that finite entities exist as the "body" of God both in its "causal" or unmanifest state and in its manifest or "effected" state, but that in the causal state they are virtually indistinguishable from the divine being. Madhva simply claimed that *Vishnu* is the efficient cause of the visible universe through his creative power (*shakti*) which is immanent in all finite entities as the source of their own existence and activity. Both of these thinkers, accordingly, were faced with the problem of reconciling belief in *Brahman* or *Vishnu* as Infinite, One without a second as claimed in the *Chandogya* Upanishad, and empirical pluralism, the fact of multiple finite entities. Both basically solved the problem by appealing to the power of *Vishnu* in controlling the existence and activity of those same finite entities. Here I would only point out that, if *shakti* or the power of *Vishnu* be regarded as the divine nature, that underlying activity by which *Vishnu* himself exists and is active in the world, then the position of Ramanuja and Madhva is unexpectedly close to my own hypothesis in this book. That is, the real Infinite is not an entity but an activity which empowers all entities (including *Vishnu* and the other gods as well as all creatures) to exist in dynamic interrelation.

Within classical Buddhism and classical Taoism, on the other hand, as we have seen in Chapters 6 and 7, there is no question of identifying the Infinite with a transcendent entity. Rather, the key question is whether it can be identified with anything at all. Is it literally incomprehensible so that my own attempt to establish the Infinite as an underlying activity which is actual only in its instantiations has to be judged as an implicit reification of that which will forever elude human attempts at explanation and analysis? For that matter, does the Infinite exist at all or is reality a purely contingent and thus ever-changing aggregate of finite things? I will answer these questions first with reference to my treatment of Taoism (in Chapter 7) and then with reference to the discussion of Buddhism (in Chapter 6).

As I indicated in my analysis of the *Tao Te Ching* and the *Chuang Tzu*, there is no question of the reality of the Tao and its subtle workings in human life, indeed, in nature as a whole. It is immanent in all things and by that very fact is transcendent of all things. Hence, it undoubtedly qualifies as the Infinite in a world of finite entities. But what it is in itself remains mysterious. As the first lines of the *Tao Te Ching* make clear, "the Tao that can be told of is not the eternal Tao; the name that can be named is not the eternal name." Likewise, in Chapter 6 of the *Chuang Tzu*, the author states: "Tao has reality and evidence but no action or physical form. It may be transmitted but cannot be received. It may be obtained but cannot be seen." He then adds: "Before heaven and earth came into being, Tao existed by itself from all time." As I indicated in Chapter 7, there are metaphysical problems connected with thinking of the Tao as a reality separate from the world if it is likewise thought to be immanent within all the concrete entities of this world. But the author at least makes eminently clear that in his mind the Tao is a supremely transcendent (and therefore non-finite or infinite) reality.

My own proposal, of course, is that the Tao is an underlying ontological activity which is actual only in its instantiations or embodiments. In this way, it is truly infinite. For it both is and is not everything in which it is instantiated. That is, it is identical with every finite entity as its principle of existence and activity. Yet it transcends each of those entities in that it is an activity, not an entity. Being operative in all of them, it is limited by none of them. Moreover, it is in principle unknowable to human beings because it has no form by which it can be distinguished from other things. Instead, it invariably takes on the form of the entity in which it is here and now instantiated. It is, accordingly, more a potentiality than an actuality. That is, as Lao Tzu and Chuang Tzu explain, it is associated more with non-being than with being. I myself would say that the Tao is more a potentiality than an actuality because it is an activity rather than an entity. For, as Aristotle proposed in Book III of the *Physics*, motion is the (ongoing) actuality of a potentiality insofar as it remains a potentiality. That is, whatever actuality it possesses here and now is destined to be superseded in terms of further stages of actualization. Only thus can it remain an activity, a dynamic rather than a fixed reality.

Furthermore, as I indicated in my analysis of various passages out of the *Tao Te Ching* and *Chuang Tzu*, the human analogies for the Tao are all best understood in terms of activities rather than entities. Admittedly, what the authors have in mind with these analogies is an ethical ideal rather than the description of an ontological reality. Yet their choice of action-oriented analogies to describe the influence of the Tao in human life is implicit testimony to their experience of its deeper ontological reality. It was no accident, for example, that they regularly conceived the Tao in terms of running water rather than standing water, since the power of the Tao lies in its constant activity, the steady pressure which it brings to bear upon the entities which lie in its path. Similarly, the ethical ideal of *wu-wei* is to be understood not as inaction but as action in line with the natural activity of nature both within and around oneself. Even the frequent references to the feminine principle in nature have less to do with female entities than with female activities such as mothering or maintaining a receptive posture in the act of sexual intercourse.

One might object, to be sure, that the Tao is likewise represented by Lao Tzu and Chuang Tzu as Emptiness or the Void in which no activity of any kind can be detected. Yet, as I commented in Chapter 7, this raises the question whether there is not an implicit reification of the Tao at work here. That is, even though the Tao can be conceived in abstraction from the things of this world as an Absolute Void, can it in reality exist as such and still be immanent within all things as their intrinsic principle of existence and activity? The Tao, when conceived as an underlying ontological activity, is not a thing and is therefore no-thing. But it is a no-thingness which is productive of things in dynamic relation with one another. If conceived as nothingness in abstraction from the things of this world, however, the Tao is literally nothing from which nothing else comes. It is then a curiously static, thing-like reality which stands in implicit contradiction to its dynamic function as potentiality or creative non-being elsewhere in the *Tao Te Ching* and *Chuang-Tzu*. Moreover, in those passages where the author refers to the Tao in terms of emptiness (as in the emptiness of a bowl), the emptiness in question is not a static but a dynamic reality. The emptiness, in other words, has a functional value in terms of some actuality to be achieved or sustained (e.g., as a bowl is designed to hold liquids or food for human consumption). The more consistent understanding of the Tao, therefore, would seem to be in terms of a dynamic nothingness, that is, as a principle for "the transformation of things" rather than as a static nothingness or emptiness in abstraction from the world.

Within classical Buddhism, on the other hand, it is decidedly more difficult to establish the reality of the Infinite, even when the Infinite, as I have contended, is considered to be an underlying activity rather than a transcendent entity. For the Buddha himself and celebrated Buddhist philosophers like Nagarjuna over the intervening centuries have cautioned against metaphysical speculation which distracts one from close attention to what is really happening within one's own consciousness and in the surrounding world. The simple fact of universal "dependent co-arising" is easily forgotten as one seeks to isolate causes and their effects within an elaborate theoretical scheme. Yet, as I pointed out at several instances in Chapter 6, the ongoing character of dependent co-arising is itself in need of further explanation. Why do entities continually arise and cease to be in mutual interdependence unless implicit within the notion of dependent co-arising is another notion, that of continuous activity? For, as Nagarjuna saw quite clearly in the *Mulamadhyamakakarika*, there is a logical inconsistency in talking about a movement from a state of rest to a state of movement or from a state of movement to a state of rest. One has to presuppose what is to be explained, namely, the reality of movement or "present moving." Hence, if talking about the Infinite as an underlying ontological activity is considered to be metaphysical speculation, it is a form of metaphysics which cannot be avoided in coming to grips with one's own experience.

Furthermore, as I urged in Chapter 6, an experience of the Infinite does not always have to be recognized as such in order to be in fact an experience of the Infinite. Precisely because the Infinite as an underlying activity is totally immanent within finite entities as their principle of existence and activity, and because, as noted above, it has no form or structure proper to itself, then one can readily overlook the presence of the Infinite in one's preoccupation with the finite. One focuses, in other words, on the specific entities that are moved here and there in strict dependence on one another and fails to note the overarching reality of unceasing movement as that from which these specific activities arise and to which they in the end return.

Yet, in describing the experience of *nirvana*, above all, in claiming that it is both the same as and yet different from the experience of *samsara*, Nagarjuna and other Buddhist philosophers give implicit testimony, as I see it, to the reality of the Infinite within the finite. For, what is it that enables them to affirm the experience of ceaseless arising and ceasing-to-be as an experience of liberation and salvation rather than an experience of bondage and depression if not that, at least at intervals, they felt the enduring presence of the Infinite within the otherwise overwhelming reality of the transient and insubstantial as represented by ceaseless arising and ceasing-to-be?[4] Moreover, the phenomenological analyses of Nishida in *An Inquiry into the Good* seem to confirm this assumption. That is, in and through his category of "pure experience," Nishida seems to be pointing to the lived experience of the Infinite within the finite. Like Shankara in his insistence on *Brahman* as the true Self of all things, Nishida is pointing to an experience of absolute Oneness in which all distinction between subjects and objects of consciousness are transcended in favor of an undifferentiated (and therefore unlimited) experience of being, consciousness, and bliss.

From a theistic perspective, of course, speculative difficulties remain. Is the Infinite, when thus understood as an underlying activity rather than as an entity, divine and thus worthy of worship? Or is it divine only insofar as it is the nature or principle of operation for a supremely intelligent and compassionate being, namely, God? As I mentioned earlier in the chapter on Taoism, the Infinite as an underlying activity is the ontological ground for everything that exists, both good and evil, thus for what brings pain as well as pleasure to all sentient beings. Hence, as an impersonal principle of spontaneity in Nature, it does not seem worthy of human worship and praise. In line with the ideal of *wu-wei*, acting in accord with nature, one may gradually learn respect for the way this principle operates both within one's own life and the lives of others. But even here one may well ask whence comes its lawfulness and predictability within human affairs if not from an intelligent being, namely, God, who continually gives order and direction to its otherwise purely spontaneous mode of operation.

Thus what seems worthy of human praise and adoration is not the Infinite as such but rather God as its subsistent principle of limitation and control. Only God is in a position to channel its native energies into a consistently productive rather than destructive direction. Even God, of course, cannot absolutely control how this energy potential will be used by the various finite entities which it empowers to exist and to act. As I indicated in the chapter on the philosophy of Alfred North Whitehead, finite entities in my judgment have a limited but still quite real power of self-determination with respect to their nature or innate energy-potential. Hence, much evil and disorder regularly come into the world as a result of the unfortunate conscious (or, in most cases, unconscious) "decisions" of finite entities. Much of the praise and worship due to God from rational creatures should be given then in at least implicit recognition of the provi-dential care of God for the world. Much more evil and disorder, in other words, would presumably take place in the universe if God were not continually present to give new order and direction to otherwise highly explosive situations.

There is, to be sure, in the theology of Meister Eckhart and other mystics in the West and certainly in the philosophical traditions of Hinduism,

Buddhism, and Taoism a deep-seated desire not for union with God as a supremely intelligent and compassionate being, but for unity with, even absorption into, the Infinite as a strictly impersonal principle of existence and activity. The appeal of *Brahman* as the all-encompassing One in classical Hinduism and of Absolute Emptiness as dependent co-arising in classical Buddhism, in other words, is grounded in a felt need for liberation from the individual self with its inherent limitations and for absorption into what is imagined as boundless existence and limitless activity. Is this to be understood as a flight from responsible selfhood or should it be considered as a form of salvation, equal or perhaps even superior to other forms of salvation in which interpersonal union with a supremely loving and compassionate God are envisioned?

It is difficult to answer this question in a purely objective manner since so much seems to hinge upon the psychological makeup of the individual human being. Perhaps this is why in the Hindu tradition the *jnana* yoga with its focus on the unity of being is not evaluated any higher or lower than *bhakti* yoga with its emphasis on devotion to a personal god, but simply offered as an alternative to the latter for those who find it more attractive.[5] My purpose in this book, moreover, has not been to indicate the superiority of one view of the Divine over the other, but rather to indicate that they are inseparable dimensions of one and the same august mystery. As the Heart Sutra in the Mahayana Buddhist tradition expresses it, "form is emptiness and emptiness is form." Form stands out against the background of emptiness; and emptiness is meaningful rather than meaningless because it is the dynamic source from which all form arises and to which all form eventually returns. As Masao Abe comments, "form is ceaselessly emptied, turning into formless emptiness, and formless emptiness is ceaselessly emptied and forever freely taking form. This total *dynamic movement* of emptying, not a *static state* of emptiness, is the true meaning of Sunyata."[6]

Activity, then, lies at the base of reality. But, as I have urged many times in this book, activity does not exist in and of itself. It is always instantiated in entities that thereby exist and are related to one another. What Masao Abe and other Buddhists refer to as "form" are entities that exist in virtue of the underlying activity. Furthermore, I would agree with Donald Mitchell that there are privileged entities, namely, the three divine persons, who exercise that underlying activity in a primordial way. That underlying activity is their common nature in virtue of which they relate to one another and through which they bring into being and sustain in being all finite entities. Mitchell refers to it as "God-Love," the Christian equivalent of what Abe calls the ceaseless self-emptying activity of Emptiness. All three divine persons empty themselves out totally in their relations to one another and thereby create the all-encompassing "energy-field" or "matrix" which is their common nature.[7]

Thus, depending upon whether one is drawn in prayer and contemplation to one of the divine persons, to all three of them together as a divine community, or to the underlying divine nature as the dynamic source of one's own being and activity, one is thereby in vital contact with Ultimate Reality or the Mystery of Being. Admittedly, in terms of the hypothesis of this book, only the underlying divine nature is infinite since it alone is absolutely formless and undifferentiated. The three divine persons as enduring subjects of that infinite activity and therefore as entities are "finite" in the sense of being fully determinate realities. But, insofar as they together constitute the limitless reality of God, they are qualitatively infinite with respect to all their creatures. As Christian, Jewish and Muslim mystics testify, conscious union with God as a personal being is an ecstatic experience which lifts one out of the bounds of the finite and into an experience of unlimited being, consciousness, and bliss, to borrow a phrase from the Hindu tradition.

Before bringing this concluding chapter to a close, I wish to emphasize the strictly provisional character of the conceptual scheme which I have used to interpret Ultimate Reality in these pages. For, unless this point is made clear, one is readily tempted to commit what Whitehead termed "the fallacy of misplaced concreteness."[8] That is, one implicitly regards certain categories or conceptual schemes as more real than the reality (realities) which they are intended to explain. As a result, one no longer adverts to the full complexity of the situation at hand and dismisses as irrelevant those empirical details which do not readily fit into one's chosen set of abstractions. Thus, to "relativize" my own conceptual scheme before bringing this book to a close, I will now review the position of a colleague in the discipline of comparative theology whose interpretative scheme both overlaps with and yet significantly differs from my own.

That colleague is Robert Neville, who in a long series of books has set forth an understanding of the God-world relationship in which the Infinite is seen to be an indeterminate rather than a determinate reality. At the same time, he does not further postulate as I do that this indeterminate reality underlying all the persons and things of creation is in fact the divine nature, the principle of existence for the three divine persons in their dynamic interrelation. Rather, he argues that the act of creation emanates from a transcendent Source which is in itself wholly indeterminate apart from the activity of creating. This Source, in other words, only becomes the biblical Creator God in and through the activity of creating just as the world becomes a determinate reality in and through that same activity. What the Source is in itself is humanly incomprehensible.[9]

There is much to recommend in this understanding of Ultimate Reality. Above all, from a Christian perspective it preserves the absolute transcendence of God and the divine freedom in creation. As Neville comments, apart from the act of creating, the Source "is not even a potentiality for creating."[10] Hence, the divine decision to create is totally without rational foundation. Furthermore, a link is thereby established with the notion of

Brahman in Advaita Vedanta Hinduism and with the concept of the Tao that cannot be named within Taoism. In both these religious traditions Ultimate Reality, like the transcendent Source of the act of creation within Neville's scheme, is totally beyond human comprehension. And yet, as I see it, what is totally transcendent and humanly incomprehensible can be readily marginalized or secularized. That is, one gradually comes to ignore the presence of the divine in one's life because one cannot understand it, or one thinks of this creative activity simply as an energy-source empowering the world process and nothing more. In both cases, at least for a Christian, Muslim, or Jew, belief in God as Creator of the world and one's personal Lord and Savior is seriously jeopardized.

Furthermore, the basic thrust of Neville's ontology can still be maintained if one thinks of this creative activity as the underlying nature of the triune God which likewise serves as the ground or source of creation. For, as an activity, it is indeterminate in itself and determinate only in the entities which it empowers to exist. Hence, in itself it is humanly incomprehensible, the mysterious source of the divine being and of all creation. Yet it is revered rather than feared because it is, in the first place, the nature common to the three divine persons in their dynamic interrelation. That is, through the self-constituting "decisions" of the three divine persons toward one another, it takes shape and direction as self-emptying love rather than purely destructive power.

Within the world of creation, to be sure, it is sometimes operative in destructive ways due to the short-sighted "decisions" of creatures vis-à-vis one another. But, because of its primordial grounding in the communitarian life of the three divine persons, the enduring thrust of creativity as the energy-source of creation is in the direction of self-emptying love and higher forms of unity among creatures in virtue of that same self-emptying love. Teilhard de Chardin was correct, therefore, in urging that love is the driving-force within cosmic evolution.[11] Yet the deeper reason for this move toward higher forms of unity within creation, in my judgment, is the ongoing exchange of life and love among the three divine persons. Creation achieves its *raison d'être* in and through progressive incorporation into the divine communitarian life.

This is, of course, an exclusively Christian vision of reality which adherents of other world religions cannot be expected to embrace. In that respect, Neville's scheme might be better suited to contemporary interreligious dialogue since it does not presuppose belief in God as triune.[12] Indeed, not even all Christians may find my approach to the doctrine of the Trinity appropriate for themselves. In any event, my overall purpose in this book will still be amply achieved if the various participants in interreligious dialogue think through and discuss among themselves the purely philosophical issues raised in these pages. All of them deal with the relationship between the finite and the Infinite in one way or another. Should the Infinite, for example, be conceived in entitative terms as the sole enduring

Reality, and, if so, how does one safeguard the at least apparent reality of the finite world? Or should the Infinite be regarded as a principle of existence and activity which is actual only in its instantiations or manifestations? If so, what is the relation of such an underlying ontological activity to God as the Supreme Being? Is there still a third way to understand in some measure the reality of the Infinite or is one necessarily reduced to silence before what transcends human imagination and/or conception?

My own understanding of the Infinite as an all-encompassing "matrix" or "energy-field" for the divine persons and all their creatures is only one possible response to these questions. But, insofar as it offers at least a somewhat plausible explanation to these vexing philosophical questions, it may encourage others out of their own religious traditions to offer alternative solutions. In this way, interreligious dialogue will be furthered as the participants come to respect both the strengths and the weaknesses of the various models proposed by the major world religions for the understanding of Ultimate Reality.

Notes

Introduction: Common Structures of Intelligibility

1. Robert Cummings Neville, *Behind the Masks of God: An Essay toward Comparative Theology* (Albany: State University of New York Press, 1991), p. 4.

2. Reference is being made here to what George Lindbeck describes as the cognitive-propositional approach and his own cultural-linguistic approach to religious doctrine. Likewise, the "liberal" position described below in the text corresponds to what Lindbeck terms the experiential-expressive approach to religious doctrine. Cf. on this point George Lindbeck, *The Nature of Doctrine: Religion and Theology in a Postliberal Age* (Philadelphia: Westminster, 1984), pp. 16-20.

3. See here a hitherto unpublished paper by James L. Fredericks, S.S., on the ambivalence of the notion of experience in contemporary interreligious dialogue. Originally presented for the Seminar on Comparative Theology at the convention of the Catholic Theological Society of America in 1992; cf. *CTSA Proceedings* 47 (1992), p. 168.

4. In this sense, I agree with many "postmodern" thinkers that a general, cross-cultural framework for interpreting reality is *currently* impossible; but I would disagree with them that this will *always* be the case. Through extensive interreligious dialogue in coming generations, something like a common philosophical framework may gradually win acceptance in most circles.

5. Alfred North Whitehead, *Process and Reality: An Essay in Cosmology*, Corrected ed., eds. David Ray Griffin & Donald W. Sherburne (New York: The Free Press, 1978), p. 7/10-11. N.B.: The second set of numbers corresponds to the pagination of the original edition of *Process and Reality*, published by Macmillan in 1929.

6. According to Whitehead, actual entities or actual occasions are "the final real things of which the world is made up." (Whitehead, *Process and Reality*, p. 18/27). Each is a momentary subject of experience which constitutes itself out of subjective representations or "prehensions" of its predecessor actual occasions in the same social context in which it too is arising. This virtually instantaneous process of self-constitution is called by Whitehead the *concrescence* of an actual occasion (cf. Whitehead's Categories of Explanation, *Process and Reality*, pp. 22-26/33-39).

7. Cf. on this point John R. Wilcox, "A Monistic Interpretation of Whitehead's Creativity," *Process Studies* 20 (1991), pp. 162-74. Wilcox summarizes nicely the controversy among Whiteheadians about the ontological status of creativity and on the basis of his own reading of the pertinent Whiteheadian texts comes to much the same conclusion about the nature of creativity as I present in this book. Cf. below, Chapter 4.

8. Whitehead, *Process and Reality*, p. 66/103.

9. Jorge Luis Nobo, *Whitehead's Metaphysics of Extension and Solidarity* (Albany: State University of New York Press, 1986), p. 256.

10. Ian Barbour, *Myths, Models and Paradigms: A Comparative Study in Science and Religion* (New York: Harper & Row, 1974), pp. 47-48.

11. David Loy, *Nonduality: A Study in Comparative Philosophy* (New Haven: Yale University Press, 1988), pp. 17-37.

12. Cf., however, A.W. Moore, *The Infinite* (London: Routledge, 1990), pp. 1-2, 34-44. Moore distinguishes between the mathematical and the metaphysical infinite, i.e., between concepts of the infinite which emphasize boundlessness, unlimitedness, immeasurability, etc., and concepts of the infinite which focus on wholeness or completeness, universality, self-sufficiency, etc. In his view, Aristotle was the first of the ancient philosophers explicitly to direct attention to the mathematically infinite rather than to the metaphysically infinite.

While this is certainly true, yet, as I shall make clear in Chapter 1, it does not exclude the possibility that Aristotle was likewise implicitly aware of the metaphysical infinity of motion; motion is complete or self-sufficient in that it has no beginning or end. Thus Moore's own argument that there really is no infinite either in the mathematical or in the metaphysical sense might be challenged as follows. Granted that there is no infinite entity (whether that entity be understood as God or in mathematical terms as the Set of all sets) because of the logical paradoxes which thereby result from the analysis of the concept, do the same arguments likewise hold true for an infinite activity which underlies the existence of all entities in the metaphysical realm and the existence of all processes of addition and division in the mathematical order? The persistence of human efforts to comprehend and even define the infinite, in other words, may well be due to a subliminal experience of the infinite as an all-pervasive activity in human life rather than simply to the experience of one's radical finitude, as Moore asserts. For that matter, how does one know the meaning of finitude except in terms of an implicit experience of infinity? (Cf. on this point Wolfhart Pannenberg, *Systematic Theology*, trans. Geoffrey W. Bromiley, Vol. I [Grand Rapids, Mich.: William B. Eerdmans, 1991], pp. 107-18.)

1. Motion and Infinity in the Philosophy of Aristotle

1. Ivor Leclerc, *The Nature of Physical Existence* (London: George Allen & Unwin, 1972), p. 41. For an analysis of Aristotle's relation to his Greek predecessors, cf. also Moore, *The Infinite*, pp. 17-44; likewise, Leo Sweeney, S.J., *Divine Infinity in Greek and Medieval Thought* (New York: Peter Lang Publishing, 1992), pp. 4-6, 143-65.

2. Aristotle, *Physics*, 200b17-19: in *The Basic Works of Aristotle*, ed. Richard McKeon (New York: Random House, 1941). N.B.: This text will be the source of all citations from Aristotle in this chapter.

3. *Ibid.*, 206a34-35. Cf. also Sweeney, *Divine Infinity*, p. 156. Commenting on this passage from Aristotle's *Physics*, Sweeney notes: "Let us suppose that a body moving around a circle from A through B to A is now actually going through B. What actually is, is the finite movement through-B, with its correspondent time. Yet although actually finite, the movement from-A-through-B is infinite insofar as it is a process which can, given certain conditions, continue without end." Sweeney adds that movement, thus understood, "is neither complete nor perfect nor intelligible" (p. 157). But, as I will argue below, this is to interpret movement in entitative terms as an incomplete being whereas its own perfection and intelligibility as an activity is to be in process, therefore, by definition never completely actualized.

4. Aristotle, *Physics*, 204a20-28. As Sweeney makes clear in *Divine Infinity*, the principal difference between Greek and medieval thinking on infinity is whether

one primarily thinks of form as limiting and determining matter or whether one likewise conceives matter as limiting and determining form. Aristotle and other Greek philosophers considered (prime) matter to be infinite because it lacked specification and/or determination through form. Aquinas, on the other hand, proposed that "form or act which is without matter and potency is also without their determination and limitation and is, thereby, both infinite and perfect" (Sweeney, *Divine Infinity*, pp. 335-36). As will be evident in this and the following chapter, I favor the Aristotelian interpretation of infinity, with the qualification, however, that the infinity of matter is not really an imperfection but rather the unexpected source of its fertility and creativity. Because it is indeterminate in and of itself, matter has the innate potentiality to produce an entire series of interconnected forms or determinations. In this sense, as a process-oriented thinker, I give priority to becoming over being (understood as a fully determinate reality).

5. Aristotle, *Metaphysics*, 1074a36-39; cf. also Leclerc, *The Nature of Physical Existence*, pp. 61-62; and Sweeney, *Divine Infinity in Greek and Medieval Thought*, pp. 163-65.

6. Aristotle, *Physics*, 204b5-9.

7. *Ibid.*, 213b30-216b22.

8. *Ibid.*, 206a15-17.

9. Aristotle, *Metaphysics*, 1048b18-34.

10. Aristotle, *Physics*, 250b11-252b7.

11. *Ibid.*, 250b11-14.

12. *Ibid.*, 266a6-9.

13. *Ibid.*, 201a10.

14. Cf. on this point Michael J. Buckley, S.J., *Motion and Motion's God: Thematic Variations in Aristotle, Cicero, Newton, and Hegel* (Princeton, N.J.: Princeton University Press, 1971), pp. 39-40.

15. Aristotle, *Physics*, 241a27f.

16. *Ibid.*, 219b16-18.

17. Henri Bergson, *Matter and Memory*, trans. Nancy Margaret Paul and W. Scott Palmer (London: George Allen & Unwin, 1950), p. 248.

18. Henri Bergson, *The Creative Mind* [original title: *Pensée et le Mouvant*], trans. Mabelle L. Andison (New York: Greenwood Press, 1968), pp. 38-39.

19. Aristotle, *Physics*, 219a22-25.

20. *Ibid.*, 234a1-3.

21. Cf. Robert Cummings Neville, *Eternity and Time's Flow* (Albany: State University of New York Press, 1993), p. 60. Neville defines eternity as "the togetherness of the modes of time—past, present, and future—so that each can be its temporal self." Eternity thus makes possible the flow of time while itself remaining at rest. Neville, to be sure, is critical of "the focus of the Kyoto School [of Buddhist philosophy] on the present as the locus of being and nonbeing" (p. 193). In my own evaluation of Buddhism in Chapter 7, however, I propose that *pratitya samutpada* or what Kitaro Nishida would call "pure experience" is an experience both of time and eternity. Otherwise, there would be no reason to think of it as an experience of salvation or liberation.

22. Aristotle, *Physics*, 260a27-29.

23. *Ibid.*, 261b27-266a9.

24. Aristotle, *Metaphysics*, 1047a30-32.

25. *Ibid.*, 1074b27.

26. John Herman Randall, *Aristotle* (New York: Columbia University Press, 1968), pp. 132-33. While noting that the being (*ousia*) of the Unmoved Mover is pure activity (*energeia*), Randall does not concur with my further assumption that such activity likewise represents an ongoing conversion of potentiality into actuality. Rather, with Aristotle, he seems to imply that it is somehow an entity or fixed reality and an activity at the same time.

27. Aristotle, *Physics*, 189b30-191a22.

28. Aristotle, *On Generation and Corruption*, 329a24-36.

29. Aristotle, *Physics*, 192a31f.

30. *Ibid.*, 252b6.

31. Randall, *Aristotle*, p. 133.

32. Aristotle, *Physics*, 194b24f.

33. *Ibid.*, 190a14f.

34. Aristotle, *Metaphysics*, 1041b6f.

35. Aristotle, *Physics*, 250b11-252b7.

36. *Ibid.*, 254b8-256a3.

37. *Ibid.*, 256a3-258b9.

38. *Ibid.*, 257b13.

39. *Ibid.*, 202a4f.

40. Cf. on this point Randall, *Aristotle*, pp. 136-44. Randall likewise proposes that the eternal Unmoved Mover is more an idealized form of motion than the ontological cause of motion in all other entities.

41. Aristotle, *Metaphysics*, 1074b34. Scholars, to be sure, argue whether the Unmoved Mover of the *Physics* is to be identified with the Unmoved Mover of the *Metaphysics*: cf. on this point Sweeney, *Divine Infinity*, pp. 161-63; likewise, Buckley, *Motion and Motion's God*, pp. 84-85. For the purposes of my argument here, I will assume that they either are the same or that, if different, the same line of thought could be basically applied to both of them: namely, that the Unmoved Mover is not itself the cause of motion but rather its primordial instantiation. Motion itself, in other words, is the primordial reality, not the Unmoved Mover of either the *Physics* or the *Metaphysics*.

42. Martin Heidegger, *Being and Time*, trans. John Macquarrie and Edward Robinson (New York: Harper & Row, 1962), pp. 21-24.

43. W.D. Ross, *Aristotle*, 3rd ed. (London: Methuen & Co., 1937), p. 183.

44. Aristotle, *Metaphysics*, 1072a19-1072b29.

45. Cf. here Sweeney, *Divine Infinity*, p. 165, n. 51: " 'becoming' and 'infinity' are two expressions for one and the same process of passing-from-potency-to-act: becoming is that process as *actual*, infinity is that same process as *potential*." I, of course, would argue that, insofar as becoming is actual, it is not only potentially but actually infinite (precisely as an ongoing activity).

46. Aristotle, *Physics*, 201b34-202a2.

47. *Ibid.*, 206a30-35.

48. *Ibid.*, 202a12-19. Cf. below, Chapter 3, for analysis of the way in which Meister Eckhart employs this same insight to describe the mystical experience of human union with God.

2. Being and Relations in the Theology of Thomas Aquinas

1. Leclerc, *The Nature of Physical Existence*, pp. 59-60.

2. E. R. Dodds, *Pagan and Christian in an Age of Anxiety* (New York: W.W. Norton, 1970), pp. 5-36.

3. *Ibid.*, pp. 69-101.

4. Plotinus, *The Enneads*, trans. Stephen MacKenna, 4th ed. (London: Faber & Faber, 1969): Fifth *Ennead*, First Tractate (pp. 369-79). For a careful study of the notion of infinity in Plotinus's thought, cf. Sweeney, *Divine Infinity*, pp. 167-241. Sweeney regards Plotinus as intermediate between ancient and medieval thinkers in his concept of infinity. On the one hand, like Aristotle and other ancient thinkers, Plotinus thinks of infinity in terms of non-being or indeterminancy. On the other hand, like Augustine, Aquinas, and other medieval thinkers, he regards infinity as a perfection rather than a defect. God as non-being is beyond being, not less than being. Cf. also on this point Moore, *The Infinite*, pp. 45-46.

5. Cf. Harry Wolfson, *Philo: Foundations of Religious Philosophy in Judaism, Christianity, and Islam*, vol. I (Cambridge, Mass.: Harvard University Press, 1947), pp. 315-16.

6. Leclerc, *The Nature of Physical Existence*, p. 64.

7. *Ibid.*, p. 66.

8. *Ibid.*, pp. 66-67. Cf. also Sweeney, *Divine Infinity*, pp. 432-37. Both Augustine and Aquinas agreed with Plotinus that infinity within God is a perfection, not a deficiency. But they disagreed with him in affirming that God is being itself, not beyond being. Thus the understanding of divine infinity common to Augustine and Aquinas is that God is fully determinate but beyond the comprehension of finite minds. Furthermore, as Sweeney points out, in Aquinas alone is this faith conviction grounded in a metaphysics of act and potency whereby matter and form mutually condition one another. That is, matter is determined by form, but form is limited by the conditions of matter. Hence, only in God is form or essence fully determinate and yet infinite, that is, unlimited by the conditions of matter and/or potentiality.

Yet, as I indicate below, there are problems with this coupling of actuality and infinity even within God. Furthermore, a much easier way to explain the infinity of God is in terms of a distinction between the divine nature and the divine persons. Each of the persons is at any given moment limited in the exercise of the divine act of being in virtue of its relations to the other two persons and to all creatures. But the divine nature common to all three persons as a principle of never-ending existence and activity is necessarily unlimited, that is, always capable of further actuation. Thus each of the divine persons at any given moment is both infinite and "finite" or determinate: infinite in that each person is the ongoing subject of a never-ending principle of existence or activity; "finite" or determinate in that each person exercises that principle of existence and activity differently both from the other two divine persons and, a fortiori, from all creatures.

9. Cf. Wolfson, *Philo*, vol. II (Cambridge, Mass.: Harvard University Press, 1962), pp. 439-60. Wolfson argues that the founder of this peculiarly medieval world view, as opposed to the world view of Plato, Aristotle, and other "pagan" thinkers of the ancient world, was Philo (457). In any event, the similarity of the basic philosophical presuppositions of Jewish, Christian, and Muslim thinkers in the Middle Ages is unmistakable.

10. St. Thomas Aquinas, *Summa Theologica*, First Part, Question 3, articles 3 & 4, response: translated from the Latin by the Fathers of the English Dominican Province and subsequently published in the United States of America (New York: Benziger Brothers, 1947). Henceforth, references to the *Summa Theologica* will be abbreviated as follows (with reference to the above citation): *S.T.*, I, Q. 3, aa. 3 & 4 resp.

11. *Ibid.*, Q. 2, a. 3 resp.

12. Cf. below, however, where I discuss the difference between the notion of *cause* and *ground* or *vital source*. In brief, while no entity (God included) can be the cause of its own existence, yet the existence of that same entity may be grounded in its nature or internal principle of existence and activity.

13. *Ibid.*, Q. 44, a. 1 resp. Cf. also L.-B. Geiger, O.P., *La Participation dans la philosophie de S. Thomas d'Aquin*, 2nd ed. (Paris: Libraire J. Vrin, 1953), p. 225: "La procession des créatures à partir de Dieu a pour cause exemplaire la procession même des divines personnes. C'est dire que toutes deux ont en quelque sorte une source commune. 'La procession temporelle des créatures procède de la procession éternelle des personnes comme un bras secondaire dérive du fleuve . . . Comme le bras se détache du cours principal, ansi la créature sort de Dieu et quitte l'unité de l'essence, en qui, comme en le cours principal, demeure contenue le flux (écoulement) des divines personnes.' " The cited material here is from Thomas's prologue to his commentary on the First Book of the Sentences of Peter Lombard: in *Opera Omnia*, vol. 6 (New York: Misurgia, 1948), pp. 1-2.

14. Aquinas, *S.T.*, Q. 44, a. 2 resp.

15. *Ibid.*, Q. 45, a. 1 resp.

16. Etienne Gilson, *The Spirit of Mediaeval Philosophy* (Gifford Lectures 1931-1932), trans. A.H.C. Downes (New York: Scribner's, 1940), pp. 64-83. Cf. also by the same author *Being and Some Philosophers*, 2nd ed. (Toronto: Pontifical Institute of Mediaeval Studies, 1952), pp. 154-89.

17. Gilson, *Spirit of Mediaeval Philosophy*, pp. 70-72.

18. *The Jerusalem Bible*, ed. Alexander Jones (Garden City, N.Y.: Doubleday & Co., 1966), p. 81 (chap. 3, note h). Cf. also John Courtney Murray, S.J., *The Problem of God: Yesterday and Today* (New Haven, Conn.: Yale University Press, 1964), pp. 8-10.

19. Heidegger, *Being and Time*, p. 31.

20. At any moment, of course, God is infinite with respect to human powers of comprehension; that is, the determinate reality of God is always infinitely beyond the limited capacity of human beings to understand. Cf. on this point, n. 8 above.

21. Aquinas, *S.T.*, I, Q. 3, a. 1 resp.

22. *Ibid.*, Q. 3, a. 4 resp.; Q. 50, a. 2 resp.

23. *Ibid.*, Q. 3, a. 8 resp.

24. *Ibid.*, Q. 4, a. 1 resp.

25. Aristotle, *Physics* , 227a10f.

26. Cf., however, Heinrich Beck, *Der Akt-Charakter des Seins* (Munich: Max Hueber Verlag, 1965), pp. 17-80, esp. p. 69. Beck argues that being understood dynamically as act signifies movement rather than simply existence in a static sense. God therefore as the fullness of the act of being is in constant movement but without passage from potentiality to actuality. While in complete agreement with Beck that the act of being signifies movement, I question whether movement even in God can take place without passage from potentiality to actuality. Beck's proposal, for example, that a dialectical movement from being to non-being and back again to being characterizes the act of being and therefore the inner reality of God (pp. 118-23) still logically involves a succession of moments and as a result a transition from potentiality to actuality in the act of succession.

27. Aquinas, *S.T.*, I, Q. 3, a. 1 resp.

28. Aristotle, *Physics* , 257a33-260a9.

29. Aristotle, *Metaphysics*, 1074b34. Cf. above, Chapter 1, n. 41, for my response

to the possible objection that the Unmoved Mover of Aristotle's *Metaphysics* is different from the Unmoved Mover of the *Physics*.

30. Still another way to make clear this key distinction between cause and ground is to recall that for Aristotle and Aquinas entities were implicitly regarded as *objects of thought*, the terms of various rationally conceived cause-effect relationships. Within the process-oriented reinterpretation of Aquinas which I am proposing here, however, entities are rather conceived in dynamic fashion as *subjects of activity* grounded in the act of being, which is itself understood as an ongoing activity rather than as a fixed perfection. Cf. also on this point below, Chapter 6, where I analyze the "existential logic" of Kitaro Nishida in his essay "The Logic of the Place of Nothingness and the Religious World View."

31. Aquinas, *S.T.*, I, Q. 7, a. 1 resp.

32. *Ibid.*, Q. 10, aa. 1 & 2 resp.

33. Aristotle, *Physics*, 219a23-25.

34. *Ibid.*, 234a1-3.

35. Cf. here Neville, *Eternity and Time's Flow*, p. 128. Neville is critical of the classical definition of eternity because it collapses the past and the future into a static present. In his own understanding of eternity, there is an ongoing transformation of potentiality into actuality: "The eternal act does not change, because it does not endure from one moment to the next. The temporal things within it change, however, actualizing efforts that add to the past and shift the future's possibilities" (p. 173). The "eternal act" in Neville's scheme corresponds roughly to the divine nature or divine act of being in my own. But in my scheme, over and above the divine act of being, there are three primordial subjects of that act, namely, the divine persons, who, like their creatures, exist in virtue of an ongoing conversion of potentiality into actuality as I indicate below.

36. Aquinas, *S.T.*, I, Q. 14, a. 4 resp.; Q. 19, a. 1 resp.

37. *Ibid.*, Q. 14, a. 6 resp.; Q. 19, a. 2 resp.

38. I place the divine names in quotation marks here and elsewhere in this book so as to make clear their metaphorical, non-sexist intent. Names like "Mother," "Daughter" and "Holy Spirit" are, in other words, likewise suitable metaphors to describe the relations between the divine persons. Cf. on this point Elizabeth A. Johnson, *She Who Is, The Mystery of God in Feminist Theological Discourse* (New York: Crossroad, 1992), esp. pp. 42-57. Cf. also the note at the end of Chapter 4.

39. Aquinas, *S.T.*, I, Q, 29, a. 4 resp.

40. The same, of course, with appropriate qualifications is true of the relation of the three divine persons to their creatures. While the divine persons as subjects of the divine act of existence *objectively* possess the perfections of all their creatures (cf. on this point Aquinas, *S.T.*, I, Q. 4, a. 2 resp.), they cannot *subjectively* exercise those perfections as their creatures do. They cannot, in other words, be both themselves and their creatures as distinct subjects of experience at the same time. They share the same basic act of existence as their creatures, but exercise it in qualitatively different ways. This is, after all, the new understanding of the infinity of God introduced by Augustine and Aquinas, namely, a qualitatively higher mode of existence than that of any creature or indeed of all creatures combined. Cf. here, n. 8 above.

41. Joseph A. Bracken, *The Triune Symbol: Persons, Process and Community* (Lanham, Md.: University Press of America, 1985), pp. 36-47.

42. Whitehead, *Process and Reality*, pp. 83-89/127-36.

43. *Ibid.*, pp. 34-35/51-52.
44. *Ibid.*, p. 99/151.

3. The Ground of Subjectivity in Eckhart, Schelling, and Heidegger

1. Cf. on this point Vladimir Lossky, *Théologie négative et connaissance de Dieu chez Maître Eckhart* (Paris: J. Vrin, 1960). Lossky focuses on the Latin works of Eckhart and the latter's relation to Thomas Aquinas. As will be noted below, his conclusions about the role of the Godhead or divine ground of being within Eckhart's thought differ significantly from my own.

2. Cf. John D. Caputo, *The Mystical Element in Heidegger's Thought* (Athens, Ohio: Ohio University Press, 1978), pp. 7-30, 140-217. Caputo's thesis is that the structural relationship between God and the soul in Eckhart's writings parallels the relationship between being and *Dasein* in the later Heidegger's thought even though what Eckhart understands by *God* is quite different from what Heidegger intends by *being* (p. 144). I will have further comments on this hypothesis later in the chapter.

3. *Ibid.*, p. 161. Lossky, on the other hand, sees the difference between Eckhart and Aquinas to lie in the different way that they think of the relationship between God and creatures in terms of existence or the act of being. For Aquinas the analogy of proper proportionality is more applicable here. That is, God's essence is to the divine existence as the creature's essence is to the creature's existence. For Eckhart, the preferred analogy is the analogy of attribution. That is, God alone is being in its fullness; creatures are said to possess being by attribution or participation in the divine act of being (cf. on this point Lossky, *Théologie négative*, pp. 251-337). But in either case one is still working within the traditional substance-oriented ontology of Plato and Aristotle rather than with a process-oriented approach to reality.

4. Cf. Reiner Schürmann, *Meister Eckhart: Mystic and Philosopher* (Bloomington, Ind.: Indiana University Press, 1978), pp. 131-213. N.B.: The book was originally published in 1972 with the title *Maître Eckhart ou la joie errante* by Editions Planete, Paris.

5. Aristotle, *On the Soul*, 430a18-25.

6. Schürmann, *Meister Eckhart*, p. 138.

7. *Ibid.*, p. 131.

8. *Ibid.*, p. 143.

9. *Ibid.*, p. 132.

10. *Ibid.*

11. *Ibid.*, p. 133.

12. *Ibid.*, p. 134.

13. *Ibid.*, pp. 135-36.

14. *Ibid.*, p. 150. Cf. also on this point Richard Woods, O.P., *Eckhart's Way* (Wilmington, Del.: Michael Glazier, 1986), pp. 58-61. Woods quotes from a German sermon of Eckhart the oft-cited phrase: "Here God's ground is my ground and my ground is God's ground." (cf. Sermon 13b in *Meister Eckhart: Sermons and Treatises*, ed. M.O'C. Walshe, 3 vols. [London: Watkins, 1985]).

15. Schürmann, *Meister Eckhart*, p. 151.

16. *Ibid.*, p. 157. Cf. on this point Lossky, *Théologie négative*, p. 360: "La génération naturelle de Fils unique et la regénération des fils adoptifs par la grâce ont le même principe formel: c'est l'Etre total de Dieu ou l'Essence divine devenue opérante, génératrice, dans la personne du Père." Hence, even though he elsewhere insists that there is no distinction between person and nature within the divine being (cf.

e.g., pp. 341-43, 364-66), Lossky here admits that the divine nature rather than anyone of the persons as such is both the ontological ground of material creation and the formal principle whereby the divine Son is eternally generated by the Father and human beings are continually remade in the image and likeness of the Son.

17. Schürmann, *Meister Eckhart*, p. 133.

18. *Ibid.*, p. 162.

19. *Ibid.*, p. 165.

20. *Ibid.* Cf. also on this point Caputo, *The Mystical Element*, pp. 130-34. Caputo argues that the images of the birth of the Son in the soul and of the breakthrough to the Godhead are complementary rather than opposed to one another within Eckhart's thought: "In Eckhart's view unity is the ground from out of which the trinity of persons flows. Thus in uniting with the ground of God, the Godhead, the soul catches the life of the Trinity at its source and so can fully enter into it. Thus for the soul to enter into the inner life of the Trinity, for it to be born as that same Son, it must unite with the ground of the Trinity, the Godhead, and then it too will give birth to the Son. Indeed in uniting with the Godhead and so with the ground of the Trinity, the soul also unites with the Father and so can itself give birth to the Son." As I indicate below, my own interpretation of Eckhart's thought closely parallels Caputo's thinking here.

21. *Meister Eckhart: The Essential Sermons, Commentaries, Treatises and Defense.* Translation and Introduction by Edmund Colledge, O.S.A., and Bernard McGinn (New York: Paulist Press, 1981), p. 187.

22. *Ibid.*, pp. 51-52. Cf. pp. 199-203 for the full text of the sermon. Cf. also Woods, *Eckhart's Way*, p. 105: "The preeminent point at which Creator and creatures meet, where the presence of God radiates through the transparency of creatures, is that spark within the human soul in which the ground of God and the ground of the soul are one ground—not fused but united."

23. Schürmann, *Meister Eckhart*, p. 164.

24. Aquinas, *S.T..*, I, Q. 29, a. 4 resp.

25. Schürmann, *Meister Eckhart*, p. 133.

26. *Ibid.* Cf. also Woods, *Eckhart's Way*, p. 133: "It is clear, first, that Eckhart said and meant that the soul and God ultimately become one without differentiation or distinction. It is equally clear that he did *not* mean that the soul *became* God or that the essential and infinite distance between Creator and creature was abrogated by the infinite immediacy they shared: 'God is in the soul with His nature, with His being, and with His Godhead, and yet He is not the soul. The reflection of the soul in God is God, and she is what she is.'" Reference is to Sermon 56 in the edition of Eckhart's sermons by M.O'C. Walshe, cited above.

27. McGinn, *Meister Eckhart*, p. 187.

28. *Ibid.*

29. *Ibid.*, pp. 51, 202.

30. *Ibid.*, pp. 202-03.

31. *Ibid.*, p. 202.

32. *Ibid.*, p. 203.

33. Woods, *Eckhart's Way*, p. 98.

34. Cf., e.g., Miklos Vetö, *Le Fondement selon Schelling* (Paris: Beauchesne, 1977), pp. 295-307; likewise, Alexandre Koyré, *La Philosophie de Jacob Boehme*, 3rd ed. (Paris: J. Vrin, 1979), pp. 483-86; finally, Xavier Tilliette, *Schelling: une philosophie en devenir*, 2 vols. (Paris: J. Vrin, 1970), 1: 534-36.

35. Koyré, *La Philosophie de Jacob Boehme*, pp. 306-20.

36. F.W.J. Schelling, *Philosophische Untersuchungen über das Wesen der menschlichen Freiheit*: in *Sämtliche Werke*, 14 vols., ed. K.F.A. Schelling (Stuttgart: Cotta, 1856ff), 7: 406. N.B.: I follow here the pagination of the original edition of Schelling's collected works which is given at the top of the page in *Schellings Werke*, ed. Manfred Schröter (Munich: C. H. Beck, 1958ff).

37. *Ibid.*, p. 408.

38. Cf. Vladimir Jankélevitch, *L'Odyssée de la conscience dans la dernière philosophie de Schelling* (Paris: Felix Alcan, 1933), pp. 40-41.

39. Schelling, *Sämtliche Werke*, 7:408.

40. *Ibid.*, pp. 363-64, 377-78.

41. *Ibid.*, pp. 385-86.

42. *Ibid.*, p. 406.

43. *Ibid.*, p. 359.

44. *Ibid.*, p. 347.

45. Cf. Michael Vater, "Heidegger and Schelling: The Finitude of Being," *Idealistic Studies* 5 (1975), 20.

46. Cf. William J. Richardson, S.J., *Heidegger: Through Phenomenology to Thought* (The Hague: Martinus Nijhoff, 1963), pp. 666, 676.

47. Cf. Martin Heidegger, *Schellings Abhandlung über das Wesen der menschlichen Freiheit*, ed. Hildegard Feick (Tübingen: Max Niemeyer, 1971), pp. 191-98.

48. Cf. Martin Heidegger, *Identity and Difference*, trans. Joan Stambaugh (New York: Harper & Row, 1969), p. 54. Cf. also by the same author, *Being and Time*, pp. 41-49.

49. Martin Heidegger, *Vom Wesen des Grundes*, 4th ed. (Frankfurt am Main: Vittorio Klostermann, 1955), pp. 18-42.

50. *Ibid.*, pp. 43-44.

51. *Ibid.*, p. 53. Cf. also Caputo, *The Mystical Element*, pp. 91-93.

52. Cf. on this point my earlier publication *Society and Spirit: A Trinitarian Cosmology* (Cranbury, N.J.: Associated University Presses, 1991), pp. 94-101, where I discuss more in detail Heidegger's reinterpretation of Schelling's notion of *Grund*.

53. Cf. on this point Caputo, *The Mystical Element*, pp. 94-96. Cf. also Richardson, *Through Phenomenology*, pp. xvi-xxiii, where in a letter to Richardson on the occasion of the publication of his book, Heidegger takes up the question of the celebrated reversal (*Kehre*) in his thought in the post-World War II years.

54. Martin Heidegger, *Der Satz vom Grund*, 2nd ed. (Pfullingen: Günther Neske, 1958), p. 188: "Nichts *ist* ohne *Grund*. Sein und Grund: das Selbe. Sein als grundendes hat keinen Grund, spielt als der Ab-grund jenes Spiel, das als Geschick uns Sein und Grund zuspielt." For an alternate translation of this text, cf. Caputo, *The Mystical Element*, p. 82.

55. Richardson, *Through Phenomenology*, p. xxviii.

56. *Ibid.*

57. Heidegger, *Der Satz vom Grund*, p. 68. He cites the following lines from Angelus Silesius, a seventeenth-century poet and mystic: "Die Ros is ohn warum; sie blühet, weil sie blühet, Sie acht nicht ihrer selbst, fragt nicht, ob man sie siehet." Translation: "The rose is without an external cause. It blooms simply because it blooms. It pays no attention to itself, nor does it ask whether anyone sees it."

58. Cf. here Caputo, *The Mystical Element*, pp. 245-57. I agree with Caputo that there are real dangers in assimilating being in Heidegger's thought to God in

Christian theology, even the hidden God of mystical theologies such as that of Meister Eckhart. Being for Heidegger is not providential or caring in its "mittences" to human beings; hence, one cannot trust being as Christians characteristically trust God. At the same time, my thesis in this book is that being is not separate from God, that it is the divine nature as a principle of existence and activity for God as well as for all creatures. Hence, even though being as a principle of existence and activity is not in itself providential or caring toward the entities which it empowers to be, it is exercised in the first place by a supremely intelligent and loving God who regulates and controls the spontaneity of being and thus guarantees that the various "mittences" of being can be trusted by humans.

59. Cf. above, n. 57.

60. Schelling, *Sämtliche Werke*, 7: 408.

61. Cf. Bracken, *Society and Spirit*, pp. 102-04, where I argue in line with the process-oriented philosophy of Alfred North Whitehead that the "actual occasion" constitutive of human consciousness at every moment cannot both make a self-constituting decision and yet be aware of itself making the decision at the same time.

4. Creativity and the Extensive Continuum in the Philosophy of Alfred North Whitehead

1. Alfred North Whitehead, *Science and the Modern World* (New York: The Free Press, 1967), p. 177.

2. Cf. Benedict Spinoza, *The Ethics*, Prop. XIV-XVIII; in *The Rationalists*, trans. R.H.M. Elwes (New York: Doubleday Dolphin, 1960), pp. 188-96.

3. Whitehead, *Science and the Modern World*, p. 178. Cf. also Lewis S. Ford, *The Emergence of Whitehead's Metaphysics* (Albany, N.Y.: State University of New York Press, 1984), pp. 119-20. Ford points out that in this early philosophical work God was not conceived as an entity but simply as a principle of limitation for the underlying substantial activity. From this perspective, *Science and the Modern World* is more monistic than *Religion in the Making* and *Process and Reality* with respect to Ultimate Reality.

4. Whitehead, *Science in the Modern World*, p. 179.

5. Alfred North Whitehead, *Religion in the Making* (New York: New American Library, 1974), p. 88. Cf. also Ford, *The Emergence of Whitehead's Metaphysics*, pp. 137-39. In *Religion in the Making*, God is conceived by Whitehead as an entity rather than simply as a principle of limitation for the underlying substantial activity (as in *Science and the Modern World*). Yet as a unique nontemporal entity, God is not affected by the operation of creativity as in *Process and Reality*. Rather, along with creativity and eternal objects, God is a "formative element" in the self-constitution of temporal actual entities.

6. Whitehead, *Religion in the Making*, p. 148.

7. Whitehead, *Process and Reality*, p. 21/31.

8. *Ibid.*, p. 18/27. Cf. also Ford, *The Emergence of Whitehead's Metaphysics*, pp. 127-33. As Ford sees it, Whitehead gradually moved in the years 1925-1929 from a monistic understanding of Ultimate Reality in terms of an underlying substantial activity with its various modes of realization to a pluralistic understanding of Ultimate Reality in terms of discrete actual entities (including God as the transcendent actual entity). While this is presumably true, given Ford's careful analysis of the pertinent texts, it still leaves open the question whether metaphysical pluralism does not carry the opposite danger of metaphysical atomism. As I make clear later

in this chapter, what is likewise needed in Whitehead's world view is a better understanding of what he calls *societies*, namely, groupings of actual entities which possess some sort of objective ontological unity and thus correspond to the macroscopic realities of common sense experience.

9. Cf. on this point two essays in the collection entitled *Whitehead's Metaphysics of Creativity*, eds. Friedrich Rapp & Reiner Wiehl (Albany, N.Y.: State University of New York Press, 1990): Jan Van der Veken, "Creativity as Universal Activity" pp. 178-88; and Reto Luzius Fetz, "Creativity: A New Transcendental?" pp. 189-208. Both authors emphasize that creativity is not simply an empirical generalization derived from particular instances of self-actualization among actual occasions but a transcendent reality operative in those actual occasions empowering them to exist. Cf., for example, Van der Veken, "Creativity as Universal Activity," pp. 182-84; Fetz, "Creativity: A New Transcendental?" pp. 191-93. Neither author, to be sure, explicitly identifies creativity with the underlying nature of God as I do in the second half of this chapter. But, from my perspective, both authors could profit from this further qualification. Van der Veken could better distinguish between God and creativity if creativity were seen as the divine nature operative in both God and creatures enabling them to exist in dynamic interrelation. Likewise, Fetz could better assert the reality of creativity as a new transcendental if creativity as linked with the act of being (p. 191) were likewise understood to be the underlying nature of God (the Supreme Being, Subsistent Goodness, Perfect Truth, etc.).

10. Whitehead, *Process and Reality*, p. 88/135.

11. *Ibid.*, p. 225/344; cf. also p. 244/374.

12. *Ibid.*, p. 348/528.

13. John B. Cobb, Jr., *A Christian Natural Theology* (Philadelphia: Westminster, 1965), pp. 203-14.

14. Wilcox, "A Monistic Interpretation," pp. 162-74. Cf. also Wilcox, *A Monistic Interpretation of Creativity* (Ann Arbor, Mich.: University Microfilms International, 1986): DAI 47-03A (8613007).

15. Donald Sherburne, *A Whiteheadian Aesthetic* (New Haven: Yale University Press, 1961), p. 21.

16. *Ibid.*, p. 20.

17. Wilcox, "A Monistic Interpretation," pp. 164-65.

18. Robert C. Neville, *Creativity and God: A Challenge to Process Theology* (New York: Seabury, 1980), pp. 8, 38.

19. Whitehead, *Process and Reality*, pp. 24/36-37, 43/68.

20. Neville, *Creativity and God*, pp. 41-43.

21. *Ibid.*, pp. 44-45. Cf. below, Conclusion, for further explanation of Neville's theory, in particular, of his hypothesis that Ultimate Reality is not simply God as a divine being but rather the transcendent Source or Ground which through the ongoing activity of creating becomes the Creator God of Biblical revelation.

22. Whitehead, *Process and Reality*, pp. 87-88/134-35: "(i) The 'primordial nature' of God is the concrescence of a unity of conceptual feelings, including among their data all eternal objects . . . (ii) The 'consequent nature' of God is the physical prehension by God of the actualities of the evolving universe. (iii) The 'superjective nature' of God is the character of the pragmatic value of his specific satisfaction qualifying the transcendent creativity in the various temporal instances." Each of these divine "natures," as I see it, is a special type of divine activity and therefore a further specification of creativity as the ontological ground of the divine being.

23. *Ibid.*, p. 18/28.

24. *Ibid.*, p. 225/344.

25. *Ibid.*, p. 348/528.

26. Ivor Leclerc, *Whitehead's Metaphysics* (London: George Allen & Unwin, 1958), pp. 83-84.

27. Whitehead, *Process and Reality*, p. 21/32.

28. Charles Hartshorne, "The Compound Individual," *Philosophical Essays for Alfred North Whitehead*, ed. F.S.C. Northrup (New York: Russell and Russell, 1936), pp. 193-210.

29. Jorge Luis Nobo, *Whitehead's Metaphysics*, p. 255.

30. *Ibid.*, p. 256.

31. Cf. on this point William A. Christian, *An Interpretation of Whitehead's Metaphysics* (New Haven: Yale University Press, 1959), pp. 395-96. Yet Christian also contends that there are good reasons in support of the opposite position, namely, that God *not* be considered as in space and time. For example, God has no spatial or temporal boundaries like finite actual occasions existing in space and time. If, however, not just God but every actual entity both exists somewhere in the extensive continuum and "is everywhere throughout the continuum" (Whitehead, *Process and Reality*, 67/104), this particular objection seems to lose much of its force. The mere fact that Whitehead himself did not explicitly make God's "region" within the extensive continuum co-terminous with the extensive continuum as a whole (Christian, *An Interpretation*, p. 394) does not seem to invalidate my extension of his thought in this new direction.

32. Whitehead, *Process and Reality*, pp. 348-49/528-29.

33. William A. Christian, "The Concept of God as a Derivative Notion," *Process and Divinity*, ed. William L. Reese and Eugene Freeman (LaSalle, Ill.: Open Court, 1964), pp. 181-203.

34. Whitehead, *Process and Reality*, p. 21/32.

35. *Ibid.*, p. 66/103.

36. Cf. on this point Wolfhart Pannenberg, *Systematic Theology*, I, 382-84. Pannenberg likewise conceives the underlying nature of the triune God as a "force-field" although his reasoning is not based on Whiteheadian metaphysics but rather on a modern adaptation of the ancient notion of the divine Spirit as *pneuma* rather than *nous*.

37. *Ibid.*, p. 31/46.

38. Cf., e.g., Bracken, *Society and Spirit*, pp. 42-49.

39. Here I consciously take issue with Charles Hartshorne's understanding of this same kind of "structured society" within Whitehead's metaphysics. Cf. here Hartshorne, "The Compound Individual," pp. 215-17; likewise, Bracken, *Society and Spirit*, pp. 42-49.

40. Whitehead, *Process and Reality*, pp. 350-51/532.

41. *Ibid.*, p. 90/138.

42. *Ibid.*, pp. 90-91/139.

43. To be more specific, in and through the structure constitutive of this common field of activity, each of the divine persons appropriates at every moment not only the objectification of its own past "decisions" but also the objectifications of the past "decisions" of the other two persons. The only difference between them is that each divine person appropriates its own subjectivity differently from the way in which it appropriates the subjectivity of the other two persons. That is, in appropriating

the structural objectification of its own past "decisions" within the common field of activity, each divine person identifies with the subjectivities therein represented. But, in appropriating the structural objectifications of the "decisions" of the other two divine persons within the common field of activity, it knows them exhaustively but does not identify with them as its own. Thus each of the divine persons *objectively* understands the subjectivity of the other two persons without *subjectively* identifying with it. In this way, each of the divine persons retains its own subjective identity within the field of intentional activity common to them all, which is their reality as one God.

44. Once again, the traditional divine names are given in quotation marks so as to indicate their purely metaphorical, non-sexist intention.

45. As should be evident to students of both Whitehead's and Hartshorne's philosophy, I am mixing features of their respective notions of God within my own Trinitarian scheme here.

From Hartshorne, as noted above, I borrow the idea that God is not an ever-developing actual entity (as with Whitehead) but a sequential series of actual occasions (technically, a personally ordered society of living actual occasions). My adaptation is to the effect that, since God is triune, each of the divine persons is such a sequential series of actual occasions.

Yet I borrow from Whitehead the idea that God first exists in terms of the primordial nature and then in terms of the consequent nature. The movement of the divine life, in other words, is from the mental pole to the physical pole rather than (as with all creatures) from the physical pole to the mental pole. In this way, God unlike creatures does not need an "initial aim" or some other extrinsic stimulus to be "lured" into the realization of new possibilities. My Trinitarian adaptation of Whitehead's notion of the primordial nature of God is to the effect that, while all three divine persons survey the panoply of possibilities available to them at any given moment, the "Father" alone decides on the possibility to be realized even as it devolves upon the "Son" and the "Spirit" respectively first to say "Yes" to this proposal from the "Father" and then to bring it to fruition. Here, too, of course, I am consciously mixing Whitehead's and Hartshorne's separate concepts of God. For, while Whitehead conceives the primordial nature of God as the result of a single primordial decision, I follow Hartshorne's lead in thinking of divine possibilities as emergent out of the ongoing actuality of the divine life in conjunction with creation. Finally, I use Whitehead's solitary reference to a "superjective nature" of God (Whitehead, *Process and Reality*, p. 88/135) so as to describe the function of the "Spirit" within the divine communitarian life. This, too, distinguishes me from other attempts to give a Trinitarian interpretation to Whitehead's notion of God (cf., e.g., Lewis S. Ford, *The Lure of God: A Biblical Background for Process Theism* [Philadelphia: Fortress, 1978], pp. 99-111, esp. p. 110, n. 8).

46. In speaking of the "Father" as the subsistent principle of potentiality, of the "Son" as the subsistent principle of provisional actuality, and of the "Spirit" as the subsistent principle of ultimate actuality, I am clearly making reference to Aristotle's definition of motion as already discussed in Chapter 1 and to the way in which I reinterpreted Aquinas's understanding of God as *Ipsum Esse Subsistens* in Chapter 2. That is, I envision each of the divine persons as an ongoing subject of one and the same underlying activity, namely, creativity or, in Thomistic language, the act of being. Each of them thus embodies one of the necessary dimensions of the act of being, but only all three working together constitute the fullness of that same

activity. Furthermore, as I indicate below, human beings initially only experience God as an integrated set of activities in their lives. Only upon reflection do they realize that these activities are proper to different divine persons.

47. Cf. above, n. 46. Likewise, cf. Joseph A. Bracken, S.J., "The issue of panentheism in the dialogue with the non-believer," *Studies in Religion/Sciences Religieuses* 21 (1992), 207-18.

48. Cf. Bracken, *Society and Spirit*, pp. 140-60.

49. *Ibid.*

50. Whitehead, *Process and Reality*, p. 66/103; cf. also Nobo, *Whitehead's Metaphysics*, p. 208.

51. Cf. above, n. 43.

52. Aristotle, *Physics*, 204a20-28.

53. Whitehead, *Process and Reality*, p. 66/103: "The reality of the future is bound up with the reality of this continuum. It is the reality of what is potential, in its character of a real component of what is actual."

54. Cf. above, Chapter 3.

55. Cf. Johnson, *She Who Is*, pp. 124-87.

56. Whitehead, *Process and Reality*, p. 34-35/51-52.

Part II: Introductory Note

1. Cf. Paul Ricoeur, *Interpretation Theory: Discourse and the Surplus of Meaning* (Fort Worth: Texas Christian University Press, 1976), p. 30: "The text's career escapes the finite horizon lived by its author. What the text means now matters more than what the author meant when he wrote it."

5. The Dynamic Identity-in-Difference of *Brahman* and *Atman*

1. Frank R. Podgorski, *Hinduism: A Beautiful Mosaic*, 3rd ed. (Bristol, Ind.: Wyndham Hall Press, 1985), pp. 1-2. Reference is made to Thomas Berry, *Religions of India* (New York: Bruce Publishing Co., 1971), p. ii.

2. Cf. on this point Michael von Brück, *The Unity of Reality: God, God-Experience, and Meditation in the Hindu-Christian Dialogue*, trans. James V. Zeitz (New York: Paulist Press, 1991), pp. 88, 127-28, 157, 247, 270. Von Brück repeatedly points out that for Advaita Vedantins only the One is ultimately real; the Many exist only on the level of *maya* or illusion. For himself and other Trinitarian thinkers, however, the Many, beginning with the divine persons but also including all creatures, are real but are incorporated as "moments" into the dynamic unity of the One. Thus non-duality as understood by Advaita Vedantins is necessarily somewhat different from non-duality as understood by Trinitarian theologians.

Likewise, both von Brück and I locate the unity of the Trinity in the *perichoresis* of the divine persons, i.e., in their activity of mutual coinherence and dynamic interrelation, rather than in the Godhead as somehow distinct from the divine persons (von Brück, *The Unity of Reality*, pp. 132-40; 144-47). Cf., however, n. 40 below.

3. *The Vedic Experience: Mantramanjari, an Anthology of the Vedas for Modern Man and Contemporary Celebration*, edited and translated with introduction and notes by Raimundo Panikkar (Berkeley: University of California Press, 1977), p. 650.

4. *Chandogya* Upanishad VI, 2, 1-2: in *The Thirteen Principal Upanishads*, trans. Robert Ernest Hume, 2nd ed. (London: Oxford University Press, 1975), p. 241.

5. Panikkar, *The Vedic Experience*, p. 653.

6. *Chandogya* Upanishad VI, 2, 2: *Thirteen Principal Upanishads*, p. 241. Cf. on this point Hume's introductory essay, "An Outline of the Philosophy of the Upanishads," p. 11, where he notes that in other Upanishadic texts non-being is said to precede the existence of being. Cf. also below, my citations from the *Rig Veda* and commentary thereon.

7. Eliot Deutsch, *Advaita Vedanta: A Philosophical Reconstruction* (Honolulu: University Press of Hawaii, 1973), p. 18.

8. *Rig Veda* X, 129, 1-3: in Panikkar, *The Vedic Experience*, p. 58. For an alternate translation, cf. *The Rig Veda: An Anthology*, ed. Wendy Doniger O'Flaherty, (New York: Penguin Books, 1981), p. 25.

9. *Ibid.*, X, 121, 1: in Panikkar, *The Vedic Experience*, pp. 71-72; cf. also *Rig Veda: An Anthology*, pp. 27-28.

10. Panikkar, *The Vedic Experience*, p. 68.

11. *Ibid.*

12. *Ibid.*, pp. 50, 68.

13. Cf. on this point Loy, *Nonduality*, pp. 17-37.

14. Cf. above, Chapter 1, where I discussed Aristotle's notion of time as the measure of motion according to before and after. Where there is no beginning or end of activity, movement as an ongoing or continuous reality is indistinguishable from a state of rest. Thus, though logically opposed to one another, pure being and pure becoming are indistinguishable in experience.

15. *Aitareya* Upanishad III, 5, 3: in *Thirteen Principal Upanishads*, p. 301. N.B.: I am following here the sequence set forth by Panikkar in *The Vedic Experience*. But, to the best of my knowledge, there is no textual evidence in the Upanishads to demand that the *mahavakyas* be ordered in precisely this way; they are rather six independent statements, drawn from different documents, all of which deal with the nature of Ultimate Reality.

16. *Ibid.*, p. 300.

17. *Ibid.*, p. 301.

18. R.C. Zaehner, "Introduction," *Hindu Scriptures*, translated and edited by R.C. Zaehner (London: J.M. Dent, 1966), p. viii.

19. Panikkar, *The Vedic Experience*, p. 672.

20. Cf. above, Chapter 1, where in connection with Aristotle's notion of movement as eternal and unchanging, I made reference to Bergson's notion of duration as a continuous flow which one experiences concretely and immediately through intuition before one reflectively analyzes it into discrete moments (e.g., into before and after).

21. Panikkar, *The Vedic Experience*, p. 669.

22. Deutsch, *Advaita Vedanta*, p. 9.

23. Von Brück, *The Unity of Reality*, p. 22.

24. *Ibid.*, pp. 51-52. Von Brück analyzes the Hindu notion of *prana* or life-energy and concludes: "In summary we can say that *prana* is either *brahman* itself or its manifestation in life-energies. *Prana* is not a principle alongside *brahman*, but the Absolute, understood as the efficacious energy behind everything that happens" (p. 52).

25. *Mandukya* Upanishad, 2: *Thirteen Principal Upanishads*, p. 391.

26. *Ibid.*, 12: *Thirteen Principal Upanishads*, p. 393. Cf. also Hume, "An Outline of the Philosophy of the Upanishads," *Thirteen Principal Upanishads*, pp. 42-52, where Hume makes clear that in this final state the individual self is "unconscious," that

is, simply experiencing an activity prior to the distinction of self and object in terms of the activity.

27. Panikkar, *The Vedic Experience*, p. 698. Cf. also Hume, "Outline," pp. 14-32, for a more detailed study of the gradual development of the notions of *Brahman* and *Atman* in the Upanishads.

28. Podgorski, *Hinduism*, p. 3.

29. Panikkar, *The Vedic Experience*, p. 701.

30. *Brhadaranyaka* Upanishad, I, 4, 10: in *Thirteen Principal Upanishads*, pp. 83-84.

31. Panikkar, *The Vedic Experience*, p. 725.

32. *Brhadaranyaka* Upanishad, I, 4, 10: in *Thirteen Principal Upanishads*, pp. 83-84.

33. Hume, "An Outline," pp. 21, 30.

34. Panikkar, *The Vedic Experience*, p. 727.

35. *Ibid.*, p. 728.

36. *Ibid.*, p. 729. Cf. also on this point an earlier book by Panikkar, *The Unknown Christ of Hinduism*, rev. ed. (Maryknoll, N.Y.: Orbis, 1981), pp. 134-48. In this work, Panikkar recognizes that there is a difference between God as the transcendent Other and *Brahman* as the immanent One. If *Brahman* is "*ens commune*, the quiddity of all beings, it cannot be identified with *ens realissimum*, the living God, source of all beings, absolute reality that is not only *in* everything but also *above* all things" (p. 138). Yet, says Panikkar, they both point to the same reality; they are "*materialiter* the same reality, but *formaliter* different" (p. 143). This earlier conception of the relation between *Brahman* and God or the cosmic Self I find to be strikingly similar to my own theory in this chapter. For me, too, God is *ens realissimum*, the transcendent Other, whereas *Brahman* is *ens commune*, the universal substratum, that out of which all individual entities emerge. Likewise for me, God and *Brahman* are *materialiter* the same and *formaliter* different. They are one concrete reality even though they are logically distinguishable as person and nature.

37. *Chandogya* Upanishad VI, 8, 7: in *Thirteen Principal Upanishads*, p. 246.

38. Panikkar, *The Vedic Experience*, p. 752.

39. *Brhadaranyaka* Upanishad II, 5, 1-19: in *Thirteen Principal Upanishads*, pp. 102-05.

40. Cf. here von Brück, *The Unity of Reality*, pp. 197-202. Von Brück speaks of God as *persona personans*, i.e., "the principle of being a person, as well as its highest instantiation" (p. 199). Thus God appears to be, in von Brück's eyes, both a transcendent person and a "person-making" activity. While I agree with von Brück that God is at work everywhere in creation to constitute ontological totalities in the divine image (p. 198), I prefer to think of God not as a "transpersonal person" (p. 200) but as a primordial community of persons. Thus the unity of reality is not the unity of a transcendent person, as von Brück seems here to imply, but the unity of a cosmic community in which the members are linked with one another in virtue of a common *unifying activity*. As noted above (n. 2), von Brück himself seems to affirm this when he speaks of *perichoresis* as the dynamic activity of the Godhead linking the divine persons to one another. But, in reference to creation, he seems to think of God in the singular as the equivalent of the Hindu *Purusha*, with the consequence that ontological totalities in creation are then likewise conceived as individual entities (after the manner of persons) rather than as specifically social realities (e.g., as Whiteheadian "societies" or communities of dynamically interrelated members).

41. *Taittiriya* Upanishad I, 8: in *Thirteen Principal Upanishads*, p. 279; cf. also

Panikkar, *The Vedic Experience*, pp. 768-69.

42. Panikkar, *The Vedic Experience*, p. 771.

43. Surendranath Dasgupta, *A History of Indian Philosophy*, 5 vols. (Delhi: Motilal Banarsidass, 1988), I, 429.

44. *Vedanta-Sutras with the commentary by Sankaracarya and Ramanuja*, II, 2, 1-10: trans. George Thibaut, 3 vols. (Delhi: Motilal Banarsidass, 1962), I: 363-81.

45. *Ibid.*, 11-17: I, 381-400.

46. *Ibid.*, 18-23: I, 400-411.

47. *Ibid.*, 28-32: I, 418-28.

48. *Ibid.*, 37-41: I, 434-39.

49. *Ibid.*, I, 1, 2: I, 16.

50. *Ibid.*, II, 1, 14: I, 323.

51. *Ibid.*, II, 2, 28: I, 420.

52. Deutsch, *Advaita Vedanta*, p. 32.

53. *Vedanta-Sutras*, II, 1, 14: I, 320.

54. *Ibid.*, II, 1, 14: I, 328-30; II, 1, 27: I, 352.

55. *Ibid.*, I, 4, 22: I, 282-83.

56. Deutsch, *Advaita Vedanta*, p. 9.

57. T.R.V. Murti, "The Two Definitions of Brahman in the Advaita," *K.C. Bhattacharya Memorial Volume* (Amalner, India: Indian Institute of Philosophy, 1958), pp. 135-50.

58. Deutsch, *Advaita Vedanta*, p. 9.

59. *Vedanta-Sutras*, II, 1, 14: I, 328-30.

60. R. Balasubramanian, "Advaita: An Overview," *Perspectives of Theism and Absolutism in Indian Philosophy*, eds. M. Narasimhachari, V.A. Devasenapathi, and R. Balasubramanian (Madras: Ramakrishna Mission, Vivekananda College, 1978), pp. 50-51.

61. *Vedanta-Sutras*, II, 1, 33: I, 356-57.

62. Cf. on this point Toshihiko Izutsu, *Sufism and Taoism: A Comparative Study of Key Philosophical Concepts* (Berkeley: University of California Press, 1984), pp. 482-85. Izutsu proposes that the notion of existence as the pure act of being represents the Absolute in Sufism and Taoism (cf. below, Chapter 7). But his remarks are likewise pertinent here with reference to *Brahman* in Advaita Vedanta Hinduism.

63. *Vedanta-Sutras*, II, 2, 2: I, 369. Shankara argues here that *Brahman* is superior to *prakrti* (unconscious matter) as first principle of the universe because, although non-moving itself, it moves the universe through the power of *maya*. Admittedly, this is still a provisional understanding of *Brahman* on the level of cause-effect relationships, but it at least makes clear that *Brahman* is for Shankara a living rather than an inert reality (even on the level of absolute knowledge).

64. Deutsch, *Advaita Vedanta*, p. 13. This last point is most evident in Kashmir Shaivism where spontaneity *(spanda)* is considered essential to the divine being. Likewise, within Kashmir Shaivism the things of this world, though only transient manifestations of the power *(shakti)* of *Shiva*, yet are real in themselves, not unreal as in Advaita Vedanta. Cf. on these points Mark Dyczkowski, *The Doctrine of Vibration: An Analysis of the Doctrines and Practices of Kashmir Shaivism* (Albany: State University of New York Press, 1987), pp. 51-57, 77-98.

65. *Vedanta-Sutras*, II, 1, 9: III, 424: "Any substance which a sentient soul is capable of completely controlling and supporting for its own purposes, and which stands to the soul in an entirely subordinate relation, is the body of that soul . . . In

this sense, then, all sentient and non-sentient beings together constitute the body of the Supreme Person, for they are completely controlled and supported by him for his own ends, and are completely subordinate to him." Cf. also on this point John Braisted Carman, *The Theology of Ramanuja: An Essay in Interreligious Understanding* (New Haven: Yale University Press, 1974), pp. 115-16.

66. Cf. I. Puthiadam, *Visnu the Ever Free: A Study of the Madhva Concept of God* (Madurai: Arul Anandar College, 1985), pp. 164-83.

67. *Vedanta-Sutras*, I, 1, 2: III, 156. Cf. also I, 1. 1 (III, 4): "The word 'Brahman' denotes the highest Person (*purushottama*), who is essentially free from all imperfections and possesses numberless classes of auspicious qualities of unsurpassable excellence."

68. Madhva, *Anuvyakhyana*, nn. 89-91 (*Vedanta-Sutras*, I, 1, 2): in *Les Noms védiques de Visnu dans L'Anuvyakhyana de Madhva*, texte avec traduction et notes par Suzanne Siauve (Pondicherry: Institut Français d'Indologie, 1959), p. 3.

69. *Vedanta-Sutras*, II, 1, 15: III, 458-59.

70. Cf. on this point Carman, *The Theology of Ramanuja*, p. 124: *Brahman* is the "Inner Controller" (*antaryami*) of all finite selves and through them of all inanimate entities as well.

71. *Vedanta-Sutras*, II, 1, 14: III, 428. Cf. also Satischandra Chatterjee and Dhirendramohan Datta, *An Introduction to Indian Philosophy*, 8th ed. (Calcutta: University of Calcutta, 1984), p. 419.

72. *Vedanta-Sutras*, II, 1, 33: III, 477. Cf. also on this point Carman, *The Theology of Ramanuja*, pp. 117-22.

73. Madhva, *Anuvyakhyana*, nn. 186-91 (*Vedanta-Sutras*, I, 1, 14): in *Les Noms védiques de Visnu*, pp. 59-61. Cf. also Puthiadam, *Visnu the Ever Free*, pp. 184-85.

74. Thibaut, "Introduction," *Vedanta-Sutras*, I, cxxii-v.

75. *Ibid.*, pp. cxxvi-vii.

76. Cf. above, Chapter 2, in which I discuss the notion of divine infinity within the philosophy of Thomas Aquinas.

77. Cf. above, n. 70.

78. *Vedanta-Sutras*, I, 1, 1 (III, 138): "all intelligent and non-intelligent beings are thus mere modes of the highest Brahman, and have reality thereby only." Cf. also I, 2, 12 (III, 271).

79. Puthiadam, *Visnu the Ever Free*, p. 193.

6. The Buddhist Doctrine of Dependent Co-Arising

1. Huston Smith, *The World's Religions* (New York: HarperCollins: 1991), pp. 112-13.

2. Cf., e.g., Denise Lardner Carmody and John Tully Carmody, *Ways to the Center: An Introduction to World Religions*, 3rd ed. (Belmont, Calif.: Wadsworth Publishing Co., 1989), p. 128.

3. Cf. David J. Kalupahana, *Buddhist Philosophy: A Historical Analysis* (Honolulu: The University Press of Hawaii, 1976), p. 28.

4. *Ibid.*, p. 29.

5. Cf. above, Chapter 4, where I make basically the same argument about the ontological status of creativity within the philosophy of Whitehead. That is, creativity is not simply a logical abstraction from specific instances of creativity within innumerable actual occasions. Rather, it is an underlying activity which, to be sure, never exists in itself but which provides the necessary ontological ground or *raison*

d'être for successive generations of actual occasions and thus for the ongoing reality of the world process.

Cf. also Malcolm David Eckel, *To See the Buddha: A Philosopher's Quest for the Meaning of Emptiness* (New York: HarperCollins, 1992), p. 43: "As an abstraction, Emptiness is difficult to respond to with devotion, no matter how much freedom the logic of Emptiness may allow a philosopher in the world of ordinary experience. But Emptiness comes down to earth when it is embodied in a particular person . . . When the analysis of Emptiness has moved to its conclusion, it is a natural conse- quence of the argument for Bhavaviveka [a sixth century Mahayana Buddhist philosopher] to turn his attention from Emptiness itself to the Buddha, the being in whom Emptiness is perfectly embodied." The same thought-pattern, therefore, seems to emerge in Eckel's careful study of the various "bodies" of the Buddha. The *Dharmakaya* or *Tathagata* Body of the Buddha is identical with Emptiness (p. 170); as such, it is opposed to the Form Body or Manifestation Body of the Buddha which is seen with the senses or pictured in the imagination. Thus "to see the Buddha" is not a matter of sense perception but of insight into the Emptiness of all things or, as I would express it, insight into the activity of self-emptying which underlies all occasions of arising and ceasing to be.

6. Here I am consciously setting myself in opposition to Frederick Streng and other scholars of Buddhist philosophy who propose that there is no objective referent to the term "dependent co-arising" (cf., e.g., Frederick J. Streng, *Emptiness: A Study in Religious Meaning* [Nashville, Tenn.: Abingdon Press, 1967], pp. 146-48). Equivalently, then, they are suggesting that the term is nothing more than a logical abstraction from particular instances of dependent co-arising occurring within human experience. My argument is that the logical abstraction must correspond to an extramental reality which accounts for the regular occurrence of the instances and thereby for the possibility of such an abstraction in the first place.

Cf. here Joanna Macy, *Mutual Causality in Buddhism and General Systems Theory: The Dharma of Natural Systems* (Albany: State University of New York Press, 1991), p. 54. She first cites a saying of the Buddha with respect to dependent co-arising ("Whether, brethren, there be an arising of Tathagatas, or whether there be no such arising, this nature of things just stands, this causal status, this causal orderliness." [*Samyutta Nikaya*, II, 25]), and then adds: "The enlightened ones do not invent it or infer it, but rediscover it. More than a private interpretation of reality, it led the Buddha to speak of it in terms of 'the nature of things.'"

7. Cf. David J. Kalupahana, *Nagarjuna: The Philosophy of the Middle Way* (Albany: State University of New York Press, 1986), pp. 10-11. A slightly different translation is provided in *Sacred Texts of the World: A Universal Anthology*, ed. Ninian Smart and Richard D. Hecht (New York: Crossroad, 1982), p. 244.

8. David Loy, *Nonduality*, p. 217.

9. *Ibid.*, p. 234.

10. Joanna Macy comments that, although language itself constrains us to enumerate these conditioning factors of human experience in sequential fashion, in point of fact they arise and cease to be simultaneously in terms of mutual causality (cf. Macy, *Mutual Causality*, p. 55).

11. Cf. here Raimundo Panikkar, *The Silence of God: The Answer of the Buddha*, trans. Robert R. Barr (Maryknoll, N.Y.: Orbis, 1989), p. 42. Panikkar quotes from the *Itivuttaka* (part of the *khuddakanikaya* of the *Sutta-Pitaka*), p. 43: "'There is, O monks, something not born, non-existent, not made, not compounded. If there were not this

something not born, non-existent, not made, not compounded, there would not be known here deliverance from what is born, existent, made, and compounded.' . . . To this effect spake the Blessed One, and hereupon said the following: 'It is not possible to delight in that which is born, which has existence, is produced, is made, is compounded, not stable, subject to Old Age and Death, a nest of diseases, fragile, and owing its operative cause to the current of subsistence. The destruction of this is a state that is tranquil, that hath passed beyond conjecture, that is not born and not produced, that is griefless and passionless—the annihilation of the conditions of Misery, a happy cessation of Doubt.'"

12. Kalupahana, *Nagarjuna*, pp. 5-6. Cf. also Gadjin Nagao, *The Foundational Standpoint of Madhyamika Philosophy*, trans. John P. Keenan (Albany: State University of New York Press, 1989), p. 5. N.B.: While Kalupahana and Nagao are opposed to one another on certain points in the interpretation of Nagarjuna's thought, they seem to be in agreement on still other points, such as the present one.

13. Nagarjuna, *Mulamadhyamakakarika*, I, 1: Kalupahana, *Nagarjuna*, p. 105. N.B.: I adopt here and elsewhere the translation of the *Mulamadhyamakarika* (hereafter *MMK*) provided by Kalupahana in his commentary.

14. *MMK*, I, 5: *Nagarjuna*, p. 109.

15. Cf. here Nagao, *The Foundational Standpoint*, p. 7: "Dependent co-arising does not indicate any essentialistic causal relationship in which some substantial entity with its own being acts upon another equally substantial entity. Rather, the true meaning of dependent co-arising is found in the negation of all substantial reality, of all subjective selfhood . . . Dependent co-arising refers to a causal relationship wherein no essence is present at any time in either cause or result."

16. *Ibid.*, II, 1: Kalupahana, *Nagarjuna*, p. 118.

17. *Ibid.*, 2: Kalupahana, *Nagarjuna.*, p. 119.

18. *Ibid.*, 5: Kalupahana, *Nagarjuna.*, p. 121.

19. *Ibid.*, 12, 17: Kalupahana, *Nagarjuna*, pp. 124, 127.

20. *Ibid.*, XXII, 1: Kalupahana, *Nagarjuna*, p. 302.

21. *Ibid.*, 11: Kalupahana, *Nagarjuna*, p. 307.

22. Kalupahana, *Nagarjuna*, p. 308. Nagao would add that the experience of dependent co-arising is simultaneously an experience of emptiness, hence, that the two can never be separated: "If one loses sight of emptiness and claims that the pervasive principle of Buddhism is dependent co-arising, one has departed from Mahayana. Likewise, if one chooses to overemphasize emptiness and thus concentrate on the overthrowing and refutation of falsehood in the manner of the San-lun sect, one falls into a dogmatism that attempts to evade the conventionality of being in the world. Emptiness and dependent co-arising must be understood together as an identity of absolute contradictories" (*The Foundational Standpoint*, p. 10). This is one of the points of interpretation on which Kalupahana and Nagao appear to diverge. Kalupahana gives far less attention to the doctrine of emptiness in the thought of Nagarjuna than Nagao does.

23. *MMK*, XXII, 16: Kalupahana, *Nagarjuna*, p. 310.

24. *Ibid.*, XXIV, 8: Kalupahana, *Nagarjuna*, p. 331.

25. *Ibid.*, 10: Kalupahana, *Nagarjuna*, p. 333.

26. Cf. Nagao, *The Foundational Standpoint*, p. 32: "The two truths mean that the truth, as ultimate meaning, is also worldly and conventional. There is no manifestation of ultimate meaning apart from the manifestation of the truth of conventional language, just as there can be no emptiness apart from dependent co-arising." Thus,

in interpreting Nagarjuna's notion of the Two Truths, I follow Nagao more than Kalupahana.

27. Kalupahana, *Nagarjuna*, p. 340.

28. Cf. above, nn. 15, 22, 26.

29. *MMK*, XXIV, 40: Kalupahana, *Nagarjuna*, pp. 353-54.

30. Cf. Nagao, *The Foundational Standpoint*, p. 27: "The world of dependent co-arising is not simply the birth-death cycle, but at the same time leads to liberation. It is not simply a transcendent 'going beyond,' but at the same time involves itself again in the world. Yet such reengagement cannot but be worldly and conventional."

31. *MMK*, XXV, 1-2: Kalupahana, *Nagarjuna*, pp. 355-56.

32. *Ibid.*, 3: Kalupahana, *Nagarjuna*, p. 357.

33. *Ibid.*, 4-8: Kalupahana, *Nagarjuna*, pp. 358-60.

34. *Ibid.*, 19: Kalupahana, *Nagarjuna*, p. 366.

35. Kalupahana, *Nagarjuana*, p. 366.

36. *MMK*, XXV, 17-18: Kalupahana, *Nagarjuna*, p. 365.

37. *Ibid.*, XXVII, 29: Kalupahana, *Nagarjuna*, p. 390.

38. Kalupahana, *Nagarjuna*, p. 390.

39. Cf. above, n. 11.

40. Cf. Smart and Hecht, *Sacred Texts of the World*, p. 246.

41. Cf. on this Ha Tai Kim, "The Logic of the Illogical: Zen and Hegel," *Philosophy East and West* 5 (1955-56), 23-24; cf. also Robert E. Carter, *The Nothingness beyond God: An Introduction to the Philosophy of Nishida Kitaro* (New York: Paragon House, 1989), pp. 54-55. The context for both these authors is Zen Buddhism, to which we will turn momentarily. But the ideas likewise apply to the interpretation of the Heart Sutra.

42. Cf. on this point Richard Rorty, *Philosophy and the Mirror of Nature* (Princeton, N.J.: Princeton University Press, 1979), pp. 17-69.

43. Carter, *The Nothingness Beyond God*, pp. 77-80; cf. also Macy, *Mutual Causality*, pp. 131-32. Likewise among systems philosophers, there is recognition that "objectless knowing" or heightened awareness of the knowing process itself is the key to understanding the "mentality" immanent within the entire universe as an all-encompassing system.

44. Kitaro Nishida, *An Inquiry into the Good*, trans. Masao Abe and Christopher Ives (New Haven: Yale University Press, 1990), p. 3.

45. *Ibid.*, p. 4.

46. *Ibid.*, p. 6. Cf. also on this point Toshihiko Izutsu, *Toward a Philosophy of Zen Buddhism* (Tehran: Imperial Iranian Academy of Philosophy, 1977), p. 81: "Often when we are absorbed in listening to an enchanting piece of music, a state of artistic *samadhi* is actualized. In such a state there is Music pure and simple. The Music fills up the whole field of existence. It is only after the music has come to an end and when we 'come back' to ourselves that we realize with a feeling of surprise that we have been completely 'identified with' music. But when we actually realize it, the I and the music are already split apart into two different things." Izutsu's analysis of the philosophical presuppositions of Zen Buddhism thus closely corresponds to my own analysis of the thought of Nishida.

47. Nishida, *An Inquiry into the Good*, pp. 7-8.

48. *Ibid.*, p. 47.

49. *Ibid.*, p. 56.

50. *Ibid.*, p. 59.
51. *Ibid.*, p. 70.
52. *Ibid.*, p. 72.
53. *Ibid.*, pp. 79-83; cf. also pp. 28, 161-62.
54. *Ibid.*, p. 170.
55. *Ibid.*

56. Kitaro Nishida, "The Logic of the Place of Nothingness and the Religious World View," *Last Writings*, trans. David A. Dilworth (Honolulu: University of Hawaii Press, 1987), p. 47.

57. *Ibid.*, p. 49.
58. *Ibid.*, p. 51.
59. *Ibid.*, p. 52.
60. *Ibid.*, p. 57.
61. *Ibid.*, p. 57.
62. *Ibid.*, p. 56.
63. *Ibid.*, p. 58.
64. *Ibid.*, p. 66.
65. *Ibid.*, p. 67.
66. *Ibid.*
67. *Ibid.*, p. 69.
68. *Ibid.*, pp. 70, 75.
69. *Ibid.*, p. 74.
70. *Ibid.*
71. *Ibid.*, pp. 99-100.
72. *Ibid.*, p. 74.

73. Donald W. Mitchell, *Spirituality and Emptiness: The Dynamics of Spiritual Life in Buddhism and Christianity* (New York: Paulist Press, 1991), p. 16.

74. *Ibid.*, p. 26.

75. Izutsu, *Toward a Philosophy of Zen Buddhism*, pp. 32-33: "For the Mind as understood by Zen is not the minds of individual persons. What is meant by the word Mind is Reality before it is broken up into the so-called 'mind' and 'thing'; it is a state prior to the basic dichotomy of 'subject' and 'object.'" This primordial "state," as Izutsu makes clear in the same context, is a state of pure activity, "ever-active, ever-creative Act" (p. 32).

76. *Ibid.*, p. 32. Speaking of the way in which the subject and object of ordinary experience disappear into a Void of Nothingness as a result of the experience of enlightenment, Izutsu continues: "But this very description of Nothingness clearly tells us that the Nothingness which is experienced in this way is by no means 'nothing' in the purely negative sense as the word is liable to be understood. . . . True, at this stage none of the individual existents exists self-subsistently. But this is not the same as saying that they are simply nil. On the contrary, they are there as concrete individuals, while being at the same time so many actualizations of the limitless, 'aspect'-less aspect of an ever-active, ever-creative Act." Thus Izutsu likewise believes that Ultimate Reality for Buddhists consists in an underlying ontological activity which is operative within a Void or all-encompassing Field and which is constitutive of both the subject and the object of ordinary experience (cf. also pp. 45-46).

7. The Secret of the Tao

1. Wing-tsit Chan, *A Source Book in Chinese Philosophy* (Princeton, N.J.: Princeton University Press, 1963), p. 137.

2. Holmes Welch, *Taoism: The Parting of the Way*, rev. ed. (Boston, Mass.: Beacon Press, 1966), p. 5.

3. Chan, *Source Book*, p. 137; cf. also Max Kaltenmark, *Lao Tzu and Taoism*, trans. Roger Greaves (Stanford, Calif.: Stanford University Press, 1969), pp. 16-18.

4. Chan, *Source Book*, p. 139.

5. Cf. above, Chapter 1, Aristotle's definition of motion in Book III of the *Physics*: "the fulfillment of what exists potentially, insofar as it exists potentially" (Aristotle, *Metaphysics*, 201a10). Likewise, see Ellen Marie Chen, "The Origin and Development of Being (Yu) from Non-Being (Wu) in the *Tao Te Ching*," *International Philosophical Quarterly* 13 (1973), 403-404.

6. Cf. Chan, *Source Book*, p. 138; Welch, *Taoism*, pp. 1-3; and Kaltenmark, *Lao Tzu and Taoism*, pp. 12-15, for a summary of the controversy surrounding Lao Tzu's alleged authorship of the *Tao Te Ching*.

7. Cf. Sung-peng Hsu, "Lao Tzu's Conception of Ultimate Reality: A Comparative Study," *International Philosophical Quarterly* 16 (1976), 215.

8. Chan, *Source Book*, p. 140.

9. Cf. on this point Chen, "The Origin and Development," p. 406.

10. Cf. here Robert C. Neville, *The Tao and the Daimon: Segments of a Religious Inquiry* (Albany: State University of New York Press, 1982), p. 51: "Apart from creating, God cannot be said to have a character, to be determinate, to be existent, one, good, true, beautiful distinguishable from nothingness or 'God' in any sense. This claim itself is a logical implication of the hypothesized creation relation—namely, that God creates everything determinate," including God's own character as Creator. In the conclusion, I will try to show how Neville's highly original understanding of God better corresponds to the underlying nature of God or the Godhead than to God in a purely indeterminate sense as Neville himself proposes.

11. Chan, *Source Book*, p. 160.

12. *Ibid.*

13. Chen, "The Origin and Development," p. 410.

14. *Ibid.* Cf. also Sung-peng Hsu, "Lao Tzu's Conception," p. 204.

15. Chen, "The Origin and Development," p. 411.

16. Cf. on this point Fetz, "Creativity: A New Transcendental," pp. 201-02. Fetz notes that in the relatively static Aristotelian-Thomistic world view forms are created by God *ex nihilo* at the beginning of creation and reproduced throughout history; within an evolutionary world view such as Whitehead and (at least in my judgment) the author of the *Tao Te Ching* espoused, new forms are continually being produced out of pre-existent materials by the creative process itself. Thus in an evolutionary perspective, contrary to the presuppositions of Aristotle and Aquinas, potentiality is ontologically prior to actuality.

17. Chan, *Source Book*, p. 141.

18. Cf. above, Chapter 6.

19. Chan, *Source Book*, p. 152.

20. Cf., e.g., Kaltenmark, *Lao Tzu and Taoism*, p. 37: The Tao "is none other than the primordial unity of chaos, the unity anterior to the formation of the world." Cf. also Izutsu, *Sufism and Taoism*, p. 481; T. P. Kasulis, *Zen Action: Zen Person* (Honolulu: University Press of Hawaii, 1981), pp. 29-30.

21. Chan, *Source Book*, pp. 144-45.

22. *Tao Te Ching*, chap. 8: Chan, *Source Book*, p. 143.

23. *Tao Te Ching*, chap. 78: Chan, *Source Book*, p. 174.

24. Chan, *Source Book*, p. 143.

25. *Tao Te Ching*, chap. 32: Chan, *Source Book*, p. 156.

26. Chan, *Source Book*, p. 136.

27. *Tao Te Ching*, chap. 30: Chan, *Source Book*, p. 154.

28. Welch, *Taoism*, p. 20.

29. Chan, *Source Book*, pp. 154-55.

30. *Tao Te Ching*, chap. 31: Chan, *Source Book*, p. 155.

31. Welch, *Taoism*, p. 25.

32. *Tao Te Ching*, chap. 30: Chan, *Source Book*, p. 155.

33. *Tao Te Ching*, chap. 61: Chan, *Source Book*, p. 168.

34. *Tao Te Ching*, chap. 10: Chan, *Source Book*, p. 144; cf. also *Tao Te Ching*, chap. 51: Chan, *Source Book*, pp. 163-64, where such activity is attributed directly to the Tao.

35. Cf., e.g., *Tao Te Ching*, chaps. 1, 20, 25, 52 & 59; Chan, *Source Book*, pp. 139, 150, 152, 164, 167.

36. Cf., e.g., *Tao Te Ching*, chaps. 6, 10: Chan, *Source Book*, pp. 142, 144.

37. Ellen Marie Chen, "Nothingness and the Mother Principle in Early Chinese Taoism," *International Philosophical Quarterly* 9 (1969), 401-05.

38. Cf., e.g., Chan, *Source Book*, pp. 137-38; Welch, *Taoism*, pp. 3-4; Fung Yu-Lan, *A Short History of Chinese Philosophy*, ed. Derk Bodde (New York: The Free Press, 1966), pp. 93-94.

39. Chen, "Nothingness and the Mother Principle," pp. 396-98.

40. *Ibid.*, p. 395. Chen adds that the commonly accepted interpretation of *wu* as pure nothingness is due to the influence of Buddhism in China, above all, the notion of emptiness within classical Buddhism. But, as I have indicated in the preceding chapter, within the writings of Nagarjuna and other classical Buddhists emptiness is identified with "dependent co-arising" or constant activity. Hence, even within Buddhism, emptiness is not pure nothingness but rather an underlying activity, formless or undifferentiated in itself but differentiated in all its sensible manifestations.

41. For this reason, I disagree with Sung-peng Hsu in his statement that the "Tao in its essence is unchanging, absolute, and eternal, but in its function it is ever moving according to constant principles" (Sung-peng Hsu, "Lao Tzu's Conception," p. 212). How can the essence be unchanging and its function be constantly changing? Rather, I would agree with Ellen Marie Chen that the Tao is pure change and that its unchanging character is due to the fact that it never rests but is constantly active.

42. Cf., e.g., *Tao Te Ching*, chaps, 15, 20, 28: Chan, *Source Book*, pp. 147, 150, 154.

43. Kenneth Kramer, *World Scriptures: An Introduction to Comparative Religions* (New York: Paulist Press, 1986), p. 124.

44. *Tao Te Ching*, chap. 40: Chan, *Source Book*, p. 160.

45. Cf. on this point Izutsu, *Sufism and Taoism*, pp. 322-23. The "reversion" in question here can be simply the ongoing transformation of various entities into their logical opposites (e.g., hot into cold and vice versa), but on a deeper level it is the reversion of all beings into non-being as their dynamic source.

46. Cf. here Neville, *The Tao and the Daimon*, p. 137.

47. *Tao Te Ching*, chap. 16: Chan, *Source Book*, p. 147.

48. Lao Tzu, to be sure, questions the distinctions between "good" and "evil" which ordinary people make: cf. here *Tao Te Ching*, chap. 20: Chan, *Source Book*, pp. 149-50; cf. also Chap. 2: Chan, *Source Book*, p. 140. But he, too, implicitly exercises a value judgment as to what is right or wrong at least for himself in submitting to the workings of the Tao.

49. Welch, *Taoism*, p. 36.

50. *Tao Te Ching*, chap. 49: Chan, *Source Book*, pp. 162-63.

51. *Tao Te Ching*, chap. 5: Chan, *Source Book*, p. 141.

52. Chan, *Source Book*, p. 142.

53. Welch, *Taoism*, p. 46.

54. Alfred North Whitehead, *Science and the Modern World*, p. 179.

55. Chan, *Source Book*, pp. 3-4.

56. Fung Yu-Lan, *A Short History*, p. 104: The *Chuang Tzu* "is, in fact, a collection of various Taoist writings, some of which represent Taoism in its first phase of development, some in its second, and some in its third. It is only those chapters representing the thought of this third climactic phase that can properly be called Chuang Tzu's own philosophy, yet even they may not all have been written by Chuang Tzu himself."

57. Chan, *Source Book*, pp. 182-83.

58. *Chuang Tzu: Taoist Philosopher and Chinese Mystic*, trans. Herbert A. Giles, 2nd ed. (London: George Allen & Unwin, 1961), p. 37.

59. Cf. above, Chapter 6.

60. Chan, *Source Book*, p. 190.

61. Chang Chung-yuan, *Creativity and Taoism: A Study of Chinese Philosophy, Art and Poetry* (New York: Harper Torchbook, 1970), p. 20.

62. *Ibid.*, p. 24.

63. *Ibid.*, pp. 40-41, 49.

64. *Ibid.*, p. 50.

65. Chan, *Source Book*, p. 189.

66. Cf. above in Chapter 6, Nishida's discussion of "pure experience."

67. *Chuang Tzu*, chap. 2: Chan, *Source Book*, p. 189.

68. Chan, *Source Book*, p. 194.

69. *Ibid*.

70. *Chuang Tzu*, Chap. 2: Chan, *Source Book*, pp. 185-86.

71. Cf. above, Chapter 1.

72. Kuang-Ming Wu, *Chuang Tzu: World Philosopher at Play* (New York: Crossroad, 1982), p. 86.

73. *Chuang Tzu*, chap. 12: Chan, *Source Book*, p. 202.

74. Chan, *Source Book*, p. 790; cf. also Welch, *Taoism*, pp. 83-87.

75. Chou Tun-I, *An Explanation of the Diagram of the Great Ultimate*: Chan, *Source Book*, p. 463.

76. Chan, *Source Book*, p. 460.

Conclusion: The Divine Matrix

1. Chung-yuan, *Creativity and Taoism*, p. 99.

2. Aristotle, *On Generation and Corruption*, 327b23-27.

3. The implications of this statement for the Christian doctrine of the Incarnation of the "Son" of God in Jesus of Nazareth lie beyond the parameters of this book.

But it in any event makes clear in retrospect why Church authorities have always insisted that Jesus was truly human as well as divine. That is, as I interpret it, Jesus possessed a human subjectivity which was in ongoing relation not only with the "Father" but also with his own deeper Self as the "Son" of God. Only thus could he be genuinely free to respond to the "Father's" initiatives and to be one with the "Son" in the "Son's" own unending response to the "Father." Cf. on this point my earlier publication *The Triune Symbol*, pp. 48-57.

4. Cf. the following passage attributed to the Buddha out of the *Itivuttaka*, 43: "There is, O monks, something not born, non-existent, not made, not compounded. If there were not this something not born, non-existent, not made, not compounded, there would not be known here deliverance from what is born, existent, made, and compounded. Since, indeed, O monks, there is something not born, non-existent, not made, and not compounded, therefore there is known deliverance from what is born, existent, made, and compounded" (cited in Panikkar, *The Silence of God*, p. 42.

5. Cf. on this point Smith, *The World's Religions*, pp. 26-29.

6. Masao Abe, "Kenotic God and Dynamic Sunyata," *The Emptying God: A Buddhist-Jewish-Christian Conversation*, ed. John B. Cobb, Jr. and Christopher Ives (Maryknoll, N.Y.: Orbis, 1990), p. 28.

7. Cf. Mitchell, *Spirituality and Emptiness*, p. 26.

8. Whitehead, *Science and the Modern World*, pp. 58-59.

9. Neville, *Behind the Masks of God*, pp. 13-17.

10. *Ibid.*, p. 15.

11. Pierre Teilhard de Chardin, *The Phenomenon of Man*, trans. Bernard Wall (New York: Harper Torchbook 1965), pp. 264-68.

12. Cf., however, Ninian Smart and Steven Konstantine, *Christian Systematic Theology in a World Context* (Minneapolis, Minn.: Fortress, 1991), esp. pp. 173-178. These authors argue for a social or communitarian understanding of the doctrine of the Trinity (much akin to my own) as the best way "to give a coherent account of the major types of religious experience and the kinds of doctrines correlated with them" (p. 173). Thereby they have in mind not simply the religious experience of Christians but that of the devotees of all the other major world religions.

Select Bibliography

Books

Aquinas, St. Thomas. *Summa Theologica.* Translated from the Latin by the Fathers of the English Dominican Province. New York; Benziger Brothers, 1947.

Aristotle. *The Basic Works of Aristotle.* Edited by Richard McKeon. New York: Random House, 1941.

Barbour, Ian. *Myths, Models and Paradigms: A Comparative Study in Science and Religion.* New York: Harper & Row, 1974.

Beck, Heinrich. *Der Akt-Charakter des Seins.* Munich: Max Hueber Verlag, 1965.

Bergson, Henri. *Matter and Memory.* Translated by Nancy Margaret Paul and W. Scott Palmer. London: George Allen & Unwin, 1950.

_____. *The Creative Mind (Pensée et le Mouvant).* Translated by Mabelle L. Andison. New York: Greenwood Press, 1968.

Berry, Thomas. *Religions of India.* New York: Bruce Publishing Co., 1971.

Bracken, Joseph A. *Freiheit und Kausalität bei Schelling.* Munich: Karl Alber, 1972.

_____. *The Triune Symbol: Persons, Process and Community.* Lanham, Md.: University Press of America, 1985.

_____. *Society and Spirit: A Trinitarian Cosmology.* Cranbury, N.J.: Associated University Presses, 1991.

Buckley, Michael J., S.J. *Motion and Motion's God: Thematic Variations in Aristotle, Cicero, Newton, and Hegel.* Princeton, N.J.: Princeton University Press, 1971.

Caputo, John. *The Mystical Element in Heidegger's Thought.* Athens, Ohio: Ohio University Press, 1970.

Carman, John Braisted. *The Theology of Ramanuja: An Essay in Interreligious Understanding.* New Haven: Yale University Press, 1974.

Carmody, Denise Lardner and John Tully Carmody. *Ways to the Center: An Introduction to World Religions.* 3rd. ed. Belmont, Calif.: Wadsworth Publishing Co., 1989.

Carter, Robert E. *The Nothingness beyond God: An Introduction to the Philosophy of Nishida Kitaro.* New York: Paragon House, 1989.

Chan, Wing-tsit. *A Source Book in Chinese Philosophy.* Princeton, N.J.: Princeton University Press, 1963.

Chatterjee, Satischandra, and Dhirendramohan Datta. *An Introduction to Indian Philosophy.* 8th ed. Calcutta: University of Calcutta, 1984.

Christian, William A. *An Interpretation of Whitehead's Metaphysics.* New Haven: Yale University Press, 1959.

Chuang Tzu: Taoist Philosopher and Chinese Mystic. Translated by Herbert A. Giles. 2nd ed. London: George Allen & Unwin, 1961.

Chung-yuan, Chang. *Creativity and Taoism: A Study of Chinese Philosophy, Art, and*

Poetry. New York: Harper Torchbook, 1970.

Cobb, John B., Jr. *A Christian Natural Theology*. Philadelphia: Westminster, 1965.

Dasgupta, Surendranath. *A History of Indian Philosophy*. 5 vols. Delhi: Motilal Banarsidass, 1988.

Deutsch, Eliot. *Advaita Vedanta: A Philosophical Reconstruction*. Honolulu: University of Hawaii Press, 1973.

Dodds, E.R. *Pagan and Christian in an Age of Anxiety*. New York: W.W. Norton, 1970.

Dyczkowski, Mark. *The Doctrine of Vibration: An Analysis of the Doctrines and Practices of Kashmir Shaivism*. Albany: State University of New York Press, 1987.

Eckel, Malcolm David. *To See the Buddha: A Philosopher's Quest for the Meaning of Emptiness*. New York: HarperCollins, 1992.

Ford, Lewis S. *The Lure of God: A Biblical Background for Process Theism*. Philadelphia: Fortress, 1978.

_____. *The Emergence of Whitehead's Metaphysics, 1925-1929*. Albany, N.Y.: State University of New York Press, 1984.

Geiger, L.-B., O.P. *La Participation dans la philosophie de S. Thomas d'Aquin*. 2nd ed. Paris: Libraire J. Vrin, 1953.

Gilson, Etienne. *The Spirit of Mediaeval Philosophy*. Translated by A.H.C. Downes. New York: Scribner's, 1940.

Hartshorne, Charles. *Man's Vision of God and the Logic of Theism*. Hamden, Conn.: Archon Books, 1964.

Heidegger, Martin. *Being and Time*. Translated by John Macquarrie and Edward Robinson. New York: Harper & Row, 1962.

_____. *Der Satz vom Grund*. 2nd ed. Pfullingen: Günther Neske, 1958.

_____. *Identity and Difference*. Translated by Joan Stambaugh. New York: Harper & Row, 1969.

_____. *Schellings Abhandlung über das Wesen der menschlichen Freiheit*. Edited by Hildegard Feick. Tübingen: Max Niemeyer, 1971.

_____. *Vom Wesen des Grundes*. 4th ed. Frankfurt am Main: Vittorio Klostermann, 1955.

Hindu Scriptures. Translated and edited by R. C. Zaehner. London: J. M. Dent, 1966.

Izutsu, Toshihiko. *Toward a Philosophy of Zen Buddhism*. Tehran: Imperial Iranian Academy of Philosophy, 1977.

_____. *Sufism and Taoism: A Comparative Study of Key Philosophical Concepts*. Berkeley: University of California Press, 1984.

Jankélevitch, Vladimir. *L'Odyssée de la conscience dans la dernière philosophie de Schelling*. Paris: Felix Alcan, 1933.

The Jerusalem Bible. Edited by Alexander Jones. Garden City, N.Y.: Doubleday & Co., 1966.

Johnson, Elizabeth A. *She Who Is: The Mystery of God in Feminist Theological Discourse*. New York: Crossroad, 1992.

Kaltenmark, Max. *Lao Tzu and Taoism*. Translated by Roger Greaves. Stanford, Calif.: Stanford University Press, 1969.

Kalupahana, David J. *Buddhist Philosophy: A Historical Analysis*. Honolulu: The University of Hawaii Press, 1976.

_____. *Nagarjuna: The Philosophy of the Middle Way*. Albany: State University of New York Press, 1986.

Kasulis, T. P. *Zen Action: Zen Person*. Honolulu: University of Hawaii Press, 1981.

Koyré, Alexander. *La Philosophie de Jacob Boehme*. 3rd ed. Paris: J. Vrin, 1979.

Kramer, Kenneth. *World Scriptures: An Introduction to Comparative Religions*. New York: Paulist Press, 1986.

Leclerc, Ivor. *Whitehead's Metaphysics*. London: George Allen & Unwin, 1958.

_____. *The Nature of Physical Existence*. London: George Allen & Unwin, 1972.

Les Noms védiques de Visnu dans L'Anuvyakhyana de Madhva. Texte avec traduction et notes par Suzanne Siauve. Pondicherry, India: Institut Français d'Indologie, 1959.

Lindbeck, George. *The Nature of Doctrine: Religion and Theology in a Postliberal Age*. Philadelphia: Westminster Press, 1984.

Lossky, Vladimir. *Théologie négative et connaisance de Dieu chez Maître Eckhart*. Paris: J. Vrin, 1960.

Loy, David. *Non-Duality: A Study in Comparative Philosophy*. New Haven: Yale University Press, 1988.

Macy, Joanna. *Mutual Causality in Buddhism and General Systems Theory: The Dharma of Natural Systems*. Albany: State University of New York Press, 1991.

Meister Eckhart: The Essential Sermons, Commentaries, Treatises and Defense. Translated and with an introduction by Edmund Colledge, O.S.A., and Bernard McGinn. New York: Paulist Press, 1981.

Meister Eckhart: Sermons and Treatises. Edited by M.O'C. Walshe. 3 vols. London: Watkins, 1985.

Mitchell, Donald W. *Spirituality and Emptiness: The Dynamics of Spiritual Life in Buddhism and Christianity*. New York: Paulist Press, 1991.

Moore, A. W. *The Infinite*. London: Routledge, 1990.

Murray, John Courtney, S.J. *The Problem of God: Yesterday and Today*. New Haven, Conn.: Yale University Press, 1964.

Nagao, Gadjin. *The Foundational Standpoint of Madhyamika Philosophy*. Translated by John P. Keenan. Albany: State University of New York Press, 1989.

Neville, Robert C. *Creativity and God: A Challenge to Process Theology*. New York: Seabury, 1980.

_____. *The Tao and the Daimon: Segments of a Religious Inquiry*. Albany: State University of New York Press, 1982.

_____. *Behind the Masks of God: An Essay toward Comparative Theology*. Albany: State University of New York Press, 1991.

_____. *Eternity and Time's Flow*. Albany: State University of New York Press, 1993.

Nishida, Kitaro. *An Inquiry into the Good*. Translated by Masao Abe and Christopher Ives. New Haven: Yale University Press, 1990.

Nobo, Jorge Luis. *Whitehead's Metaphysics of Extension and Solidarity*. Albany: State University of New York Press, 1986.

Pannenberg, Wolfhart. *Systematic Theology*. Translated by Geoffrey W. Bromiley. Vol. I. Grand Rapids, Mich.: William B. Eerdmans, 1991.

Panikkar, Raimundo. *The Unknown Christ of Hinduism*. Rev. ed. Maryknoll, N.Y.: Orbis, 1981.

_____. *The Silence of God: The Answer of the Buddha*. Translated by Robert R. Barr. Maryknoll, N.Y.: Orbis, 1989.

Plotinus. *The Enneads*. Translated by Stephen McKenna. 4th ed. London: Faber & Faber, 1969.

Podgorski, Frank R. *Hinduism: A Beautiful Mosaic*. 3rd ed. Bristol, Ind.: Wyndham Hall Press, 1985.

Puthiadam, I. *Visnu the Ever Free: A Study of the Madhva Concept of God*. Madurai, India: Arul Anander College, 1985.

Randall, John Herman. *Aristotle*. New York: Columbia University Press, 1968.

Richardson, William J., S.J. *Heidegger: Through Phenomenology to Thought*. The Hague: Martinus Nijhoff, 1963.

Ricoeur, Paul. *Interpretation Theory: Discourse and the Surplus of Meaning*. Fort Worth: Texas Christian University Press, 1976.

The Rig Veda: An Anthology. Edited by Wendy Doniger O'Flaherty. New York: Penguin Books, 1981.

Rorty, Richard. *Philosophy and the Mirror of Nature*. Princeton, N.J.: Princeton University Press, 1979.

Ross, W. D. *Aristotle*. 3rd ed. London: Methuen & Co., 1937.

Sacred Texts of the World: A Universal Anthology. Edited by Ninian Smart and Richard D. Hecht. New York: Crossroad, 1982.

Schelling, F.W.J. *Sämtliche Werke*. 14 vols. Edited by K.F.A. Schelling. Stuttgart: Cotta, 1856ff: in *Schellings Werke*. Edited by Manfred Schröter. Munich: C. H. Beck, 1958ff.

Schürmann, Reiner. *Meister Eckhart: Mystic and Philosopher*. Bloomington, Ind.: Indiana University Press, 1978.

Sherburne, Donald. *A Whiteheadian Aesthetic*. New Haven: Yale University Press, 1961.

Smith, Huston. *The World's Religions*. New York: Harper & Row, 1991.

Spinoza, Benedict. *The Ethics*. In *The Rationalists*. Translated by R.H.M. Elwes. New York: Doubleday Dolphin, 1960.

Streng, Frederick J. *Emptiness: A Study in Religious Meaning*. Nashville, Tenn.: Abingdon Press, 1967.

Sweeney, Leo, S.J. *Divine Infinity in Greek and Medieval Thought*. New York: Peter Lang Publishing, 1992.

Teilhard de Chardin, Pierre. *The Phenomenon of Man*. Translated by Bernard Wall. New York: Harper Torchbook, 1965.

The Thirteen Principal Upanishads. Translated by Robert Ernest Hume. 2nd ed. London: Oxford University Press, 1975.

Tilliette, Xavier. *Schelling: une philosophie en devenir*. 2 vols. Paris: J. Vrin, 1970.

Vedanta-Sutras with the Commentary by Sankaracarya and Ramanuja. Translated by George Thibaut. 3 vols: I & II (Sankaracarya), III (Ramanuja). Delhi: Motilal Banarsidass, 1962.

The Vedic Experience. Edited and translated with introduction and notes by Raimundo Panikkar. Berkeley: University of California Press, 1977.

Vetö, Miklos. *Le Fondement selon Schelling*. Paris: Beauchesne, 1977.

von Brück, Michael. *The Unity of Reality: God, God-Experience, and Meditation in the Hindu-Christian Dialogue*. Translated by James V. Zeitz. New York: Paulist Press, 1991.

Welch, Holmes. *Taoism: The Parting of the Way*. Rev. ed. Boston, Mass.: Beacon Press, 1966.

Whitehead, Alfred North. *Adventures of Ideas*. New York: The Free Press, 1967.

_____. *Science and the Modern World*. New York: The Free Press, 1967.

_____. *Religion in the Making*. New York: New American Library, 1974.

_____. *Process and Reality: An Essay in Cosmology*. Corrected ed. Edited by David Ray Griffin and Donald W. Sherburne. New York: The Free Press, 1978.

Wolfson, Harry. *Philo: Foundations of Religious Philosophy in Judaism, Christianity, and Islam*. Vol. I. Cambridge, Mass.: Harvard University Press, 1947; Vol. II. Cambridge, Mass.: Harvard University Press, 1962.

Woods, Richard, O.P. *Eckhart's Way*. Wilmington, Del.: Michael Glazier, 1986.

Wu, Kuang-Ming. *Chuang Tzu: World Philosopher at Play*. New York: Crossroad, 1982.

Yu-Lan, Fung. *A Short History of Chinese Philosophy*. Edited by Derk Bodde. New York: The Free Press, 1966.

Articles

Abe, Masao. "Kenotic God and Dynamic Sunyata." *The Emptying God: A Buddhist-Jewish-Christian Conversation*. Edited by John B. Cobb, Jr. and Christopher Ives. Maryknoll, N.Y.: Orbis, 1990.

Balasubramanian, R. "Advaita: An Overview." *Perspectives of Theism and Absolutism in Indian Philosophy*. Edited by M. Narasimhachari, V. A. Devasenapathi, and R. Balasubramanian. Madras: Ramakrishna Mission, Vivekananda College, 1978.

Bracken, Joseph A., S.J. "The issue of panentheism in the dialogue with the non-believer." *Studies in Religion/Sciences Religieuses* 21 (1992), 207-18.

Chen, Ellen Marie. "Nothingness and the Mother Principle in Early Chinese Taoism." *International Philosophical Quarterly* 9 (1969), 391-405.

_____. "The Origin and Development of Being (Yu) from Non-Being (Wu) in the *Tao Te Ching*." *International Philosophical Quarterly* 13 (1973), 403-17.

Christian, William A. "The Concept of God as a Derivative Notion." *Process and Divinity*. Edited by William L. Reese and Eugene Freeman. LaSalle, Ill.: Open Court, 1964.

Fetz, Reto Luzius. "Creativity: A New Transcendental?" *Whitehead's Metaphysics of Creativity*. Edited by Friedrich Rapp and Reiner Wiehl. Albany, N.Y.: State University of New York Press, 1990.

Hartshorne, Charles. "The Compound Individual." *Philosophical Essays for Alfred North Whitehead*. Edited by F.S.C. Northrup. New York: Russell and Russell, 1936.

Hsu, Sung-peng. "Lao Tzu's Conception of Ultimate Reality: A Comparative Study." *International Philosophical Quarterly* 16 (1976), 197-218.

Kim, Ha Tai. "The Logic of the Illogical: Zen and Hegel." *Philosophy East and West* 5 (1955-56), 19-29.

Murti, T.R.V. "The Two Definitions of Brahman in the Advaita." *K.C. Bhattacharya Memorial Volume*. Amalner, India: Indian Institute of Philosophy, 1958.

Nishida, Kitaro. "The Logic of the Place of Nothingness and the Religious World View." *Last Writings*. Translated by David A. Dilworth. Honolulu: University of Hawaii Press, 1987.

Van der Veken, Jan. "Creativity as Universal Activity." *Whitehead's Metaphysics of Creativity*. Edited by Friedrich Rapp and Reiner Wiehl. Albany, N.Y.: State University of New York Press, 1990.

Vater, Michael. "Heidegger and Schelling: The Finitude of Being." *Idealistic Studies* 5 (1975), 20-58.

Wilcox, John R. "A Monistic Interpretation of Whitehead's Creativity." *Process Studies* 20 (1991), 162-74.

Index

Abe, Masao, 111, 137, 167(n. 6)
act of being: as divine nature, 29-30, 32-33, 37,
    43, 154(n. 46); as conversion of
    potentiality into actuality, 26, 29, 31-33,
    34, 37, 147(n. 35)
activity: always instantiated in entities, 78, 84,
    88, 91-92; as actually infinite, 17-24, 29-30,
    33-34, 42-43, 66, 142(nn. 12, 3); as
    equivalent to prime matter, 17-20; as
    ground of being, 102, 110, 160(n. 5); as
    immanent within entities, 4, 116, 117-18,
    122-23, 124, 125; as principle for existence
    of things, 113, 125; hypostatized activity,
    17; never-ending and unchanging, 20-22,
    78; not an abstraction from concrete
    reality, 53-56, 152(n. 14), 160(n. 6);
    transcends its instantiations, 6, 116, 124,
    126, 127; underlying, 3, 5, 18, 52, 54, 55,
    58-60, 65, 75-76, 78, 84, 88, 91-92, 94, 98,
    99, 100, 102, 103-05, 108-10, 112-13, 117,
    119, 122-27, 129, 130, 131, 133-35, 137-40,
    159(n. 5), 161(n. 11), 163(nn. 75-76), 165(n.
    40); unifying, 84, 104-05, 110, 157(n. 40),
    159(n. 5) (cf. also creativity, motion)
actual entity (cf. actual occasion)
actual occasion, 3, 36-37, 51, 52-66, 141(n. 6),
    151(n. 61); and agency, 60-62; and
    subjective immortality, 64-65, 66
actuality vs. potentiality, 18, 31-33, 37, 113-14,
    125-26, 129, 134, 143(n. 4), 144(n. 26),
    145(n. 8), 146(n. 26), 147(n. 35) (cf. also
    objectivity vs. subjectivity)
Advaita Vedanta, 4, 5-6, 73, 74, 75, 76, 78, 79,
    81, 82-83, 86-89, 116, 139, 155(n. 2), 158(n.
    62)
Aitareya Upanishad, 78-79, 156(n. 15)
antaryami (divine controller), 89, 91, 159(n. 70)
appearance and reality, interpenetration of,
    128
Aristotle, 5-6, 11-24, 25-28, 31-32, 34, 37, 39-40,
    42-43, 53, 105-06, 110, 112, 115, 125, 129,
    134, 142(nn 3-4), 144(n. 26 & 41), 145(nn.
    4 & 9), 147(n. 30), 154(n. 46), 156(nn. 14 &
    20), 164(nn. 5 & 16)
Atman, 75-92, 93, 98; as Self or subject of
    consciousness, 80-82, 82-85, 131; identity
    with *Brahman*, 78-79, 80-82, 82-85, 131

atomism, metaphysical, 151(n. 8)
Augustine, 25-26, 129, 145(nn. 4 & 8), 147(n.
    40)
avidya (ignorance), 87, 88
Balasubramanian, R., 158(n. 60)
Barbour, Ian, 5
Beck, Heinrich, 146(n. 26)
being: and non-being, 73, 77-78, 87-88, 113,
    116-17, 120, 121, 123, 125-26; as activity,
    17, 23 (cf. also activity); as the act of
    existence, 26, 28-29, 33-34, 76-77, 78, 89,
    145(n. 8), 146(n. 26), 147(n. 30), 158(n. 62);
    as ground, 49-50, 66-67, 148(n. 2), 150 (nn.
    54 & 58); as nature of God, 42, 50, 148(n.
    2), 150(n. 58); as Tao that can be named,
    113, 126; ontological priority over
    non-being in the West, 114-15, 125, 164(n.
    16)
Bergson, Henri, 15, 23, 156(n. 20)
Berry, Thomas, 155(n. 1)
Boehme, Jacob, 45, 49, 51, 67
Brahma-sutras, 86, 87, 89
Brahman, 4-5, 68, 73, 75-92, 112; as Absolute
    or sole Self, 87-89, 132; as *ens commune* or
    ens realissimum, 157(n. 36); as Highest
    Self, 89-92, 132; as non-dual reality, 75-92,
    131; as One without a second, 76, 88, 91,
    131, 137, 139, 155(n. 2), 157(n. 36); as true
    Self, 132, 136; as underlying activity,
    78-80, 80-85, 88-89, 91-92, 131; as
    unchanging Being and ceaseless
    Becoming, 80, 89, 158(n. 63)
breakthrough into the Godhead, 41, 45, 149(n.
    20)
Brhadaranyaka Upanishad, 82, 84-85
Buckley, Michael J., 143(n. 14)
Buddhist schools of metaphysics, 86-87
Caputo, John, 148(n. 2), 149(n. 20), 150(n. 58)
Carman, John Braisted, 159(nn. 65 & 70)
Carmody, Denise and John, 159(n. 2)
Carter, Robert E., 162(n. 41)
cause and effect relation, 94, 95, 97-98, 122
Chan, Wing-tsit, 112, 117, 121, 126
Chandogya Upanishad, 76, 83-84, 133
Chatterjee, Satischandra, 159(n. 71)
Chen, Ellen Marie, 114, 119, 165(nn. 40 & 41)
Christian, William A., 153(n. 31)

Other Titles in the Faith Meets Faith Series